MW01194607

THE STORY OF MAGIC

THE STORY OF MAGIC

MEMOIRS OF AN AMERICAN CRYPTOLOGIC PIONEER

FRANK B. ROWLETT

WITH FOREWORD AND EPILOGUE
BY
DAVID KAHN

AEGEAN PARK PRESS

Copyright © 1998   Thomas M. Rowlett

All rights reserved. No part of this book may be reproduced in any form or by any means, electronic or mechanical, including photocopying, recording, or by any information storage and retrieval system, without permission in writing from the Publisher.

Aegean Park Press
P.O. Box 2837
Laguna Hills, CA 92654-2837

Library of Congress Catalog No. 98-073252

ISBN: 0-89412-273-8

FIRST EDITION

Printed in the United States of America

It may be roundly asserted that human ingenuity cannot concoct a cipher which human ingenuity cannot resolve.

— Edgar Allan Poe

CONTENTS

FOREWORD

FRANK ROWLETT LIVED his life in shadow. His work as a codebreaker was done in deepest secrecy. His exploits remained unknown to all but a few. His great triumph, as the leader of the team that broke the Japanese PURPLE diplomatic cipher machine, was obscured when his boss, William F. Friedman, became known as "The Man Who Broke Purple." His $100,000 Congressional award for cryptographic inventions was barely mentioned in the press. His award of the National Security Medal by President Lyndon Johnson in person was little noted.

Yet Rowlett is one of the key figures of American cryptology. Though he followed in the footsteps of Friedman, his older, pathbreaking mentor and boss, he made great contributions of his own. His PURPLE solution helped Allied troops lodge themselves in Normandy. His cryptographic inventions, particularly the idea of using keying rotors to irregularize the rotation of enciphering and deciphering rotors, rendered high-level American secrets invulnerable. He organized and inspired hundreds of World War II draftees in cracking Japanese army codes. His work saved thousands of lives. His administration put U.S. cryptology on a sound and efficient basis.

But his story has never been publicly told. Now, at last, the U.S. government has withdrawn its objections to the publication of the memoir he set down a decade or two ago, and Aegean Park Press is issuing it.

It is a fundamental contribution to the history of American cryptology. Nothing like it has been written, and nothing like it will be: The other persons involved are all deceased, and the documents in the archives do not record the personalities, the anecdotes, the human reasons behind many decisions, as recounted here.

Through the eyes of a major participant, this book tells how, after the State Department withdrew its funding from Herbert O. Yardley's joint Army-State American Black Chamber, effectively abolishing it, the United States Army went beyond Yardley to build a modern, mathematical cryptologic unit — except for Poland's, the only agency on such a basis in the world. This basis was needed because, in a worldwide shift, cryptography was abandoning code systems, which were best solved by linguists and classics scholars, for cipher systems, which, based on letters and therefore subject to statistical regularities, could best be attacked by mathematicians. Rowlett, a boyish young mathematics teacher from Virginia, was the first of the new breed to be hired. That was on 1 April 1930, a month and a day before he turned 22. The life in shadow had begun.

Rowlett tells how, under Friedman, he and his fellow recruits learned the terms and techniques of this once occult, now rapidly modernizing, science. And gradually they began breaking foreign cryptosystems.

He narrates his story well. He eschews technicalities, probably as much for security reasons as for rhetorical. Some will regret this, but it is all but made up for by the humanity of his book — which is peopled by men and women who, like himself, labored in obscurity and silence to serve their nation. Likewise, some will regret that he did not base his book on documents but wrote from memory — that, for example, he sets down whole conversations from memory. These objections do not much damage a pathbreaking memoir. Many technical documents exist in the archives and may be consulted by whoever compiles the definitive history. The conversations would have been lost if Rowlett had not set them down, and since their exact phraseology matters less than their substance, they contribute greatly to history. Moreover, these objections fall before Rowlett's modesty, refusal to stray beyond firsthand knowledge, and restraint in judgment, all of which anchor faith in his honesty.

For some reason, Rowlett stopped his memoir *in medias res*. It could not be published truncated thus. With the approval of the author, and on the bases of his oral history interview with National Security Agency historians, though it has been heavily redacted, and of newly available documents, I have sought to round out this work. The author has read and approved my supplement.

In this wonderful book — revelatory and well written — Frank Rowlett has told the story of the morning of American cryptology. It brings the man who lived in shadow into the sunlight. It deserves to be read not only by historians of cryptology, but also by historians of intelligence, of war — and of America.

DAVID KAHN

CHAPTER 1

THE CODE DESTRUCTION MESSAGE

I T WAS ALMOST NOON on December 3, 1941. I was hurrying down the long corridors of the Navy and Munitions buildings in Washington, D.C., returning to my office on the third floor of the Munitions Building. I was the cryptanalyst in charge of the Army's codebreaking effort on Japanese diplomatic intercepts. I was also deeply involved in the preparation of keying systems for the new electromechanical cipher machine to be used for the most secret military communications of the United States.

During the past two years the Army and Navy had joined in the development and production of an advanced cipher machine called the ECM by the Navy and the M-134C, later SIGABA, by the Army. Enough of these machines to equip the more important Navy fleet and shore installations and the Army commands down to division level were being built. The production of these machines had only recently been started and some of them now were ready to be issued. With these machines, the United States military forces would possess the most secure and efficient cipher machine in the world.

I had just attended a meeting with the Navy machine cryptographers in which we had worked out the final details for a keying system that would permit the new cipher machine to be used for joint communications between Army and Navy units, as well as within each of the two services. Each service had already completed its preparation of cipher machine keys for internal service communications, and these were now in full production. With the completion of the keying system for joint usage, we would be ready to use the new cipher machine throughout the United States military establishment.

While in the Navy Building, I had visited the Navy cryptanalytic group in OP-20-G responsible for the Navy's work on Japanese diplomatic intercepts. This work was shared between the Signal Intelligence Section in the Army, which worked on the Japanese diplomatic intercepts originating on even days, and OP-20-G in the Navy, which worked on the intercepts for the odd days. Our processing arrangements were kept flexible so that we could quickly and effectively respond to any changes in communications security introduced by the Japanese Foreign Service cryptographers. The combined intelligence output of the two organizations was known by the cover name MAGIC.

The intelligence from MAGIC was considered so sensitive that, outside of the Signal Intelligence Section and OP-20-G personnel and the intelligence analysts of G-2 and ONI, only a few key individuals in the State Department and the White House had access to it. If the Japanese should learn that we had broken their most secure diplomatic codes and ciphers, replacements would inevitably be issued and the vital MAGIC intelligence information would be lost.

There had never before been such intense interest in the Japanese diplomatic intercepts as we were now experiencing. The White House and the State Department had explicitly asked for expeditious handling of all Japanese diplomatic intercepted messages dealing with the discussions between the United States and Japan which were then in progress. G-2 and ONI were demanding immediate exploitation of all Japanese diplomatic messages intercepted on the Tokyo-Rome and Tokyo-Berlin circuits. The daily keys used by the Japanese for their most important cipher machine system, the system that we called PURPLE, and the transposition keys for their most secret code system, known to the Japanese as the "OITE" system, had to be expeditiously recovered. All messages between Tokyo and Honolulu had to be solved and studied for reports of Japanese espionage.

For weeks those of us who had access to the translations of Japanese diplomatic intercepts had become more and more convinced that war between the United States and Japan was inevitable, and it was only a matter of time before it would start. Among other indications, unusual developments in Japanese Foreign Office communications had been noted. The Japanese had recently started to use voice codes on the international radiotelephone circuits between Tokyo and Washington.

On November 19, 1941, they had put into effect a special code to be used in the news and information broadcasts made from Tokyo by the Japanese Foreign Office in case regular commercial radio channels could no longer be used. We referred to this special code as the "Winds Code" because it was to be used in the middle and at the end of a weather forecast, and it employed wind reports as a signal for authorizing the destruction of codes and other important secret information on its receipt.

In a message dated November 27, 1941, the Japanese Foreign Office had issued yet another code for emergency use. They referred to this code in their messages as the INGO DENPO or "Hidden Word" code. This code had a more extensive vocabulary than the "Winds Code," and it was intended to be used for reporting on the state of relations between Japan and other world powers, including the United States and Great Britain, in case the regular commercial radio communications channels were not available.

When I arrived at my office in the Munitions Building, I planned to report the results of my meetings with the Navy to my supervisor, William F. Friedman, the Army's chief cryptanalyst and the head of the Signal Intelligence Section. He was not in his office and his secretary told me that he would not return until later. She then added that Miss Louise Prather, the supervisor of the group that prepared our MAGIC translations for distribution, had left an important item on my desk, and she suggested that I read it immediately. When I reached my desk I found a single-page translation of a Japanese PURPLE machine intercept placed neatly in its center. The translation read as follows:[1]

```
FROM: Tokyo TO: Washington December 2, 1941 #867.


    1. Please destroy by burning all of the codes you
have in your office, with the exception of one copy
each of the codes being used in conjunction with the
machine, the OITE code and the abbreviation code.
(This includes other Ministries' codes which you may
have in your office.)
    2. Also in the case of the code machine itself, one
set is to be destroyed.
    3. Upon completing the above, transmit the one word
HARUNA.
    4. Use your discretion in disposing of all texts
of messages to and from your office, as well as other
secret papers.
    5. Destroy by burning all of the codes brought to
your office by telegraphic courier Kosaka.
(Consequently, you need not pursue the instructions
contained in my message #860, regarding getting in
touch with Mexico.)
Army 25640


Translated 12-3-41
```

---

1. *The "Magic" Background of Pearl Harbor*, Volume IV Appendix, page A-122, Department of Defense, United States of America.

I had never before seen a Japanese message with code instructions like this one. I had difficulty in believing that the Japanese would order the destruction of almost all of their diplomatic codes held in Washington, and — what was most remarkable — that they would order the destruction of one of their PURPLE cipher machines. I could understand their replacing a PURPLE machine, but not destroying one. It was obvious to me that this message had implications much broader than merely providing operating instructions for the Washington code room personnel.

While I was reading the translation a second time to ensure that I fully understood it, I heard the voice of Colonel Otis K. Sadtler, the Officer in Charge of Operations Branch, Office of the Chief Signal Officer, in the outer office asking for Friedman. The Signal Intelligence Section was a unit of the Operations Branch and under Colonel Sadtler's command. When Colonel Sadtler was told that Friedman was not in, he asked for me. On learning that I was at my desk, he came directly into my office.

"Rowlett, what is the meaning of this message from Tokyo telling Washington to destroy codes?" he excitedly asked as he handed me a copy of the translation I was studying.

"I have just read the message for the first time," I answered as I returned his copy to him.

"Have the Japs ever done anything like this before?" he asked me, without allowing me to say anything further.

"I've never before seen a code instruction message like this one," I answered. "It just doesn't make sense for them to order the destruction of most of the codes held in Washington as well as one of their two PURPLE machines, when they need both machines for their normal communications."

"Do you think that they may have learned that we have broken their codes and that they're getting ready to replace them?" he asked.

"That is a possibility," I answered, "but I don't think it is a likely one."

I then described the normal Japanese practices for changing codes, explaining that the Japanese consistently introduced their new codes on the first day of the month, and that such changes were conducted in a very orderly fashion with not just one, but all holders, being notified well in advance that the new codes would be put into effect on a specified date. I also pointed out that the message we were discussing obviously did not deal with a general change in codes, since no other holders of the systems it mentioned had been notified. I added that if they considered their codes compromised, they probably would not order their destruction.

Colonel Sadtler then asked me to explain the effect the destruction of the systems would have on the ability of Washington and Tokyo to communicate with each other. I responded that Washington's capacity for enciphering and deciphering messages would be seriously curtailed and that only a fraction of the normal traffic in and out of Washington could be handled. I also mentioned that if they had only one cipher machine and it failed, they would be forced to use the OITE system, which was much slower to operate. I added that from my understanding of their communications practices I could think of no communications security reason for Tokyo to issue such instructions to Washington.

Colonel Sadtler became increasingly agitated as he listened to my explanations. Suddenly, a conviction seemed to strike him, and his whole demeanor changed. He pulled himself up to his full stature as if he were standing at attention and, with his dark eyes flashing excitely, exclaimed: "Rowlett, do you know what this means? It can mean only one thing, and that is that the Japanese are about to go to war with the United States!"

Without saying another word, he spun around and dashed through the office door into the corridor outside. I followed him, and when I got to the door, I could see him actually running down the corridor, evidently heading for the G-2 offices.

As I stood in the doorway thinking over Colonel Sadtler's remarks and conclusions, I was certain that he was right and that war with Japan could break out at any moment. It was clear to me that the Signal Intelligence Service must now assume the full wartime role its founders had visualized for it when it was brought into being in early 1930, at the time I had joined it. How well it would meet the requirements of this role could not be known until the war was over.

If I could have looked ahead approximately four and a half years to the late spring of 1945, I would have seen myself reading another historic item of MAGIC from a PURPLE machine intercept. This time the end and not the beginning of World War II was predicted. In a message from Tokyo to Moscow, the Japanese Ambassador in Moscow was instructed to approach the Russian authorities with a request that they intercede for an "honorable peace" with the Allies on the behalf of the Japanese Government. The terms proposed by the Japanese in that message were tantamount to an unconditional surrender; the only caveat was that the "integrity of the Imperial household be maintained." This intercepted Japanese diplomatic message was the first hard intelligence evidence received by the Allies that the Japanese had accepted defeat and were willing to surrender.

CHAPTER 2

OUR GROUP ASSEMBLES

I T WAS A FEW minutes before eight o'clock on the morning of the first of April — All Fool's Day — 1930. I was standing in front of the main entrance to the Munitions Building at 21st and "B" Streets in Washington, D.C. In my hand was a letter telling me to report at eight a.m. to Room 3406 in that building. I was to be employed as a Junior Cryptanalyst in the Signal Service at Large, Office of the Chief Signal Officer, War Department.

I walked through the main entrance to the Munitions Building. Inside the door stood a uniformed guard, and I went up to him and said: "I have a letter telling me to report for work here today. How do I get to Room 3406?"

He pointed through a second doorway to a flight of stairs and said: "Take those stairs to the third floor. When you get to the third floor, turn to your right on the front corridor. Room 3406 is down the first corridor to the right from there."

"Thank you," I said, and I joined the trickle of people passing through the second doorway. I climbed the two flights of stairs to the third floor. At the top of the second flight I turned right and almost immediately I found myself at the entrance to a wing of the building. A short flight of steps led downward to a wide double doorway.

When I went down the steps I found myself in an open wing about sixty feet wide. The center of this wing was clear, but along each side dozens of desks and file cabinets were arrayed. Some employees were at their desks and seemed to be settling in for the day's work; others were removing their hats and coats or hurrying down the middle of the wing, evidently just arriving.

Along each side of the cleared middle of the wing stood a number of square columns. On each column was painted what appeared to be a room number.

I walked along looking for the column bearing the number 3406. When I found it, there were two desks, a table, and a number of file cabinets alongside it. On top of the nearest file cabinet was a neatly lettered sign which read: Civilian Personnel, OCSigO. I concluded that I had reached my destination.

A woman, seated at one of the desks, was using the telephone. As I approached her, she noted the envelope I was carrying and motioned for me to take the chair at the front of her desk. I sat down and waited for her to complete her conversation. When she finished, she smiled at me and said, "Good morning. Are you Mr. Rowlett?"

"Yes ma'am," I said and handed her the letter.

"I'm Mrs. Leahy," she said as she took the letter. "We were expecting you to report this morning." She looked at the letter long enough to identify it and added, "Mrs. Kuntz has your file and will handle your processing for employment. She just stepped over to the mail room and should be back at her desk very soon. Please sit down while you are waiting for her."

I looked about the wing. It was the first time — except for Post Offices — that I had ever been inside a government building. I was curious to see what it was like. Everyone seemed busy and, except for a couple of late arrivals, the atmosphere was one of quiet efficiency.

I soon noticed a man approaching Mrs. Leahy's desk. He appeared to be about fifty years old and was dressed in a neat, well-tailored, black suit. He carried himself erectly with a great show of authority. As he walked, he squared his shoulders and swung his arms rhythmically from his sides to his front so that his hands clasped momentarily and then were immediately released and returned to his sides. He had such a splendid air of authority that I wondered if he might not be the Chief Signal Officer himself. When he got to Mrs. Leahy's desk, she said, "Good morning, Mr. Flynn."

He did not respond to her greeting but instead turned so that he could get a good look at me. After giving me a careful scrutiny, he gruffly asked, "Who's this?"

Mrs. Leahy arose from her desk and moved over to where I was sitting. I stood up and faced Mr. Flynn.

"Mr. Flynn," she said, "this is Mr. Rowlett. He is the first of the group we are hiring for Mr. Friedman. Mrs. Kuntz will process him for employment."

This answer seemed to satisfy Mr. Flynn. He turned to Mrs. Leahy and said, "When you finish with him, call me. I'll take him down to 3416." With these words he left us and continued down the middle of the wing toward the rear of the building, squaring his shoulders and swinging his arms in cadence with each step that he took.

Mrs. Leahy looked at me and smiled. "That was Mr. Flynn," she said. "He is the Chief Clerk for the Office of the Chief Signal Officer and — incidentally — my boss." In a few minutes Mrs. Kuntz appeared. Mrs.

Leahy introduced us, and Mrs. Kuntz seated me at the table. She gave me a number of forms which she helped me to complete. Using the typewriter on her desk, she transferred some of the information to other forms. When she finished them, she had me check the typed information to be sure that it was correct. After that, she had me sign the forms.

When I finished signing the last one, she said, "There's only one more thing to do, and Mrs. Leahy normally does that." She took me to Mrs. Leahy's desk and said, "Mr. Rowlett is ready to be sworn in."

Mrs. Leahy said, "Please raise your right hand and repeat after me the oath of employment." When we finished this process, she smiled at me and said, "Congratulations. You are now an employee of the Office of the Chief Signal Officer. Please sit down and wait for Mr. Flynn." She then called Mr. Flynn's office as he had instructed her and told him I was finished.

I had been so busy working with Mrs. Kuntz that I had not had an opportunity to ask her about my duties. I had been identified on the forms as a Junior Cryptanalyst, but she had not volunteered any information about the duties of a cryptanalyst. "Now I'll find out what I'll be doing," I thought as I waited for Mr. Flynn.

In a few minutes Mr. Flynn strode into the area, swinging his arms as he had earlier, and came to where I was sitting. He stopped directly in front of me and, as he came to a halt, his arms automatically stopped their movement. I got up from my chair and his pale gray eyes met mine directly.

He raised his right hand, crooked his forefinger at me, and said, "Come with me, Rowlett." Without further explanation he turned and began his arm-swinging, hand-clasping march down the middle of the wing toward the rear of the building. I followed a couple of steps behind him, wondering where I was being led and if Mr. Flynn had some concealed mechanism installed under his jacket which forced his arms and hands to move as they did each time he took a step.

When he came to the first enclosed office, he stepped up to its swinging half-door, grasped its handle, opened it, and then motioned for me to follow him inside. Behind one of the three desks in the room sat a middle-aged man, neatly dressed in a light gray suit and wearing rimless eyeglasses. Behind the eyeglasses a pair of friendly grayish blue eyes twinkled.

Mr. Flynn stepped up to the desk and stiffly announced, "Major Crawford, Sir, this is Rowlett, the man you were expecting today. The personnel office has finished with him and he is ready to go to work."

Major Crawford arose from his chair and graciously extended his hand across the desk.

"Mr. Rowlett," he said, "I am pleased to welcome you. We have been looking forward to your arrival for some time. I hope you will enjoy working for the Army Signal Corps."

Mr. Flynn excused himself and left the office. Major Crawford returned to his chair.

"Please sit down," he said as he motioned for me to take a seat beside his desk. I suppose he must have sensed my feeling of uncertainty, and, obviously trying to put me at ease, he asked, "Is this your first visit to Washington?"

"Yes, sir," I answered.

"Do you have satisfactory living arrangements?" he asked.

"Yes, but only for a short time," I answered. "I am staying for a few days with my cousin who has a house in Arlington."

"Good," he said. "If you need to look for a room, I'll be glad to excuse you for the rest of the day."

"Thank you," I answered, "but I plan to look for a place this weekend. I thought it would be better for me to learn something about what I will be doing and where I will be working before I choose a place to live."

"You will be working here in the Munitions Building," he said, "but we had better wait for Mr. Friedman, your boss, to tell you about your duties. You and two other young men who are due to arrive later this month will be doing some very special work under Friedman's direction. I personally can't tell you much about it, but I'm sure you will find it most fascinating. It is a new field of activity for which the Signal Corps has only recently been made responsible. Certain operations which were separately managed by several branches of the War Department have been centralized, and the Chief Signal Officer has been given the responsibility for them. All of us who have been involved — and especially the Chief Signal Officer — are anxious to get the new work under way. Your reporting for duty today is the most significant step that we have yet taken toward getting the new organization started."

"Why doesn't someone tell me what I'll be doing? Do they really have a job for me?" I thought.

"Sir," I asked, "could you please tell me something about the nature of the work?"

"Billy Friedman will take care of that when he returns," Major Crawford answered. "He had to attend a meeting at the Adjutant General's office this morning. Billy should return soon, and I am sure he can tell you all about your duties. This is also his office, and he works at the desk just behind where you are sitting. You can temporarily use the unoccupied desk in this room."

He then handed me a copy of the Washington Post and suggested, "Why don't you catch up on today's news while you are waiting for Billy. I have some business which will keep me away for the remainder of the day, and you can have this office all to yourself until he returns."

With that he gathered some papers from his desk, put them into a brief-case, took his hat from the rack, and prepared to leave the room. As he went through the office door he turned to me and said, "Please make your-self comfortable until Billy returns."

It was now almost eleven o'clock. I was more interested in my sur-roundings than I was in the newspaper. From where I sat, I carefully exam-ined the office. It was a fairly large room, simply furnished with three desks and a table located in one corner against the wall. In another corner stood two file cabinets on which were neatly piled some radio magazines. Two of the walls had slatted, cafe-like half doors, evidently to provide both privacy and ventilation. The third wall had four large, steel-framed windows which opened onto a court between the wings of the building. The fourth wall was the most interesting; in its middle a large steel door with a combina-tion lock was mounted. The door was closed. I wondered what might be behind it, for it was the most formidable door I had ever seen outside of a bank vault.

After giving my surroundings a good looking over from the chair in which I was seated — I didn't dare get up and walk about the room — I started to look at the newspaper. It had very little attraction for me, for I was growing more and more curious about what I would be doing. I felt a little disappointed at being left by myself in an empty room with nothing to do but read a newspaper; I was all keyed up to start working.

About half an hour later I heard voices just outside the door through which Mr. Flynn had brought me. One of the voices I recognized as belonging to Mr. Flynn, who was saying, "I brought him here just about an hour ago, and he ought to be in here with the Major."

Just then the swinging half-door opened, and a neatly dressed — almost dapper — individual carrying a briefcase entered, followed by Mr. Flynn. Flynn pointed to me and said, "Mr. Friedman, this is Rowlett, the man who reported this morning. Civilian Personnel has finished with him, and he is ready to go to work."

As I got up from my chair, the new arrival walked up to me, extended his hand, and said, "I'm Friedman. Welcome to the Signal Intelligence Sec-tion of the Army Signal Corps. I'm glad you're here."

I took his hand and answered, "Thank you. I'm glad to be here." Mr. Flynn, apparently having done his duty with respect to me a second time, excused himself and departed. Friedman settled himself at his desk and said, "Please sit down." I sat down at the desk Major Crawford had told me to use, and he rolled his chair out from his desk and turned so that he faced me directly.

"I am sorry that I wasn't here to welcome you when you finished with the personnel office," he said. "On the first of each month we have this regularly scheduled meeting in the State, War and Navy Building at the Adjutant General's Office. Since I have been designated as the official representative of the Chief Signal Officer, I have to attend. Mr. Flynn tells me that you have met Major Crawford. Major Crawford is our chief and reports directly to the Chief Signal Officer. I am the chief of the Signal Intelligence Section, and I report to Major Crawford. At the moment, the Signal Intelligence Section consists of three individuals: me, my secretary, and you. You are the first of three young men whose employment has only recently been authorized. I expect the other two to arrive before the end of the month. They are also mathematicians who have been hired as Junior Cryptanalysts."

Friedman's remarks had little meaning for me. I did not know who the Chief Signal Officer was, I had never heard of the Signal Intelligence Section before, and no one had offered to tell me what a Junior Cryptanalyst was supposed to do. I was tired of being mystified, and I thought that the time had arrived to do something about it.

"Mr. Friedman," I asked, "could you please tell me what a Junior Cryptanalyst is supposed to do?"

My direct question seemed to take him by surprise. He looked at me quite curiously as if he might be thinking that I should have known this before I accepted the job. After a slight hesitation he asked, "Why do you ask that question?"

"I've asked several people, both down in Virginia and here in Washington, about the duties of a Junior Cryptanalyst, and not one of them knew. I have tried to find a definition of the work 'cryptanalyst' in several dictionaries, but not one of them lists it. Frankly, I am puzzled and curious, and I would like to have some idea of the kind of work I will be doing."

My answer amused Friedman. He smiled and said, "I suppose you are puzzled. I suspect that there are only a very few persons who might know what the word 'cryptanalyst' means. In fact, the words cryptanalyst and cryptanalysis were officially adopted by the War Department only a few weeks ago, although I started using them several years ago. The first official use of these words was in the description of the duties of the staff of the Signal Intelligence Section, and you have the honor of being the first individual to be employed by the U.S. Government as a Junior Cryptanalyst. By the way, are you familiar with the works of Edgar Allen Poe?"

"Yes," I replied, puzzled by this question.

"Do you recall his story about the Gold Bug?" he asked.

For the first time the light began to dawn. "Do you mean the story of how a cipher was broken?" I asked.

Friedman seemed pleased at my answer. "Yes, that is the one," he said. "Now, in our terminology, the secret writing described by Poe is called a cryptogram; and one who solves cryptograms is a cryptanalyst. In other words, a cryptanalyst is one who reads code messages or cryptograms without knowledge of the keys or the means used to disguise their plain-texts. We are going to train you to be a cryptanalyst. Have you ever tried to solve a code message?"

"Outside of reading the story by Poe, I have never given any thought to breaking code messages," I answered. "I have read that many governments use codes to protect their secrets, but I know nothing about codes or how they are used."

"We will soon change that," Friedman said. "I have prepared a special course of study for you and the other young men we are expecting. As soon as they arrive, your training will start. Meanwhile, I think you should look over what little has been written about cryptography and cryptanalysis and acquaint yourself with some of the basic information on these subjects. Unfortunately, the best books are not in English. Please wait here while I get some examples of the books we have in our collection."

Friedman left his chair and walked over to the vault door. Positioning his body so it blocked my view of the combination dial, he unlocked the door and opened it. Beyond the steel door I could see a second barrier of two steel panels which met in the center of the doorway. Taking a key from his pocket he unlocked the panels, pushed them aside, and disappeared into the area behind them. In a short time he returned carrying four books.

"I recall that your language is German," he said as he moved toward the desk at which I was sitting. "I have here two books in German which I think are the best ones written in that language on cryptography. I have also two books by French experts which are more up to date than the books in German. By the way, do you read French?"

My spirits dropped at these remarks. I had studied German in college only because two years of a modern language was required for a degree, and I had no confidence in my ability to read and understand the language. I had taken only one year of French in high school. I feared that if Fried-man was expecting me to learn about cryptography and cryptanalysis by reading books in German and French, I would soon be on my way back to southwest Virginia looking for another job in the state school system.

"I am not sure of my German, and I only had one year of French in high school," I said apologetically.

Friedman handed me two of the books, saying "These two are in Ger-man. One of them was written several years ago by a German cryptogra-pher named Kasiski. It contains some good explanations of a variety of cipher systems. The other is more recent, and it is by an Austrian military cryptographer, Andreas Figl. I will also leave the two books in French for you to examine at your leisure."

I thanked him as I thumbed through the book by Kasiski. Each page contained a number of words that I did not recognize. "I will need a dictionary," I said.

"I will see that you get one," he said. "It is now time for lunch. I suggest that you eat at the Navy cafeteria."

He gave me directions for reaching the cafeteria, and explained that he had a luncheon engagement elsewhere in Washington. "I may not return until mid-afternoon. Your first assignment will be to read Kasiski," he said. "You can start when you return from lunch."

As I walked down the long corridors of the Munitions and Navy buildings, I began to feel some concern about my new job. I feared my knowledge of German was not good enough for me to be able to understand the two books Friedman had given me to study, and this gave me a feeling that I was involved in something that might be more than I could handle. At that moment I strongly wished that I was back in Rocky Mount, Virginia, having lunch with the other members of the teaching staff of the Franklin County High School.

When I returned to Room 3416 after lunch, I found it empty. On my desk were four dictionaries — two in German and two in French.

I picked up the book by Kasiski and started to work my way through the first chapter. I soon lost my fear of the language; the grammar was easy, but the text was replete with words I had never before encountered. I soon found that with the dictionary I could penetrate the mysteries of Kasiski's prose. After devoting about an hour to Kasiski's first chapter, which was a long exposition of his philosophy of cryptography, I got bored and started to search through the remainder of the book for examples of the cipher systems Friedman had told me it contained. These were much more interesting; and I soon discovered that if I limited my attention to the descriptions of code and cipher systems, I could get a good idea of how they operated without becoming bored by the discussions of their virtues and shortcomings. My interest began to mount, and I thought to myself that this was more like fun than work. I could see from my short examination of Kasiski that the study of codes and ciphers might be a most fascinating undertaking.

Friedman returned about four o'clock. He almost burst through the swinging door, hurried to his desk on which he deposited his briefcase, and as he hung his hat on the rack we turned to me and asked, "How are you getting along?"

"Fine," I answered. "I had no idea that there were so many different kinds of codes and ciphers."

"Are you having any trouble with the language?" he asked.

"Only with the vocabulary," I answered. "Kasiski uses terms that I have never encountered before."

Friedman picked up the book from my desk and noticed that it was opened at a point about three-fourths of the way through it.

"Have you read all of this," he asked.

"No sir," I answered. "I got bored with parts of the text and skipped over them. I have been concentrating on the descriptions of the codes and how they are used. I thought possibly the remainder of the text would be easier to deal with if I got some understanding of the systems."

"A good idea," said Friedman. "I also found some passages rather uninteresting when I read this book for the first time. However, the examples have been very useful to me in my preparation of texts on military cryptography and cryptanalysis. How would you like to translate Kasiski into English so it could be used as collateral reading for our courses?"

I did not like this suggestion, for I could see myself spending weeks and weeks laboring over a translation of Kasiski. I did not think that I would be able to produce anything I would be proud of if I had to try it. I ventured a counter proposal.

"It might be a lot more useful if only the examples were extracted and simply presented in English," I suggested.

Friedman showed little interest in this proposal. "Please continue with your study of these books, and after you have finished them, we'll give some further thought to the question of their translation," he said. "Since it is almost time for closing the office, I suggest that you prepare to leave now. I will return the books to the vault. You will of course report to this room tomorrow morning. You can continue your study of Kasiski then."

These were welcome words, for I was beginning to feel tired. "I will report here tomorrow morning," I replied.

He took the books from my desk and turned to the vault door, saying, "Good night, Mr. Rowlett."

"Good night, Mr. Friedman," I answered as I left the office.

✂   ✂   ✂

I spent the rest of the week plowing through the deadly prose of Kasiski and Figl. It was a boring exercise, and I was beginning to think that I was not meant to be a cryptanalyst. Friedman seemed to be content to have me spend all my time studying the German and French books on cryptography he had given me on the day I had reported for work. From the limited discussions I had with him, it became evident that he was waiting for the arrival of the other two Junior Cryptanalysts before starting me on the training program he had mentioned earlier.

I found the environment in the office quite pleasant. Major Crawford was amiable and most considerate, and he took the initiative in introducing me to the other members of his staff when they had business with him in his office. Everyone seemed friendly and cooperative. I did sense some curiosity about my duties in the attitude of some members of the staff, all of whom had their desks in the area adjacent to the office occupied by Crawford and Friedman, but who never entered it except on business.

I got my first introduction to the need for secrecy about my work on Monday morning when Major Crawford came into the office carrying a newspaper. After saying good morning in his usual friendly manner, he asked me if I had seen the article on codes and ciphers in the Washington Sunday Star of the day before. I answered that I had, and that I had read the article with considerable interest.

"It is remarkable how many individuals are fascinated by cryptography," he observed. "Yet there are only a very few persons in this country who really know anything about the subject. This article in the Sunday Star is only a superficial treatment and is hardly worth the paper it is printed on. But if one of these feature writers learned of our plans to establish a cryptanalytic group in the Office of the Chief Signal Officer, he could turn out an article which would attract a lot of attention throughout the world."

"Such widespread attention to what we are planning would certainly be to our disadvantage," he continued. "I think that Billy and I need to work out some plans for ensuring that knowledge of your group is carefully held within the Signal Corps and certainly kept out of the newspapers or any other form of the press."

When Friedman arrived, Crawford immediately launched into a discussion of the Sunday Star article with him. Crawford described his concept of keeping the existence of our group a secret and stated that all information about the group ought to be held closely within the Office of the Chief Signal Officer.

Friedman argued that it would be impossible to hide completely the existence of the group. The Civil Service Commission and the Personnel Office of the War Department had already been involved in the recruitment of its members, and it was now too late to remedy the situation insofar as the personnel actions already taken were concerned. Crawford acknowledged this point, but he pointed out that there would be continuing instances where information about the group might leak to the public and ultimately into the press.

"Mr. Rowlett," he asked me, "what do you tell your cousin and your friends when they question you about your work?"

"I tell them I am a cryptanalyst," I answered.

"And if they persist in asking you further questions, what else do you tell them," he continued.

"So far I have not been able to tell them anything, except that when they ask me what a cryptanalyst does, I answer that he works with codes and ciphers. I am not able to tell them any more for that is about all I know about it myself."

Crawford then addressed Friedman, saying, "Now, Billy, here is the sort of thing that worries me. People are going to be curious about each member of this group we are organizing, and will be asking questions of each about the nature of his duties. In the absence of instructions to the contrary, Rowlett gave straightforward answers to the question which were asked him. But when he and the other members of the group become more deeply involved in the duties we have planned for them, we could find that an embarrassing situation has developed. I think that we ought to formulate some guidelines about the kind of information that must not be discussed outside the office by the members of the group. If we do not provide proper guidelines for our cryptanalysts to follow, each will have to develop his own responses to questions about his work. Not only would this be unfair to them, but also it could result in personal embarrassment to them as well as damage to our efforts."

"I agree with you that it would not be fair to require each member of the group to establish his own guidelines, "Friedman replied.

"Good," Major Crawford responded. "I think we ought to instruct Rowlett that he should not discuss the nature or the details of his duties with any outsider and that he should not reveal the existence of his group to such outsiders. And above all, he should avoid any discussion of his duties with representatives of the press."

"Also," Major Crawford continued, "because he will inevitably be questioned by his friends, we should provide him in advance with answers which will satisfy the questioner without stimulating further curiosity. For example, if Rowlett indicates that he is not allowed to discuss the nature of his duties or the type of work he is doing, he will only encourage the questioner to become more curious and thereby generate more embarrassing questions."

"I agree," Friedman answered. "Since all the members of the group have been selected from the Junior Mathematicians Register of the Civil Service Commission, they could state, when pressed by a questioner, that they are conducting a statistical analysis of War Department communications. But under no circumstances should they give any indication that they are being trained as cryptanalysts, or that they have anything at all to do with codes and ciphers. In fact, I think we ought to instruct each member of the group to deny any knowledge of cryptography or cryptanalysis in case a direct question of that sort is put to them."

I had followed the discussion with interest, for it was giving me a new perspective on the nature of my job. Up to this point I had not felt any need for secrecy about my work. While I did not now understand why secrecy about my duties was important, I was intrigued with learning that it was. I began to sense that there might be something dramatically exciting about being a cryptanalyst. I continued to listen to the discussion, hoping to learn more about this aspect of my work.

"On Friday I learned that our second employee for the group will arrive at the end of this week," Friedman stated. "I have not yet learned when the third is expected. Originally, I had hoped that all three of them would report at the same time so that they could start their training program as a group. Now this seems impossible, so I have decided that Mr. Rowlett should immediately start working on some of the extension courses on cryptography. There is a spare copy of the draft of my text for the course in military cryptography which he can use. Since he eventually will be studying and working in the vault, I think he should start occupying it today."

"Excellent," said Crawford, "but we should make it clear to him that he is not to have access to the file cabinets that are now stored in the vault."

"Certainly," Friedman responded. "If you are in agreement he can start working in the vault immediately."

"I agree," Crawford said, looking at me with a friendly smile. "Let's unlock the vault and show him what parts of it are off limits to him."

Friedman unlocked the vault door, and opened the steel panels. "This rooms needs ventilating," he remarked as he entered the vault.

While Friedman opened the vault windows, Crawford ushered me through the doorway. Almost half of the vault was filled with filing cabinets, but in the area nearest the windows there were two large tables. Crawford took me by the arm and, pointing to the area containing the file cabinets, addressed me in a very serious tone of voice.

"These cabinets and the space they occupy are off limits to you," he said to me. "You can study and work at the tables, but you are to stay out of the area where those files are located. Under no circumstances are you to open the files or examine their contents. Do you understand me, Mr. Rowlett?"

"Yes, sir," I answered. "I will stay out of that area."

"Billy will give you your other instructions," he remarked as he turned toward the vault door.

"Billy," he said, "I think we ought to leave the vault door open while Rowlett is working in it so that there will be sufficient ventilation, especially on these warm spring days."

He then added with a twinkle in his eye, "Also, we can keep an eye on him to make sure that he keeps away from the file cabinets."

Crawford again turned his attention to me. "Young man," he said, "I'll have you shot next morning at sunrise if I catch you near those file cabinets." He then left the vault.

Friedman pointed to the two large tables near the windows. "For the time being you may work at any spot that suits you," he suggested. "Now, let me get you a copy of your first assignment, Special Text No. 165."

While Friedman opened one of the off-limits file cabinets, I selected a chair and placed it at one of the tables. Friedman took a manila folder from the file cabinet and brought it to the table I had selected. We both sat down and he explained what I was expected to do with the material.

"This is the first course in cryptography ever to be offered by the Signal Intelligence Service, and you are to be its first student," he explained. "It consists of a text and lesson assignments. I suggest that you first read the complete text very carefully before you start working on the lesson assignments. Please work as neatly as you can in preparing your answers to the questions in the lesson assignments, and you should use what we call 'cross-section' paper for working out the examples. If you have any questions about any part of the text or the lesson assignments, please do not hesitate to call on me."

I thanked him, and he left the vault, leaving the door open. I made myself comfortable at my table, and before I started working on the materials he had left with me, I satisfied my curiosity about the vault by looking it over carefully from the table at which I was sitting. After Major Crawford's remarks, I was not about to get close to the forbidden area.

The vault was evidently a typical Munitions Building room which had been converted to a secure area by the installation of a double steel door in its only entrance. The outer door was of heavy steel and was secured by a combination lock-and-bar arrangement. The inner door was formed of two lighter steel panels which folded to each side of the entrance, and these were secured by a lock operated by a key.

Only one of the walls had windows and these opened over an areaway between the fourth and fifth wings of the building. Each window was protected by a grillwork of one-half-inch diameter steel bars. The room itself was about twenty-four feet square, and the space farthest from the windows was filled with rows of filing cabinets. In the area nearest the windows were two large work tables, evidently so located in order to take fullest advantage of the ventilation and daylight. On the wall opposite the entrance door two large blackboards had been mounted. Two four-shelf bookcases occupied the wall space between the entrance door and the windows. These were filled with a variety of books, some of which were exceptionally large in size, bearing such titles as *International Code of Signals*, *ABC Code*, *Universal Trade Code*, and the like. A few chairs and a typing table completed the furnishings.

By the time I had finished sizing up my surroundings, Friedman reentered the vault carrying a quantity of large sheets of paper and a some pencils which he placed on the other of the two tables.

"I suggest you use these sheets of cross-section paper for working out the examples for the course in military cryptography that I have given you," he said. "The quarter-inch squares are a convenient size for recording the letters of a cryptogram, and I can assure you that by using it you will avoid many errors."

When Friedman left the vault, I examined the typewritten pages in the manila folder he had given me. It was about the fifth carbon copy of the manuscript, and in some spots it was almost illegible. "I ought to be a pretty good cryptanalyst if I make any sense out of this copy," I thought as I started to read the text.

I soon discovered that while Friedman's prose was not the most inspiring I had ever encountered, it was far superior to that of Kasiski and Figl. Although the style was clear and the subject matter not very difficult, the text was replete with terms and expressions which I had never before encountered. "Mono-alphabetic substitution," "multiple alphabetic substitution," "digraphic substitution," "transposition ciphers," "additives," "subtractives," and other specialized cryptologic terms were scattered throughout the text. For me it was a new vocabulary, but fortunately none of the examples in the text were complicated, and I had no difficulty at all with them. I vainly looked for some discussion of cryptanalysis, hoping to satisfy my curiosity about how codes and ciphers were broken.

By noon I had finished reading the text in spite of its poor legibility, and I was ready to start work on the lesson assignments which formed a part of the course. As I walked down the corridors of the Munitions and Navy Buildings for lunch at the Navy cafeteria, I speculated about the sort of work I would be doing. The conversation between Crawford and Friedman had given me a new perspective on the job I had taken. Evidently our work was looked on as a highly secret endeavor, for Crawford's concern about publicity was certainly genuine. Although I had really no good idea of the type of information I would be dealing with and thereby had no basis for making a judgment, I thought that being a cryptanalyst might after all be an interesting experience.

After lunch I started on the lessons, and I found that they were surprisingly easy. All I needed to do was to read the question and then search through the text for the answer, which was usually explicitly stated in the text as a sentence or a paragraph. Evidently the student was expected to copy the relevant portion of the text in formulating the answers to the questions. Although it struck me as a fairly stupid exercise, I carefully copied the answers from the text onto my lesson work sheets. The exercises in cryptography required a little more thought but only enough to ensure that I was making no clerical errors in the enciphering or deciphering processes. By the end of the day I had finished two of the lessons, and was working on the third.

Just before closing time, Friedman came into the vault and sat down at the table at which I was working. He asked about my progress. I handed him the lessons which I had completed, and he gave them a careful scrutiny.

"Very good," he commented, "but there is one fault you must promptly correct. Your printing is very poor, and many of your letters are ambiguous. For example, observe the way you form the letters 'U' and 'V'. They are barely distinguishable from each other."

As he made these remarks, he pointed to several examples in the exercise. He was right, for even I, who had printed the letters, could not tell the difference between my printed versions of the two letters.

"Except for your printing, you have done very well on these assignments. There is a small instruction booklet which will help you improve your printing," he said. "It is a Signal Corps publication which is issued to all message center clerks and shows how to form each letter of the alphabet in a standard and unique manner so it can be accurately identified. I will provide you with a copy of it tomorrow morning.

"It is now time to close the office and I will show you how the vault is to be secured for the night. It will be your responsibility to close all the windows and to lock them and to throw the bolt on the steel door to the vault and secure the combination on the lock when you depart at the end of the work day. For the time being, either Major Crawford or I will open the vault door each morning."

Friedman watched me as I locked the windows and turned out the lights. When we both stepped outside the vault door, he demonstrated for me the manner in which the vault door was to be locked. He then told me to lock the door and watched me closely as I followed the procedure he had described to me. After I had thrown the bolt and twirled the combination dial, he tested the door handle and gave the dial an additional spin.

Next morning when I arrived at the office, neither Friedman nor Crawford was there, and I had to wait until one of them came in before I could get into the vault. I was eager to complete the exercises in the course in elementary cryptography, for I wanted to learn something about cryptanalysis.

Friedman soon arrived and unlocked the vault for me. I promptly started to work on the third lesson. In a short while Friedman brought me a small, thin pamphlet.

"This is a Signal Corps Training Pamphlet," he explained. "It is used in the training of message center clerks. It contains a great deal of information about the clerical processes involved in preparing messages for electrical transmission. You should study it very carefully, especially the section which explains how the letters of the alphabet are to be printed. I suggest that you look it over before you continue with your lesson assignments."

I spent the next hour studying the training pamphlet and practicing the exercises in printing which Friedman had pointed out to me. These exercises were accompanied by diagrams indicating how each stroke of the pencil should be made in printing each of the letters of the alphabet by hand. There was also a section which emphasized the need for accuracy in the transcription of code messages. After absorbing all that seemed to be useful from the pamphlet, I went back to work on the cryptographic course and finished another two lessons before lunchtime.

When I returned from lunch Friedman came into the vault and looked over the two lessons I had finished. He seemed to be more interested in the appearance of the lesson sheets than in their content. He selected one of the lessons I had finished the day before, evidently to determine if I had made any improvement in my printing. He seemed pleased with what he found.

"You will probably finish this course by tomorrow afternoon," he remarked. "I will have your next assignment ready for you when you complete the last lesson."

As Friedman predicted, I did finish the course by midafternoon of the next day. When I gave him my lessons he handed me another typewritten manuscript to read.

"This is a draft of Special Text No. 166, Advanced Military Cryptography," he explained. "The lesson materials for this subcourse have not yet been prepared. I would like for you to read this manuscript both for content and editorial purposes. I have gone through it once, and I have noted that some parts are missing and there are a great many typographical errors. I want you to keep note of all the errors you discover in the manuscript, and I would appreciate any suggestions you have for clarifying the text."

The manuscript was merely a continuation of the subcourse I had just completed. It dealt with more complex substitution and transposition ciphers and included some information on codes and how they were to be used, but still there was nothing in the text about cryptanalysis.

➳   ➳   ➳

On Wednesday, Friedman told me that Abraham Sinkov, a young man from New York City and a graduate of City College, would report for duty on the next day. I was pleased to hear this, for not only was it an indication that the start of the training program in cryptanalysis was getting closer, but also I was finding it somewhat lonely working in the vault by myself.

The next day just before lunch I heard Mr. Flynn's voice in the outer office saying, "Mr. Friedman, here is Sinkov. He has just finished with Civilian Personnel and is ready to go to work." For the next half hour I could hear Friedman in conversation with the man that Mr. Flynn had brought to his office. I concluded that the second member of the group had now arrived and I wondered if Friedman would bring him into the vault, or have him work outside for few days just as I had done.

My curiosity was soon satisfied, for Friedman came into the vault bringing with him a young man about my age. Friedman introduced us and then explained in general terms the nature of the work of the Signal Intelligence Section, just as he had for me, except that he cautioned Sinkov not to discuss our work with anyone outside our office. He then gave Sinkov the Signal Corps training pamphlet for message center clerks and Special Text No. 165 to study as his work assignment for the afternoon. Finally, he suggested that it would be a good idea for us to have lunch together, so that Sinkov could get acquainted with the cafeteria facilities in the Navy Building.

After Friedman left us, I led the way to the Navy cafeteria. I could readily see that Sinkov was reacting to his first day of duty much as I had. During lunch we made considerable progress in getting acquainted and generally exchanged information about our respective backgrounds. I was pleased to learn that he too had studied mathematics in college and that he had taken the same Junior Mathematician examination that I had taken in August of the summer before. When we had finished our lunch and were on our way back to the vault, he showed the same curiosity about the nature of our jobs that I had felt on my first day.

"I have been wondering about what kind of work we will be doing," he remarked. "I surmise that cryptanalysis has something to do with codes. Are we part of the Secret Service?"

"I don't think so," I answered. "From what Mr. Friedman and Major Crawford have told me, we are being trained to work in the Army Signal Corps. Actually, I have been told very little about our duties except that for several months we will be involved in a special training program. It appears that our work will be very secret and I have been cautioned by both Mr. Friedman and Major Crawford to avoid any discussion of it with anyone outside the Signal Corps, and especially to avoid any contacts with newspaper reporters."

When we got back to the office, I led the way into the vault. Sinkov chose to work at the other of the two tables, and we occupied ourselves with our respective assignments. I continued my work on Special Text No. 166, which I found to be horribly typed, and, as Friedman had indicated, in need of considerable editorial correction.

At closing time Friedman came into the vault and suggested that I explain to Sinkov the procedure for securing the vault. He then bade us good night, and we promptly put away our materials and closed the vault for the night.

The next week was rather quiet. I finished my work on Special Text No. 166, and returned it to Friedman. My next assignment was to study Signal Corps Training Pamphlet Number 3, Elements of Cryptanalysis. This was a text which Friedman had prepared some years earlier as a basis for a course in military codes and ciphers which he had conducted at Camp Alfred Vail (later to become Fort Monmouth), New Jersey, and which had been printed in 1924 at the Government Printing Office. There was an appendix to this text which consisted of a set of sixteen problems in crypt-analysis with their solutions. When Friedman gave me the text, he removed the last few pages of the appendix which contained the solutions and cautioned me not to discuss the problems with Sinkov, who would independently work on them when he finished Special Text No 166. I was delighted at last to get started on cryptanalysis and immediately plunged into the text.

It did not take me very long to find that understanding the terminology of cryptanalysis was going to be my worst stumbling block in mastering the text on cryptanalysis. Such expressions as "completing the plain component," "primary components," "secondary alphabets," "cyclic phenomena," to mention a few that I found in the text, were absolutely meaningless to me. The expression that puzzled me the most appeared in the last question of Lesson No. 1, which read as follows: "What is meant by the expression 'spatial relations and linear extensions of the crests and troughs' in a frequency table?"

In spite of the unfamiliar terminology, I finally began to make sense out of the text. I resorted to the technique I had found useful in dealing with Kasiski's book; I simply worked out the examples in the text using my own ingenuity. When I started to work on the first few problems, I merely applied the techniques described in the text. I was able to do this successfully, for the techniques were simple and the cryptograms were designed so that the student could readily solve them by direct application of the procedures described in the text. As I worked further into the assignments, the problems became more difficult and some of them required several hours of study. One of the lessons resisted my efforts for several hours before I discovered the weakness which enabled me to solve it. It was a problem involving the transposition of words, modeled after the so-called Federal Army Cipher, used extensively by the Union Army during the Civil War. When I finally recovered the plaintext of the cryptogram, the elation which I felt more than made up for the effort I had expended on solving it.

During the week, Sinkov and I became better acquainted, and I found the working day much more interesting because of his company. We regularly ate lunch together, and since our backgrounds were entirely different, we had many interesting discussions. Sinkov's stories and his description of life in New York City were revelations to me, and I am sure that my yarns about life in a small Virginia town depicted for him a strikingly different way of living from that which he had experienced in New York City.

Toward the end of the week, Friedman informed us that he expected the third member of our group to report on the following Monday. He explained that he had hoped to find a fourth member for the group, but so far he had not been successful. The original plans had called for the employment of a group of four young men, all with mathematical training, each of whom would also have studied a modern language. He noted that Sinkov and I had been selected because we had studied French and German, respectively, and that the young man who was to report on Monday had studied Spanish. He also told us that he had tried to find, as the fourth member of the group, someone with a mathematical background who had studied Japanese. But since there was no one on the Civil Service register with these qualifications, he felt it might take several months to find such an individual. Accordingly, he was planning to start the three of us on the cryptanalytic training program as soon as practical after the arrival of the third member of the group. He seemed very disappointed that he had not been able to find someone with training in Japanese.

Friedman also told us the name of the third man to report was Solomon Kullback and that he was a graduate of City College. Friedman asked Sinkov if he was acquainted with him. Sinkov responded that he was slightly acquainted with a mathematics student at City College with that name.

A short while before lunch on Monday morning, while Sinkov and I were working in the vault, we heard Mr. Flynn announce the arrival of Kullback. Friedman repeated the routine that he had followed with Sinkov when he reported and, after a short discussion with the new arrival in the outer office, brought him into the vault. After introducing Kullback to us, Friedman gave him the same briefing he had given Sinkov and provided him with the message center training pamphlet and Special Text No. 165 to study as his first assignment.

When we went to lunch, Sinkov and Kullback did most of the talking, generally comparing notes on their experiences at City College. Kullback was most curious about his new job and especially its relation to mathematics. Both Sinkov and I agreed that we had seen nothing in our assignments to indicate that mathematics was at all involved. "It is nothing more than a full-time job of puzzle solving," I told Kullback.

By the latter part of the week I had finished the training text on cryptanalysis, and, when I turned my last lesson into Friedman, he seemed a bit embarrassed that he had nothing definite for me to undertake at that time. Much to my disappointment, he again brought up the subject of Kasiski and Figl and asked me if I had finished reading both texts. I reported that I had finished the book by Kasiski and about half of the book by Figl, whereupon he immediately suggested that I finish reading the book by Figl. He must have sensed my disappointment, for he then told me that he had some other duties in mind which would occupy my time until Sinkov and Kullback had both completed the lessons of training text on cryptanalysis. Meanwhile, he would try to find some texts in English which we could read. I returned to my table and started reading Figl again.

This time, Figl did not seem so uninteresting. I suppose it was because I had by now developed some familiarity with codes and ciphers, and the processes described by Figl no longer seemed pointless or mysterious. Also, I had become more familiar with his vocabulary so that I was not required to use the dictionary as frequently as before.

That night Friedman had evidently given some thought to how he could keep me occupied until Sinkov and Kullback had completed their assignments, for next morning he produced some elegantly printed brochures which he passed around for us to examine.

"Here is a selected sampling of the Riverbank Publications," he told us. "These documents were prepared at the Riverbank Laboratories in Illinois while I was employed by Colonel George Fabyan as a researcher. Fabyan, having made a fortune in cotton, established the Riverbank Laboratories to conduct research in plant genetics in the hope that improved methods for the cultivation of cotton could be developed. While I was working for him in the field of plant genetics, he became interested in the controversy being played up in the press at that time over the authorship of Shakespeare's plays. We were discussing this subject at lunch one day, and I made the remark that the matter might best be settled by the application of scientific disciplines to the analysis of the manuscripts.

"Much to my surprise Fabyan on the spot assigned me to the task of undertaking a scientific study of the question and directed me to drop my other research and to start work on it immediately. As a result of this assignment, I had to make a comprehensive study of the field of codes and ciphers, referring to all the available sources for information on the subject and its related fields. He encouraged me to document my research, and I prepared several papers on the subject which were published as reports of the Riverbank Laboratories. I have selected some of these reports for you to read now; the remaining ones will be used as supplementary texts in your special training course and they will be issued to you at the appropriate time."

I had never before heard of any controversy about the authorship of Shakespeare's plays, and I wanted to learn more about the matter.

"What was the outcome of your research?" I asked.

"While I was working at the Riverbank Laboratories, we never really completed the task we had set for ourselves," he explained. "On one of his visits to Washington, Colonel Fabyan discovered that the War Department was in need of experts in codes and ciphers, and he sent me to Washington to assist Military Intelligence in this field. After the war began I was commissioned as a Military Intelligence officer and sent to France to work with the French unit responsible for breaking German field ciphers. After the war, I returned to Riverbank. Later, I came back to Washington to work in the Office of the Chief Signal Officer. Since I have been employed by the government, I have not been able to devote any time to the Shakespearean controversy. However, our work at Riverbank did show that there was little if any validity for the claim that Bacon was the author of the Shakespearean plays, and, in fact, we showed that many of the contentions of those who argued that Bacon was the author were without foundation."

"You will note that the publications I am leaving with you are 17, 18, and 19," he continued. "The other publications which preceded these three in the series dealt with the other fields of research undertaken by the Riverbank Laboratories and have nothing at all to do with cryptography or cryptanalysis. However, there was one publication produced by Fabyan which he took great pride in and which he kept prominently displayed in his office. It was a volume about the size of an average college textbook, elegantly bound with its title and the name of its author ostentatiously imprinted on the binding. Fabyan had made his fortune as a cotton broker, and the title of the book was *What I Know About Cotton*, by George Fabyan. Inside the binding there was nothing but blank pages."

As soon as Friedman left the vault, the three of us started to examine the publications he had left. The titles were very impressive, and the pamphlets were beautifully printed. I selected the one bearing the title of *Formulae for the Solution of Geometrical Transposition Ciphers*, hoping to find some easy way of solving the type of system which had caused me so much trouble in my study of the training pamphlet on cryptanalysis. However, when I started reading it, I was disappointed with what I found, for it dealt only with the simpler types of block transpositions which had been elaborately described by both Kasiski and Figl and which even to my untutored eye afforded little if any security against cryptanalysis. I turned my attention back to Figl, fully determined to finish once and for all my assignment to read the full text before starting on the other two Riverbank Publications, which were now being eagerly devoured by Sinkov and Kullback.

᠀   ᠀   ᠀

One afternoon toward the end of the month, Crawford and Friedman received a visitor who was escorted to their office by a member of the office staff of the Secretary of War. The vault door was open and I could clearly hear the visitor being introduced as Congressman Shaffer of Virginia. This was the name of the congressman from the Ninth District of Virginia, my home district.

I had never met the congressman, and I was most curious about his visit to the Office of the Chief Signal Officer, especially to Crawford's office. My curiosity was not to be immediately satisfied, for as soon as the introductions were completed, Major Crawford closed the vault door, effectively cutting off the possibility of my overhearing any further part of the meeting.

As I speculated about why the congressman was visiting Crawford and Friedman, I began to wonder if it had any sinister implications insofar as I was concerned. I could think of nothing that I had done that might adversely affect my working for the government, but the coincidence of the incumbent congressman from my congressional district visiting the office in which I was employed seemed to me to be something more than mere chance.

After about an hour, Friedman opened the vault door and invited me to join Major Crawford and himself. In view of my earlier thoughts about the reasons for a visit by my home district congressman, I became apprehensive. When I stepped out of the vault door, which Friedman was holding open for me, I was ready to be fired summarily. Friedman closed the door behind me and invited me to have a chair by Major Crawford's desk.

"We have just had a visit from Congressman Shaffer of your state," Crawford said. "Have you ever met him?"

"Oh boy, here it comes," I thought as I answered, "I've heard quite a lot about him, but I've never met him."

"Do you know a young man by the name of John Hurt who lives in Wytheville, Virginia?" Crawford asked.

"No, sir," I answered.

"Hurt is the nephew of Congressman Shaffer, and the Congressman had learned from Civil Service that we were looking for an expert in Japanese. It happens that his nephew is proficient in Japanese and is badly in need of a job. I had hoped that you might be acquainted with the young man and could give us some information about him," Crawford explained.

"I've never met Mr. Hurt," I answered.

"Thank you," said Major Crawford. "You may return to your work."

When I returned to the vault, both Sinkov and Kullback looked at me with curiosity written over their faces. I felt that I had to offer them an explanation of why I had been called out of the vault, so I reported the gist of the short conversation to them.

Next morning Friedman, who had developed the practice of spending some time with us each morning and afternoon, told us that he was making arrangements for a Major Creswell of G-2, who was a proficient Japanese linguist, to interview a young man who knew Japanese. He told us that even if the young man, whose name was John Hurt, was fully qualified in the language, it would be very difficult for the War Department to employ him, since he was not on the Civil Service rolls.

"We have looked into every conceivable source for a Japanese expert," Friedman informed us, "but we have not been able to find anyone. I hope that if this young man meets our requirements, we will be able to employ him."

A few days later Friedman reported to us that Mr. Hurt had come to Washington and would be interviewed that afternoon. All three of us had now become highly interested in the prospects for completing the group, and we were looking forward with more than ordinary interest to learning the results of Hurt's interview with Major Creswell.

Soon after lunch a young man was ushered into the outer office by Mr. Flynn. After a short interview with Friedman and Crawford, Friedman and the young man left the office, evidently to visit Major Creswell's office. It was a good half an hour before Friedman returned alone.

"I left Mr. Hurt with Major Creswell," he reported to Crawford. "Creswell will start with a written test and will have him translate some Japanese newspaper clippings and selections from Japanese books. When Hurt finishes the written part of the test, Creswell and one of his colleagues from G-2 will give Hurt an oral examination to determine how well he speaks and understands the language. Creswell will report to us as soon as the examinations are over."

"From the few remarks that Hurt made, I got the impression that he is not much of a mathematician," Crawford remarked. "But, if he is strong in Japanese, maybe we should consider employing him, even though he may be weak in mathematics. We could have him teach our other three Junior Cryptanalysts the language, and they could apply their mathematical talents to the Japanese work that we are planning for the group. Really, Billy, I begin to despair that we will find anyone with a mathematical education who knows Japanese."

"I am afraid that I must agree with you," Friedman answered.

Inside the vault all three of us were listening intently. I was hoping that the young man would be found qualified, for it would be very pleasant to have a fellow Virginian working with us.

It was almost closing time before we heard the results of the interview. Crawford received a telephone call, and after he completed it, we overheard him report to Friedman that the interview was finished and that Major Creswell was bringing Hurt back to their office. Friedman arranged to have

Hurt wait at the civilian personnel office while he and Crawford discussed the results of the interview with Creswell.

Fortunately, as the vault door was left standing open, we could hear Creswell's report. He was most enthusiastic about Hurt's knowledge of Japanese. "I've never met an American who is as proficient in Japanese as that young man," Creswell told Friedman and Crawford. "It is unbelievable. If you don't employ him, you will be making a great mistake. He is remarkably fluent in conversational Japanese, he can read both forms of written Japanese, and his vocabulary is fabulous. He knows Japanese much better than I, or, for that matter, anyone else in G-2. And do you know, he has never been to Japan! It is most extraordinary that he has mastered the language without having spent years in Japan. My recommendation is that he be hired."

"Did you learn anything about his ability in mathematics?" Crawford asked.

"I did not discuss his education in other fields," Creswell answered. "Hurt told me that he started learning Japanese from a neighbor who had been a missionary in Japan. Later, when he was at the University of Virginia, he arranged to have Japanese students as his roommates, and all his conversations with his roommates were carried on in Japanese. He also attended Roanoke College in Virginia and Johns Hopkins in Baltimore, where he likewise was closely associated with Japanese students. His knowledge of the language is really phenomenal. Incidentally, Mr. Hurt is also proficient in German and French, and he speaks French like a native. His German, however, is not as good as his Japanese and French, but much better than average for an American. I say, hire the young man."

"Billy, I think we should take Major Creswell's advice," Crawford remarked. "We could use an extra hand in German and French."

"If you concur, I think I had better tell him that we are interested in employing him and that we will be in touch with him as soon as we can make the arrangements to have him put on the payroll," Friedman said. "He is now waiting in Mrs. Leahy's office."

"Be sure to leave no doubt in his mind that we want him to work for us," Crawford instructed Friedman. "Meanwhile I will call Congressman Shaffer and tell him that we will employ Mr. Hurt if the Civil Service Commission will give its approval."

Friedman immediately left the office. When he returned some minutes later, he reported to Crawford that Hurt was staying with his uncle overnight and that he could be contacted at any time by calling the congressman. Both Crawford and Friedman seemed pleased with the prospect of having Hurt as the fourth member of our group.

Next morning when Friedman made his usual visit with us, he reported that personnel actions were being taken to employ Mr. Hurt as the fourth member of the group. For the first time he discussed with us the importance of language in our work, and indicated that we could expect some language instruction as a part of our training. He told us that, since there was such a scarcity of qualified Japanese linguists, he and Crawford had decided that the three of us should start studying Japanese as soon as possible after Hurt joined the group. "Today Japan is our highest intelligence priority," he informed us.

Two very important things happened to me toward the end of the month. I got my first paycheck and I rented an apartment. My pay check was for the first two weeks of work (we were paid twice a month) and was for the grand sum of $83.33, only about eight dollars less that I had received for a full month's work as a school teacher in Franklin County, Virginia.

The apartment was in the old Boulevard Apartment building at 2121 New York Avenue, N.W., within easy walking distance of the Munitions Building. If I hurried, I could have lunch at home instead of having to eat at the Navy cafeteria, in which I was now beginning to lose interest.

The apartment was the barest minimum offered for living purposes in the area. It consisted of a single room, with a so-called Murphy bed which folded up into the wall when not in use and a small kitchenette and bath. It was furnished and rented for $50.00 per month with a free month's rent if it was leased for a full year. My wife and I felt that we could make out with a one-room apartment for at least a couple of months until we could find something a bit larger but still within our means.

Sinkov soon finished the training pamphlet on cryptanalysis, and Friedman kept us supplied with a variety of odd tasks while Kullback, the last arrival, caught up with us. We prepared and checked out the exercises in encipherment and decipherment which Friedman was incorporating into his subcourse on advanced military cryptography, proofread the galley sheets for the text on elementary military cryptography which had arrived from the Government Printing Office, studied the Army regulations applicable to the Signal Corps in order to learn the duties and responsibilities of the Chief Signal Officer and otherwise occupied ourselves with a variety of odd jobs assigned to us by Friedman. During this time, Sinkov and I kept urging Kullback to get on with his studies so that we could start the next phase of our training program.

Hurt also started spending a few hours with the group each day, studying the texts that Friedman had first given us. He was not yet officially hired, but he had agreed to start work on the training courses in anticipation of his formal employment.

I found Hurt to be a most interesting individual, and we soon became very good friends. He had been born in Wytheville, Virginia, and had attended the University of Virginia, Roanoke College, and Johns Hopkins in Baltimore. Also, in pursuit of his interest in studying French, he had spent several months in Paris, where he had met a young lady from America who was also studying there. They had fallen in love, and when they returned to America, they announced to the young lady's parents their intention to be married. Their plans met with strong objections from the girl's parents, who were Jewish, and who had no desire for their daughter to marry an indifferent Protestant.

Hurt finally overcame their objections by accepting the Jewish faith, thus removing the major obstacle. The marriage, however, did not last long, and Hurt found himself at loose ends, without funds, and sorely in need of a job. He had contacted his uncle, Congressman Shaffer, who learned from the Civil Service Commission that the War Department was in need of a Japanese expert.

The day that Kullback turned in his final lesson from the text on cryptanalysis, Friedman presented each of us with a folder that contained a single lesson assignment identified as Problem No. 1. When he passed out the folders, he explained that for the time being we would individually work on each exercise as the first few lessons were relatively simple and involved very little clerical work. Later on, as the problems became more complex, we would form two teams for working on the training problems, both to speed up the preparation of the statistical data essential to the solution of the problems and to get us accustomed to working as teams. He also told us that he had learned that Hurt's employment would soon be approved, but that Hurt would not participate in the cryptanalytic training program with us until he was officially employed by the government.

"Your first assignment is to solve the cryptogram of Problem Number 1," he told us. "First try to determine if it is enciphered by a substitution or a transposition system, and after you have made this determination, you can proceed with the recovery of the text of the message and the keying system employed for the encipherment of the message."

If Crawford and Friedman wanted to stimulate a competitive spirit among the members of the group, they could not have picked a better way of doing it. Here we were, the three of us just like race horses at the starting line, waiting for Friedman to fire the starting gun. I do not remember just what sort of a system was employed to encipher the message text for our first lesson assignment, but it must not have been very secure for all three of us finished the solution within a couple of hours. For the next few days, Friedman kept us supplied with exercises which he usually handed us without giving us any information about the nature of the cryptographic system involved. He evidently felt it was good discipline for us to learn on our own to diagnose the cryptograms and identify the type of system employed. Occasionally, when he found that we had come to a dead end in our analysis, he would give us a hint or a clue as to what to look for in the cryptograms. The first eight or ten problems were soon completed, and I was pleased to find that I was able to keep pace with the others. In fact no one of us stood out in front, and although I tried hard to outstrip the others, I was pleased that I was not left behind in the competition.

I remember that one of the early problems resisted our attacks for so long that Friedman, who was watching our progress now very closely, finally decided that we should set it aside for the time being and return to it later. He seemed to be amused that we had been unsuccessful in solving the cryptogram. I was personally glad to put the message aside, for it had seemed to me that there was not enough data provided for us to determine the type of system that was being used. Kullback was the first to solve the message, but Sinkov and I did not get the solution until some time later.

Crawford moved out of the office which he had occupied with Friedman, and Friedman took the desk Crawford had been using. Friedman was soon joined by a most interesting individual, Captain Norman Lee Baldwin, who had been assigned the responsibility for organizing the Second Signal Service Company, the intercept arm of the Signal Intelligence Service.

Captain Baldwin frequently joined us for lunch and we found him to be a most delightful raconteur. His favorite stories dealt with the English, and often he would assume an imitation British accent when he was telling one of his stories. Some of them were priceless and so ribald in nature that they might not be printed even today.

Baldwin was also an avid radio amateur, and he spent a lot of his time communicating with radio amateurs all over the world. He had been sent to China by the Army shortly after World War I, and he was proud of the fact that he personally had transmitted the first radio message ever to be sent from the Chinese mainland. He had also been in Siberia and had worked with the Russians, and I found the stories he told of his experiences in Asia, with both the Chinese and Russians, to be one of the highlights of my early days with the SIS.

Captain Baldwin was also proficient in the Chinese language, and it was he who gave me my first instruction in the use of a Chinese character dictionary. I had never really understood the nature of a Chinese ideograph, and he enjoyed explaining to me the system employed in indexing the characters in Chinese dictionaries. In odd moments and spare time, I learned to identify the radicals and count the number of strokes so that I could use a Chinese character dictionary with a fair degree of facility. I found this instruction to be useful when later on we began our serious study of Japanese under Hurt.

By the end of June we had settled down to a regular and what I found to be a very pleasant routine, devoting most of out time to the study of crypt-analysis. Hurt, at the time he was officially employed, had joined us in the cryptanalytic training program. Friedman organized the four of us into two teams, with Abe and Kully on one team and Johnnie and I on the other. Occasionally, Friedman would have some other duties for us, but these usually could be disposed of without significant interference with our studies, and we were able to spend almost all of our time on the training program.

CHAPTER 3

WE DISCOVER THE BLACK CHAMBER

ONE WARM AND humid morning in late June, 1930, Friedman came into the vault and asked us, Kully, Abe, and me, to accompany him to the G-2 area of the Munitions Building. He escorted us from the third floor, fourth wing, where our office was located, down the stairs to the second-floor corridor without any explanation of the purpose of our mission. I clearly remember that I was wearing for the first time some brand-new summer clothes — a blue serge jacket, white pin-striped trousers, and white suede leather shoes. I recalled that as we walked along the second-floor corridor behind Friedman, I was feeling very proud of myself for being dressed so well for what, from Friedman's attitude, seemed to be a very special sort of mission.

When we arrived at the intersecting corridor of the seventh wing, Friedman swung to the left without missing a step. We followed closely behind. The area seemed deserted. After a few steps he turned abruptly to his right and stopped in front of a steel door, similar to the one on the vault in which we worked, located behind a wooden railing built along the corridor wall.

He took from his inside coat pocket a small card and started to operate the combination lock on the front of the steel door. We watched with high curiosity. When he had set the final number, he threw the bolt and swung open the door, exposing the second steel door behind it. He again reached into his pockets, extracted a key, and unlocked the inner door, which he opened with a flourish.

The area behind the second door was pitch dark. He now produced a small box of matches, lit one, and by its light sought out the pull cord of the switch controlling the nearest ceiling light. When the light came on, it revealed a windowless room about twenty-five feet square, almost completely filled with filing cabinets, arranged back to back in double rows with barely enough space between their fronts for the drawers to be pulled open. The only other furniture in the room was a small table and a chair just inside the vault door. Friedman's next move was to switch on the fans mounted on the walls to their highest speed and to turn on the remaining three overhead lights.

While he was going through this process, the three of us remained just outside the door, waiting for his instructions. He came back to the vault door, peered up and down the corridor, and then waved us inside the vault. When we were all inside, he set the inner steel panels slightly ajar and turned to us, saying in a solemn and very imposing manner, "Welcome, gentlemen, to the secret archives of the American Black Chamber."

I was puzzled by the seriousness with which he made the announcement. I remember that I silently thought that it had been truly dark in that room before he lit the match and turned on the first ceiling light. I had never heard of anything called the American Black Chamber, and the words meant nothing special to me. However, I said nothing and neither did Abe and Kully; we just stood, looking as impressed as we could, surveying the dust-covered contents of the room.

Friedman then explained that the room contained the working files of a highly secret cryptanalytic organization that had operated in New York for several years and which had been closed down during the previous summer. G-2, Washington, War Department, had an interest in this operation and had brought its files to the Munitions Building, where they were being held in storage. These files had been turned over to the Chief Signal Officer for the use of the Signal Intelligence Service, and it was our duty to organize and catalog them.

Friedman asked that we spend the next two hours looking over the files in order to familiarize ourselves with their contents, pointing out that as the first order of business we should try to locate all the information they contained about German Army field ciphers and Japanese diplomatic codes and ciphers. He then produced a document from one of the file cabinets which he identified as an inventory of the contents of room and which he proposed that we use as a guide to help locate the German and Japanese materials. After explaining that he would return by lunchtime, he left, carefully adjusting the steel doors so that the contents of the room were not visible from the outside corridor.

After Friedman left, Abe stretched out his arm and drew his index finger across the top of the nearest cabinet. When he noted the thick smudge of dust on his finger, he grimaced.

I removed my new blue jacket and hung it on one of the file cabinet drawers which I opened. After Abe and Kully had likewise disposed of their jackets, Kully turned to Abe with an impish grin on his face, pointing to my new and immaculate white trousers. Then they both laughed.

We now started to examine the materials in the file cabinets. In a few minutes we forgot all about the thick dust that covered everything in the room; and we forgot about the summer heat and the poor ventilation. We were completely hypnotized by what we were finding. Here were the secret records which dealt with the American code-breaking activity sponsored by the United States State Department and the Director of Military Intelligence, United States War Department. Here were copies of the secret codes and ciphers of many of the great nations of the world. Here were the work sheets used in breaking Japanese diplomatic codes. Here were the translations of Japanese messages relating to the negotiations of the Washington Naval Conference, to which were attached letters of appreciation signed by high officials of the United States government. Here were the decipherments of the German field ciphers of 1917 and 1918 with descriptions of how the cipher systems were broken. Here were hundreds of copies of unsolved code messages sent from and addressed to every important nation in the world. Here was also a wealth of other cryptologic items which could be appreciated only after hours and hours of detailed study. King Solomon's mines could have offered no greater treasure for us.

We were so entranced by the contents of the vault that we lost all track of the passage of time. Friedman's return startled us. He found three sweaty and grimy, but starry-eyed Junior Cryptanalysts. Kully had a dirty streak across his forehead. Abe's shirt was spotted with smudges of dust and soaked with perspiration. My brand-new white pin-striped trousers were no longer white — they were a dirty mess.

Friedman looked us over and, after making a remark with an amused smile about "what a dirty business cryptanalysis can be", suggested that we wash up and go to lunch. He asked for the three of us to plan to spend some time at his desk after we finished lunch, stating that we would be joined by Hurt for an important discussion about our future duties.

In the early afternoon the four of us met with Friedman in his office. He settled us in chairs around his desk and carefully closed the office doors. By the time he sat down behind his desk we were literally on the edges of our chairs, waiting for him to open the meeting, and hoping to learn more about our future activities. As for me, it was the most electric moment that I had yet experienced, and all sorts of romantic ideas were running through my mind.

Friedman began his remarks by describing the work of what he called "Yardley's Bureau" in fairly general terms. He indicated that it was a joint intelligence activity conducted by the State Department and War Department G-2, with the State Department supplying the bulk of the funds needed for its operation. This activity had been conducted in New York City instead of Washington because of legal limitations imposed on the appropriated funds from which it was financed. It was directed by Herbert O. Yardley, a former State Department cryptographer who had been commissioned and put in charge of the War Department's World War I cryptanalytic organization. It operated under the cover of a commercial enterprise known as Code Compiling Company, Inc., at 52 Vanderbilt Avenue, New York, N.Y.

In the summer of 1929, when the new Secretary of State, Mr. Henry Stimson, first learned of the nature of Yardley's activities, he had summarily issued an order abolishing "Yardley's Bureau." He further ordered that the organization be closed out in the shortest possible time and flatly laid down the rule that no other such activity would be tolerated in the State Department while he was serving as Secretary of State. G-2 had looked upon this order as a major disaster to the American intelligence effort and had tried to have it set aside. However, Stimson was adamant and G-2 finally had to accept his decision.

When the Director of Military Intelligence found that he would be unable to have the order of the Secretary of State reversed, he had consulted the Chief Signal Officer and had proposed that a code-breaking operation be set up in the War Department under the administration of the Chief Signal Officer. He had offered the funds, previously contributed by G-2 to the State Department in support of Yardley's operation, to the Chief Signal Officer for the purpose of hiring a small group of young men who would be trained in all aspects of cryptology. It was hoped that these would become the cadre of an effective cryptanalytic organization to undertake the future production of intelligence by breaking the code messages of the other great powers of the world.

The Chief Signal Officer was already charged with the responsibility for the production of codes and ciphers for the Army and, since it was perceived that this new activity would improve the cryptologic capability of the War Department, the proposal was enthusiastically received by the Chief Signal Officer. The funds made available to the Chief Signal Office were barely sufficient to provide for the employment of four Junior Cryptanalysts and one Cryptographic Clerk, and the four of us represented the realization of the first step in the implementation of the long-range plan to develop a greatly enhanced cryptologic capability in the War Department.

Friedman explained that the mission of the Signal Intelligence Service, which was the official term applied to the new organization, was two-fold. The first and most important objective was to ensure that the United States military codes, for both peacetime and wartime use, were the best and most secure that could be devised. The other objective was to undertake the peacetime interception and analysis of foreign code and cipher communications for the production of intelligence for use by the nation's top level planners and policy makers, and in the event of war, to be prepared to intercept and solve the enemy communications at all levels so that the commanders of our armed forces would be provided with the intelligence necessary for their successful prosecution of the war.

He also provided us with more information on the intercept service then being organized and told us that it would be staffed by the most competent radio operators in the Signal Corps. Some of these operators had already been assigned to the intercept organization and were currently being given special training to fit them for intercept activities. He added that the first of a world-wide network of intercept stations was in the process of being set up at Fort Monmouth, New Jersey.

He impressed on us the need for secrecy, pointing out that both the Director of Military Intelligence and the Chief Signal Officer were fearful that if officials of the State Department became aware of the new cryptanalytic activity being established the State Department might take steps at the highest level of the government to have the new organization abolished. He explained that the organization had been administratively located in the Office of the Chief Signal Officer rather than in G-2, for if its existence became known to the Secretary of State, its continuation could be justified as being essential to the support of the officially assigned responsibilities of the Chief Signal Officer to design, compile, store, and issue all cryptographic materials required by the War Department and to supervise the use of all Army cryptographic systems.

Friedman then reaffirmed that for the next several months the four of us would spend part of our time studying cryptology with the aim of mastering all that was currently known about cryptography and cryptanalysis; the remainder of our working time would be devoted to the production of improved codes and ciphers for use by the War Department. He emphasized his conviction that all currently used United States codes and ciphers were "woefully inadequate, outdated, inefficient and — worst of all — insecure." He added that it was imperative that we get started as soon as possible on the improvement of all cryptographic systems used in the War Department so that at least the Army would have adequate cryptographic security if the United States should become involved in another war.

He then advanced his conviction that cryptography would have to be mechanized if we were to achieve the security and efficiency in our military communications which modern warfare would demand. He pointed out the advantages resulting from the introduction of tanks and aircraft in the last war and argued that similar advances in communications could be achieved by introducing machines into the message center processes at all levels of the Army. He spoke disparagingly of the efficiency and security provided by the bulky codes that had conventionally been used throughout the government, elaborating on the amount of time and effort required for their replacement and the problems of secure storage and distribution inherent in the very nature of code and cipher systems. He admitted, however, that it would be several years before adequately secure and efficient cipher machines would be available and that the War Department would have to continue to employ the conventional code systems until cipher machines could be produced in sufficient quantities to supply the message centers from the top echelons of the War Department down through division level in the Army.

When we asked him if we would be spending much time with the Yardley files, he told us that for the time being we were only expected to ensure that the files were in good order. He then explained that he would from time to time select appropriate materials from them for us to study as part of our training.

As an example of how he expected to use the Yardley files, he sketched out for us the work that had been done in France during the last war on the German field army cipher known as the ADFGVX cipher. He explained that during the war no satisfactory general solution to the system had been devised. Only occasionally could the Allied cryptanalysts recover one of the keys used by the Germans, and this could be achieved only under very special circumstances. He identified this type of solution as the "Painvain Solution," named after its inventor, Captain Georges Painvain, who was a French Army cryptanalyst he had worked with during World War I, a man whose cryptanalytic ability was held in highest esteem by both the French and the Americans. He then expressed his belief that a general solution to the ADFGVX Cipher could be devised by which all messages in this type of system could be read without the need for the special conditions upon which the wartime solution had depended. He told us that he planned to have us undertake a study of the wartime traffic as one of our first research projects after we had completed our cryptanalytic training course.

He then went on to point out that in the discussions which had led up to the establishment of the Signal Intelligence Service, G-2 had assigned general priorities to be followed for the work on foreign communications. Japan was given first priority, followed by Germany and Italy in that order, with all the other nations of the world grouped together as the fourth priority. He remarked that with the limited resources available to us and with the tremendous amount of work which had to be done on the improvement of the War Department systems, we might not be able to start work on producing intelligence from Japanese intercepts for several years. "However," he added, "we are going to get our intercept service into operation and start collecting Japanese messages so that when we do get to work on the Japanese codes, we will not suffer from lack of intercepted materials to analyze."

CHAPTER 4

WAR DEPARTMENT SECURITY IN 1930

I N 1930 A MUCH-NEEDED change in the responsibility for handling communications security matters was taking place in the War Department. Before that year, the responsibility for higher echelon War Department cryptographic systems, as distinguished from the so-called Army field ciphers, was split between the Chief Signal Officer and the Adjutant General. Under the older arrangement, the Chief Signal Officer was responsible for the design and compilation of the cryptographic systems used by the War Department for departmental communications, and the Adjutant General was separately responsible for their storage, printing, and use. Early in 1930 this split in responsibility was eliminated, and the Chief Signal Officer was given full responsibility for all phases of War Department communications security. One of the most important actions resulting from this realignment was the transfer of the War Department code room from the Adjutant General's offices in the State, War and Navy Building to the War Department Message Center, which was located in the rear of the fourth wing, third floor of the Munitions Building.

All messages to and from the War Department still had to be cleared through the Adjutant General, whether classified or unclassified. Unclassified messages were transmitted in the clear, that is, without being encoded, while classified messages had to be processed through the War Department code room, where they were encoded in an appropriate cryptographic system. They were then transmitted over the War Department radio net or over commercial communications facilities such as RCA or Western Union. Normally all messages between Washington and the headquarters of the nine Corps Areas in the continental United States and between Washington and the headquarters of the three overseas departments — Panama, Hawaii and Manila — were handled by the War Department radio net operated by the Signal Corps. Messages to the various military attachés were usually handled by the commercial communications companies.

When the War Department code room was moved from the State, War and Navy Building to the Munitions Building, only two code room employees were transferred from the Adjutant General's Office to perform the code room duties; the other skilled cryptographers elected to remain with the Adjutant General's Office and were assigned to other duties. The two individuals who transferred to the Signal Corps were career cryptographers who had been working continuously in the War Department code room for nearly a quarter of a century. They had made the transfer because each had only a few months of service left before retirement, and they preferred to transfer to the Signal Corps, where they could continue their cryptographic work rather than to remain with the Adjutant General's Office and have to accept new and unfamiliar duties. The work load in the code room was more than the two employees could handle, and because no funds were available at that time for the employment of civilians for this purpose, the Chief Signal Officer planned to assign selected enlisted military personnel to complete the staffing. The selection and assignment of military personnel took longer than had been expected with the result that the code room was seriously overloaded.

When the effects of the personnel shortage in the code room became apparent, Major Crawford and the Officer in Charge of the War Department Message Center were directed to work out a solution. The only source of cryptographers trained in the War Department code rooms procedures were the individuals who had elected not to transfer to the Signal Corps, and it was out of the question, both because of bureaucratic pride and the expressed desires of those involved, to request the temporary assignment of some of these individuals until the Signal Corps could procure the additional staff required for full code room operation. The solution which was finally reached was that Sinkov, Kullback, and I would be detailed to the code room for part-time duty as required until the military personnel could be assembled and trained. Both Friedman and Crawford considered this arrangement to be advantageous because it not only alleviated the code room personnel shortage but it also provided an opportunity for the three of us to obtain practical experience in cryptography under actual code room conditions. Since the requirement for our assistance was limited to peak-load situations, which occurred only one or twice a week, the interference with our training program was tolerable.

I was more affected by this arrangement than Abe and Kully, because all the incoming and outgoing messages had to be typed in final form before they cleared the code room, and I was called on more frequently for this detail since I was the only one who was qualified as a typist. For me this was a most valuable experience, for it gave me a practical understanding of the problems associated with the code room processes. This greatly influenced my later work on our own cryptographic systems.

The two men who transferred from the Adjutant General's Office were the finest sort of persons to work with. They were most considerate and helpful and extremely patient with each of us. At first I sensed some reserve in their attitude, but after a few days this disappeared. Mr. Benjamin F. Smith, the senior of the two, regularly worked the day shift. The other cryptographer, Mr. Williams, preferred the night shift. Mr. Williams usually reported to the code room in the middle of the afternoon so he could spend some time with Mr. Smith to ensure continuity in the code room operation. Since there was no third, or graveyard, shift, Mr. Williams usually worked until all the messages which had arrived on his shift were processed. Sometimes this meant that Mr. Williams would have to work until the small hours of the morning when the traffic was heavy; when it was light and there was no backlog, he made up for the long hours he had spent on other days by leaving as soon as he had cleared the last message through the code room.

There was one facet of this detail that I particularly enjoyed. Mr. Smith took great pleasure in reminiscing about his code room experiences and especially about the happenings during the war years of 1914–1918. One of his most fascinating stories dealt with the circumstances of what he called the armistice message, the official message from the American Expeditionary Forces to Washington confirming the signing of the Armistice. According to Mr. Smith, all code room facilities on both sides of the Atlantic became heavily overloaded during the last weeks of the war. Practically all classified messages were being assigned the highest handling precedence by their originators, and the point was reached where there were so many messages with the highest precedence indicator that these were handled by the Washington code room on a first-come, first-served basis, and messages without a precedence indicator would be simply ignored. The volume of messages was so great in early November of 1918 that even the highest priority messages required several days before they cleared the code room and were delivered to the addressee.

When the armistice was signed, the American newspapers received word of it through the news reports cabled in clear from France, and immediately headlines about the event began appearing in all the leading newspapers. Reporters besieged the White House and the War Department demanding confirmation from Washington of the items that were pouring into America from the news correspondents in Europe. The Secretary of War not only was the target of all the American newspapers but also was under pressure from the White House to provide official confirmations of the news reports about the armistice. Finally, after several hours, the pressure became so great on the Secretary of War that he left his regular office and occupied a desk in the code room area so that he could personally direct the search for the official statement on the armistice from the American Expeditionary Forces.

My first assignment that had any real responsibility occurred when I was selected to work the night shift in the War Department code room. For several years Mr. Williams had taken his annual leave during the summer so that he could spend some time in his home town in the Midwest. He had made special plans for this, his last year, for on retirement he was moving back to his home town and needed to make arrangements for a place to live. The officer in charge of the message center requested that one of us be released to work in the code room for a short while so that Williams could be granted the leave which was so important to him. My ability as a typist made me the prime candidate for the detail.

When Friedman approached me with the proposal that I fill in for Mr. Williams, he assured me that I would be given commensurate time from other duties to make up for any time that I lost from my cryptanalytic training. He reaffirmed his intentions to keep all the members of the group together in the training program and indicated that the other three would be given other duties so that I would not fall behind. This most gracious promise overcame any reservations that I might have had at taking the assignment. Arrangements were made for me to spend several nights working with Mr. Williams before he started his annual leave, to ensure that I would be fully prepared to cover the night shift during his absence.

It was a pleasure to work with Mr. Williams. He was the most efficient cryptographer that I ever met. He had actually memorized the most frequent code groups in all the codes then being used, so that when he was encoding or decoding a message he needed to refer to the code book for only the most infrequently occurring groups. For example, when he decoded a message, he would insert a fresh message blank in his typewriter, place the incoming code message alongside it, and start typing the clear text of the message directly from the code text as if he were translating a foreign language. Only when he came to a group whose meaning was not known to him would he refer to the code book, and in fact he could process most of the routine messages without ever having to refer to the code book.

The first night of my new assignment, Mr. Williams did all the work, while I observed. When I reported for work the next night, he suggested that I do the work while he watched. There was only a small amount of traffic on the second night, and I was able to handle all of it without any difficulty. The next night when we tried the same approach, a large amount of traffic from the Ninth Corps Area started to arrive just after sundown when the San Francisco transmitter became active, and Mr. Williams, who I am sure was now getting bored watching me fumble through the code room procedures, processed the San Francisco messages while I handled the other traffic. The next few nights were fairly routine, and I was able to cope with the workload without undue difficulty. Mr. Williams seemed satisfied that I could handle the shift and started his leave.

I found this assignment very rewarding. I was doing important work for which I was personally responsible, and this was entirely different from being a student, where I dealt only with practice materials and theoretical situations. Another aspect which I enjoyed was the atmosphere of the War Department Message Center. During the night shift, usually after sunset in California, the transcontinental radio circuits between Washington and San Francisco became active. The radio signals were received at Fort Myers and relayed to the Munitions Building by wire circuits which terminated in the War Department Message Center, where the terminal of each circuit was manned by an operator. Usually the operators had little to do until the atmospherics cleared up and the circuits were open, but they had to work feverishly to handle all the traffic while the radio-circuit conditions were favorable.

Sometimes when the atmospheric conditions were especially favorable, it was possible for the operators in the Munitions Building to work directly with the overseas operators in Panama and Hawaii. As a youth I had become interested in all aspects of amateur radio and, since I was never fortunate enough to own my own transmitter, I found watching the operators in action at their posts, sending and receiving messages from overseas transmitters, to be most exciting.

Usually about ten o'clock in the evening an operator who could be spared would be sent to the Army mess hall in the Quartermaster Corps Barracks just a short distance from the Munitions Building. He would soon return with quantities of coffee and milk and a large basket filled with a variety of sandwiches, bread, cake, and marmalade. These would be arrayed on a large table just outside the code room area, and all the operators who were free would assemble around the table for the night shift break. Each night that I was on duty in the code room, one of the enlisted men would knock on the code room door and invite me to join them.

During the time that I was substituting for Mr. Williams, I became acquainted with an officer who was to play an influential role not only in the future of the Signal Intelligence Service but also in the formation of the national cryptologic effort after World War II. This was Captain Carter W. Clarke, who at that time was in charge of the transmitting and receiving station at Fort Myers as well as the Signal Center in the Munitions Building. He had full access to all areas, and each night when he visited the Signal Center he would spend some time with me in the code room. We soon became well acquainted, and he showed considerable interest in my personal background and education, which I felt free to discuss with him. He very circumspectly kept our conversations away from the Signal Intelligence Service activities, and I did not volunteer any information about my regular duties there. These visits marked the beginning of a series of official relations between us which continued until he retired from his last military active duty assignment with the Central Intelligence Agency in the late Fifties.

Another advantage of this assignment was the insight which I gained in code room operations and procedures. This proved to be especially valuable when I became involved in the development of cipher machines for use by the army several years later.

What I found most discouraging in this assignment was the poor security provided for the classified War Department messages by the out-dated systems and the inadequate security practices which had been followed for years and which were still in use. There were only three categories of classified messages; these were For Official Use Only, Confidential, and Secret. It was the accepted practice to transmit unclassified messages over the War Department radio circuits in clear; however, when unclassified messages were transmitted over commercial circuits where the government was charged for each word transmitted, the texts were always encoded, since the encoding process produced a much shorter telegram than if the message was sent in clear. When the message was classified, it was always encoded, regardless of whether it was to be transmitted over commercial circuits or over the War Department radio networks. With the exception of secret messages between G-2, Washington, and the military attachés, the War Department Telegraph Code was used for all classified messages transmitted over the War Department Radio nets. The classification of the message was always given by the first group of the code message, and this was the sole distinction among messages in the three categories of classified traffic.

The War Department Telegraph Code had been in use for many years and was considered compromised simply because it had been used for such a long time. The only system of any sophistication was the one used for the military attaché messages, and this was a small code of 10,000 groups that was never used unenciphered.

Even at this early point in my cryptanalytic training I was shocked by the insecurity of many of the code room practices. When I asked both Mr. Williams and Mr. Smith for their opinions about the security of the procedures which they had been following, they readily admitted that they had serious doubts about them. Smith told me confidentially that he had several times expressed his doubts about the security of the code room practices, but he had met with so much resistance to change that he had given up pursuing the subject further with his superiors. By the time my assignment to the code room ended, I had resolved to register my concern with

Friedman and recommend to him that better cryptographic systems and procedures needed to be put into effect for the War Department communications as a matter of greatest urgency.

When Mr. Williams returned to duty, the personnel situation had eased, and one enlisted man with previous code room experience was ready to start working full time on the day shift. Our training would no longer be interrupted by temporary assignments to code room duty.

I promptly reported to Friedman my concern about the systems being used and the practices being followed in the War Department code room. He listened to all I had to say with interest, and at the end of my discourse he told me that my observations confirmed his own fears.

"I have been aware of the inadequacy of the War Department cryptography for some time," he told me. "However, it is impossible to take any steps to improve our code room practices and our cryptographic systems until the full responsibility for these matters is given to the Chief Signal Officer. For the past few years I have been urging the introduction of better security practices, but because the Adjutant General has part of the responsibility for War Department cryptography, no action can be taken without his concurrence, which has become increasingly more difficult to obtain. Finally, the Director of Military Intelligence and the Chief Signal Officer, because of their concern about the security of War Department cryptographic systems and procedures, persuaded the Secretary of War that the Chief Signal Officer should be made responsible for all phases of War Department communications security, and an order to this effect was issued only a few months ago. The most important consideration at the moment is that the Chief Signal Officer has not yet received authorization to use the funds which had been budgeted for the printing of new codes and the production of better cipher systems. Until this authorization is received, which should be within the next few weeks, we are at a standstill in our actions to improve our communications security.

"I am glad that you came to me with your concern," Friedman continued. "One of the important objectives of the Signal Intelligence Service is to overhaul the outdated cryptography of the War Department and to replace the current concept of clumsy code-book systems with electro-mechanical cipher machines which will automatically encipher and decipher our classified messages. I have designed such a machine, and several are now being built. In about two years the construction of enough of these cipher machines to equip the code rooms in Washington, Panama, Manila, and Honolulu will be completed. Until these new machines are ready, we will have to continue the practices and systems that the War Department has been employing for almost half a century. But I assure you, Mr. Rowlett, that in the next few years we are going to revolutionize the security of our governmental communications and give our country the most secure code and cipher systems of all time. And you and your associates are going to be deeply involved in bringing this about."

My discussion with Friedman left me in good spirits, for I was convinced that he was fully aware of the deficiencies that had concerned me. I could understand his reasons for not taking immediate action to introduce improvements. After my experience with the code books I had been using for the past few weeks, I was intrigued with his remarks about cipher machines. I was also stimulated to speculate about the nature of the cryptographic systems being used by the U.S. Navy and the other departments of the government. I also wondered about the future of the cryptography of the other great nations of the world, and how much security their systems would provide. I remembered my discussions with Captain Baldwin and John Hurt regarding the written languages of Japan and China, and I tried to imagine what sort of cipher machines might be used for the encipherment of Chinese characters.

By the end of 1930 we had added two more names to the personnel roster of the Signal Intelligence Service. Friedman wanted to have a young chemist on his staff, who he hoped would become proficient in the field of secret inks, which at that time was one of the responsibilities of the Signal Intelligence Service. A young man by the name of Larry Clark, a chemistry major who was attending night classes at George Washington University, was hired as a clerk. The other new member of the Staff was Lieutenant Mark Rhodes, a Signal Corps officer, who was the first regular army officer to be assigned full time to the study of cryptology.

There were now eight of us in the Washington component of the Signal Intelligence Service. Captain Baldwin was spending all his time with the Second Signal Service Company. Major Crawford had been transferred to another post, and Major Spencer B. Akin had replaced him.

CHAPTER 5

THE CODE COMPILATION PROGRAM

I T WAS NOT LONG after our assignments to temporary duty in the War Department code room were finished that Friedman announced he was ready for us to start to work on the code compilation program. Evidently this was a very important action to him, for he arranged a special meeting of the entire staff of the Signal Intelligence Service, at which he outlined the program he had planned for us to follow.

Friedman opened the meeting by reviewing the state of cryptography as it was practiced at that time by the United States governmental departments. Each of the major departments and bureaus of the government had its own code-and-cipher organization, the most important ones being the State, War, and Navy departments. There was little exchange of information among the cryptographic groups of these three departments, since each regarded the security of its classified telegrams as a matter of departmental responsibility. The systems used by these three departments were based on large code books, designed mainly for the economical transmission of messages, rather than for providing cryptographic security. In some cases where the subject matter of the message was especially sensitive, the message, after being encoded, might be superenciphered to add the extra security desired. These superencipherments were applied, however, somewhat reluctantly by the code rooms, for they were time-consuming and in all cases added delays in the handling of the messages.

In peacetime, both the codes used at War Department levels and the code-and-cipher systems used in the field were printed at the Government Printing Office. In time of war, the codes and ciphers needed for field use would be produced by special printing plants located at appropriate field headquarters.

The communications security arrangements of the War Department were scheduled to be overhauled, and the Signal Intelligence Service was to perform this mission. The immediate plans called for the preparation of two series of codes, one to be designated as War Department Confidential

Codes, to be used for messages classified CONFIDENTIAL, and the other, designated as War Department Staff Codes, for messages classified SECRET. Several codes, or editions as they were called, would be prepared in each series, so that if an edition was compromised, either through loss of a copy or by excessive use of the code, the edition in use would be recalled and the next edition in the series would be put into effect.

The most important reform planned was that when the new codes were issued, none of them would ever be used without appropriate superencipherment, and secure superencipherment systems for use with the new codes would have to be prepared. Messages of the FOR OFFICIAL USE ONLY category would still be encoded in the War Department Telegraph Code, since this category was not considered sensitive enough to require cryptographic protection. The use of the Military Intelligence Code for enciphering messages between Washington and the military attachés would be continued, and it would always be enciphered.

Several editions of the codes to be used for confidential and secret messages would be prepared, so that a replacement could be issued in case one was discovered to have been stolen or otherwise compromised. The usage of each code would be carefully monitored so that when the volume of messages prepared in it was great enough for it to be recovered by cryptanalysis, the code would be replaced. The preparation of the codes to be used at army and division levels would be held in abeyance until the compilation of the departmental codes was completed.

As he displayed a copy of a manuscript for a code which he had finished preparing in late 1929, he told us our first task would be to proofread and check this manuscript for errors. When it was ready to be sent to the Government Printing Office, we would start on the compilation of the other departmental codes.

He explained that funds were now available for the publication of new codes to be used at both the War Department level and field levels. The preparation of several editions for use at both levels had been planned. The first priority was the preparation of the codes to be used at the departmental level, and after the requirements for new codes at this level had been met, the preparation of systems for use at field levels would be started.

Next he addressed his remarks to the plans for our training program in cryptanalysis. He noted that we had now reached the point where we could do some research on systems whose cryptographic security had not been properly evaluated. One of the systems that needed to be studied was the German Army field cipher used during World War I known as the ADFGVX Cipher System. Another was the U.S. Army Cipher Device, Type M-94, which was modeled after a cryptographic device invented by the French cryptologist Bazeries and which had been modified before it was adopted for U.S. military use. Friedman felt that these two systems might possibly be used by the U.S. Army for lower-echelon communications and he wanted to have them fully evaluated for possible weaknesses.

Friedman then remarked that he personally considered the use of large codes with their associated superencipherments as being only a stopgap until automatic cipher machines could be developed. He expressed his conviction that keyboard-operated electrical cipher machines would replace all other cryptographic procedures and materials and that eventually the encipherment of messages would be performed automatically by special equipment which would feed the enciphered text directly into a radio transmitter. On the receiving end the enciphered message would be fed into a similar arrangement where it would be automatically deciphered and its clear text printed on a message blank for prompt delivery to the addressee.

Friedman then told us that we would start immediately on the code compilation program by devoting one half of each day to it and the other half to the continuation of our training program. As the first step in our work on the compilation of the War Department systems, he directed us to study the Government Printing Office style manual so that we would become familiar with the requirements for making corrections to the code manuscripts which we would be checking. He also asked us to review our work on the construction of permutation tables — also called garble tables and mutilation tables — so that we would be prepared to design appropriate ones for generating the code vocabularies for the new codes which he had planned for us to compile. He then presented us with a huge manuscript which he identified as our first proofreading assignment.

I felt some disappointment with the prospects in the change of our work pattern. I was eager to finish the training course in cryptanalysis, and I feared that any interruption of it would delay our entry into what at that time I considered to be the most fascinating aspect of our work — the breaking of codes used by foreign governments. However, after my work in the War Department code room and in view of the insecure practices which I had observed being used there, I felt relieved that some positive action was now being taken to improve the security of the War Department systems. I had had enough practical experience with the use of code books to develop an instinctive dislike for them; not only were they clumsy and difficult to use, but the task of replacing a compromised code could be time-consuming and very difficult. I was captivated by Friedman's remarks about the advantages of cipher machines, yet at this point in my cryptographic knowledge I had no comprehension of the practical problems involved in their design and construction. Also, I had no concept of the degree of security they could be expected to provide, for in our training program we had not yet started the study of cipher machines.

We started our code production work by proofreading the code manuscript which had been prepared by Friedman prior to our arrival. It was a beautifully typed manuscript and had been prepared on a special typewriter. We found it to be almost error free, and we wondered if it was really necessary for us to spend the time required for proofreading the manuscript before it was sent to the Government Printing Office. There was one typing error which we found almost immediately and which amused all of us except Friedman. The error occurred on the title page of the manuscript and instead of reading "Prepared by the Code Compilation Section, Office of the Chief Signal Officer," the typist had mutilated the word "Compilation" so that it became "Complication". When this error was brought to Friedman's attention by Lt. Rhodes, he emphatically remarked: "That is no error. It was typed that way intentionally."

It took us several weeks to finish proofreading the manuscript and to prepare it in final form for submission to the Government Printing Office. We then started on the compilation of the first edition of a series of codes which were to be designated as War Department Staff Codes. These codes were to be based on the same plaintext vocabulary, which contained over 60,000 groups.

〜 〜 〜

When we finished proofreading the typed manuscript and it had been delivered to the Government Printing Office by Friedman, he started us on the preparation of further editions of codes for departmental usage. Before we started work on these additional codes, he explained to us the general procedure he expected us to follow.

Some time before 1930, he had compiled a basic code vocabulary which he planned to use in the compilation of a series of two-part codes for use at the War Department level. He had organized the plaintext elements of the code vocabulary in a file of three-by-five-inch index cards, with each card containing a single plaintext meaning. These cards had been arranged alphabetically, and they were stored in a number of filing drawers which were stacked on top of the regular files in the rear of the vault in which we worked. Each file drawer held about two thousand cards, which amounted to about thirty drawers of cards for a 60,000-group code book.

The first step in the procedure which we were to follow contemplated the rearrangement of the cards of this basic file of plaintext meanings into a random order. After the cards had been satisfactorily disarranged, a five-letter code group would be assigned to each card. Since the five-letter code group would be taken from the permutation table in alphabetical order, the decoding section would be produced automatically. Instead of having a manuscript typed from the cards, he had arranged to have the typesetters at the Government Printing Office set the type directly from the cards. After the cards had been set into type, galley proofs would be printed and the cards and galley proofs returned to us. We would then sort the cards back into their original plaintext order, thus forming the encoding section of the code. The rearranged cards would now be sent back to the typesetters, who would use them to prepare galley proofs of the encode section.

He had planned that when the galley proofs of the encode section were returned to us, we would simultaneously cross-check and proofread the galley proofs to ensure that the code elements in the encode and decode sections were identical and that there were no typographical errors.

The same set of basic vocabulary cards could then be used to prepare another edition. The cards would first have to be put in random order and then, as each new code group was assigned in alphabetical order from the permutation table, the previously assigned code group would be blocked out. The cards would then be provided to the Government Printing Office and when the cards and galley proofs for the decoding section were returned, the cards were rearranged alphabetically and sent back to the printers for the preparation of the encoding section. Subsequent editions of the codes could be prepared by repeating this procedure for each edition.

When Friedman finished his instructions to us, he then asked for our views on the procedure. Since none of us had had any experience with code compilation, and since the whole scheme seemed logical, we had nothing to suggest. However, we did raise one question which resulted in considerable discussion. This dealt with the method scrambling the 60,000 cards. Friedman's response was that he had not yet arrived at a method for scrambling such a large number of cards, and that he hoped we would be able to work out an acceptable solution for this part of the procedure. After making this remark, he then gave us the job of preparing the permutation table for the generation of the code vocabulary and suggested that we give some thought to devising an efficient procedure for thoroughly scrambling the cards.

The preparation of the permutation table took only a couple of days, and while it was in progress we spent some time discussing possible way of scrambling the huge mass of cards which seemed to assume greater and greater proportions each time we thought about them. When we presented the finished permutation table to Friedman, he accepted it but immediately asked if we had any suggestions for dealing with the scrambling of the cards. We frankly confessed that we could offer no practical suggestion as to how this might be accomplished. After some further discussion of the problem, we decided to use the vault area for the scrambling operation, since it was obvious that the cards would have to be secured every night.

Finally, more or less in desperation, we decided to rearrange the furniture in the vault so that a large area of the floor was cleared, and then dump several drawers of the cards on to the cleared area and attempt to mix them thoroughly by hand.

After trying this procedure for a while, we found that it did not mix the cards as thoroughly as we had hoped it would. To improve the procedure, we started throwing handfuls of the cards into the air, so they would be scattered over the cleared floor area. Finally, one of us got the idea of turning the electric fans mounted on the walls to full speed and throwing handfuls of cards into the streams of air generated by the fan blades. We felt that this offered some improvement, but after several hours we tested a sample and found that the results were still far from satisfactory and that the process would have to be continued for some time before an acceptable disarrangement of the cards would be achieved.

We kept at this task for several hours. The routine we followed was for each of us to pick up as many cards as we could hold in our two hands and then throw them into the streams of air from the two fans which were mounted nearest to the cleared area. While we were throwing the cards into the streams of air from the fans, we found that we had to keep the vault door and windows tightly closed so that none of the cards would be lost. There were four of us involved, and we acted like a gang of five-year-old kids playing in a sandbox.

At one point in the scrambling operation Major Louis Cansler, a member of the War Plans and Training Division staff, entered the vault to refer to some files kept in one of the secure file cabinets. When he opened the vault door and found the four of us wildly throwing cards in the air and evidently enjoying it, he stopped and stared at us in amazement.

"What in the world is going on here?" he exclaimed.

Friedman, who was seated at his desk near the vault door got up and came inside the vault where Cansler was standing.

"They are randomizing a code vocabulary for a two-part code," he explained to Cansler.

"Do you mean to say they are doing this as a part of their job?" Cansler asked.

"Yes, it is a necessary part of our code compilation procedure," Friedman answered.

Cansler slowly shook his head as he watched us. "I thought for a moment that this code business had gotten to them," he remarked in mock seriousness.

After a couple of days of throwing cards into the air we became convinced that it would not produce a satisfactory mixing of the cards. We finally hit upon the idea of clearing our worktables and forming places for as many stacks of cards as possible on the table tops. We then dealt a card on each place, following a haphazard pattern, from the cards picked out of the mass of cards on the floor. This procedure enabled all of us to move about the tables adding a single card at a time to the several dozen piles of cards which the broad tops of the tables would accommodate. By carefully avoiding any regular pattern of distributing the cards, and by repeating the process several times, we were at last able to achieve an acceptable randomization of all of the plaintext cards.

The next step was to assign a five-letter code group to each card, Each of the code groups had to be selected from the permutation table which we had prepared, and in this process we had to be especially careful that we did not assign the same code group to two different plaintext elements. If we missed a group and failed to assign a plaintext meaning to it, no harm was done, for there were more code groups than plain-language equivalents.

Assignment of code groups to the cards was a straightforward operation. Each of us selected a section of the permutation table; our task was to write a single five-letter code group on each of the plaintext cards. Of course, the five-letter code groups had to be clearly printed so that no mistakes would be caused by ambiguous letters when the typesetting was done. This process developed into a tedious, monotonous job which none of us liked. It would have become unendurable if we had to work at this task all day long, day after day. Fortunately, the arrangement for spending half a day on our study of cryptanalysis provided us with a welcome relief.

After code groups had been assigned to several thousand cards, Friedman took the first lot to the Government Printing Office, where they were to be set in type and galley proofs prepared. Meanwhile, we continued our assignment of code groups to the remaining cards, which Friedman passed on to the typesetters. By the time we had finished the assignment of code groups to the plaintext cards, the first group of cards Friedman had taken to the Government Printing Office had been returned and we were ready to start the process of creating another edition of the code.

Because of our lack of experience with code compilation, we had expected this step to be a simple and somewhat mechanical procedure. After only a couple of days we discovered that this operation was the most tedious that we had yet encountered. The typing on the cards had been done in small type in order to save space, and not only was the process boring by its very nature, but the eyestrain which resulted from trying to discriminate the alphabetic differences between two cards, some of which carried two or three hundred letters of information, was extremely tiring.

There was one good result which came of this experience. We resolved that once we had arranged the cards correctly into their proper alphabetic order, we would number them serially. Then, instead of using the letters of the plaintext meaning to alphabetize the cards, we would merely have to arrange them according to the serial numbers assigned to each card. Indeed, we bemoaned our lack of foresight in not having thought of serially numbering the cards while they were in proper alphabetic order before we first started to rearrange them.

When we completed our task of rearranging the entire set of cards, they were returned to the printers for setting the encoding section into type. There was little we could do now on the code but await the return of the galley proofs, for the important steps of cross-checking and proofreading could not be started until the first galley proofs of the encode section were ready.

While we were waiting for the completion of the galley proofs, we worked on a variety of tasks related to the code compilation program. One of these was the regular preparation and distribution of cipher tables for the current edition of the military intelligence code which was used by G-2 for communication with the various military attachés assigned to the major U.S. diplomatic installations abroad. These tables were used for superenciphering all messages prepared in the military intelligence code and were issued on a quarterly basis. If one of the tables was lost or suspected to be compromised, it would be replaced by a special table held as a reserve in secret storage by each holder and all copies of the compromised table would be destroyed.

Prior to the realignment of the cryptographic responsibilities in the War Department in 1930, the compilation and issue of the military intelligence codes and the enciphering tables used with them was performed by G-2 and not by the Adjutant General. When the Chief Signal Officer was given the total responsibility for War Department cryptographic matters, G-2 agreed to transfer the military intelligence code and cipher-table preparation to the Signal Intelligence Service. Originally, the cipher tables had been prepared by using multigraph drums with movable type, and each new table was prepared by rearranging the movable type pieces for the cipher equivalents. After watching us try to master the multigraph process, Friedman vetoed its further use, and we adopted the far simpler mimeograph stencil process.

We prepared several editions of the enciphering tables at a time. Kullback and Sinkov would prepare the handwritten drafts of the new tables, and I would type the stencils from their drafts. After the stencils were typed, each of us would individually cross-check them to ensure that they were free of errors. I would then run off the stencils on the mimeograph machine, and we would assemble and verify each table and assign it a serial number for accounting purposes. As each edition was completed, it was held in secret storage until it was needed for issue. Only the necessary number of copies of each edition was retained, and all extra copies were destroyed along with the work sheets and stencils. Usually one of us had to accompany the materials to be destroyed — we called it secret trash — to the incinerator and actually watch it burn to ensure that not even charred scraps which might contain legible portions of the tables were left in the ashes. This meant that during the burning process we had to stir the contents of the incinerator with a long metal rod to ensure that even the tiniest scrap of paper was entirely consumed. This was not an assignment that any of us looked forward to during the hot Washington summers.

Since the enciphering tables were regularly changed, we had to schedule their distribution well in advance to ensure that each table was received by its intended user prior to the effective date of the table. To achieve this, we required each holder to acknowledge receipt of the table immediately upon its delivery. The tables which were distributed overseas were acknowledged by cabling a single five-letter code word, which was later confirmed by a signed receipt from the holder. For those tables which were distributed within the continental United States a telegraphic receipt was not required, and the receipt of the tables was acknowledged by mail. Cipher tables were never sent to an overseas installation by international mail, but were always distributed by an authorized courier of the military attaché system. Those which were distributed within the United States were handled by registered mail.

The receipts for the cipher tables had to be carefully monitored to ensure that all tables had been received by their holders prior to their effective date. On several occasions, when we failed to receive an acknowledgment for a table from one of the holders, we sent a query in code to the delinquent holder asking if the table had been received. In most of these cases, the failure to acknowledge occurred as an oversight on the part of the holder, who had sent in the mail receipt but had failed to transmit the cable acknowledgment.

There was one case which caused us considerable concern. The G-2 mail room inadvertently placed two cipher tables intended for different holders in the same package. The package containing the two tables was delivered and the recipient, without noting the address on the second envelope, assumed he had been sent an extra table. He dutifully sent a single cable acknowledgment and just as dutifully filled out and returned both mail receipts. When the effective date of the new table approached and we noted that one of the tables had not been acknowledged, we cabled a query to the military attaché who had not responded, asking if he had received a new table. When he reported that the table had not been received, we sent cables to all holders of the code authorizing the use of the reserve table on the date scheduled for the new table, and declared that the new table had been compromised and forbade its use. Both G-2 and the Signal Intelligence Service were greatly concerned about this development until the mail receipts were finally received and we noted the two receipts signed by the military attaché who had been sent the second table by mistake. To my knowledge no cipher table to be used with the military intelligence code was ever reported lost or compromised by the field.

In due course the galley proofs were received from the Government Printing Office. Proofreading a two-part code is quite a different matter from proofreading a regular manuscript. We were required to take each plaintext meaning of the encode section of the code and locate its appearance in the decode section. Our purpose was to ensure that not only was the type correctly set for both the code group and its plaintext equivalent, but also that there was an exact letter-by-letter correspondence between the two appearances, one in the encode section and the other in the decode section.

In performing this checking operation, each of us was given a complete set of galley proofs for the decode section. The galley proofs for the encode section were parceled out among us, and we carefully looked up each of the encoding section elements in the decoding section to ensure that the code group and its equivalent were identically represented in each section. This combined proofreading and cross-checking process took time. By now we had become somewhat philosophical about our code compilation efforts, and each day we put in four solid hours at the task.

Some days during the Washington summer we would get a break — we would be excused from work because of the unbearable heat. The Office of the Secretary of War, which had the authority for excusing the employees in the Munitions Building because of the heat, relied on the Meteorological Section of the Office of the Chief Signal Officer for providing information on the comfort index of the building. When it promised to be an unusually hot day, it was always a welcome sign during the later hours of the morning to see the sergeant who was the chief clerk of the Meteorological Section walking down the corridor of the fourth wing with his hygrometer and thermometer, testing the temperature and humidity in order to arrive at the comfort index. As soon as the announcement that we would excused for the afternoon was received, Kully and I would call our wives and arrange for the four of us to meet at the first tee on the West Potomac Golf Course, which was located within a short distance from the Munitions Building, and we would then spend the remainder of the afternoon playing golf.

When the galley proofs for the first code we compiled had been set in type, we started the compilation of the next edition. As planned by Friedman, we used the same set of three-by-five-inch cards and followed the same general process, except that we serially numbered the cards before their alphabetical order was disturbed. We continued the application of this procedure until we had satisfied the requirements for both the War Department Staff Code and the War Department Confidential Code.

It took several months for us to bring the code compilation program to the point where new and more secure codes were available for protecting War Department communications. Our training in cryptanalysis had continued, and we had completed the study of the more elementary cipher devices and had started on the analysis of the more sophisticated electro-mechanical cipher machines. It was in the study of these that I found the greatest intellectual challenge, and it became clear to me that the solution of some of the more complex systems would have been almost impossible without some knowledge of mathematics.

CHAPTER 6

THE CIPHER DEVICES WE STUDIED

The Wheatstone Cipher Device

Very early in 1931 we started the study of cipher machines. The first one we studied was called the Wheatstone Cipher Device after its inventor, Sir Charles Wheatstone, the famous English scientist. Years later, a British engineer officer named Pletts, employed in the War Office during the first World War as a cryptanalyst, produced a version of the device which was much more reliable mechanically and operationally than the original model constructed by Wheatstone. The British Army was ready to adopt the Pletts design as a field cipher device because the War Office cryptanalysts thought it offered greater cryptographic security and reliability of operation than any other device or system available at that time. Yardley's assessment of the device was sought, and he in turn submitted the device to Friedman, who at that time was working at the Riverbank Laboratories, asking for Friedman's opinion of its security. Friedman responded that he considered the device insecure and advised against its adoption by the U.S. Army as a field cipher system. Friedman's findings were met with disbelief by the cryptanalysts who had devised the system and by Yardley, who had already concluded that the device was acceptable for U.S. Army usage. Since Friedman had only expressed his opinion of the security of the device, he was challenged to solve a set of messages enciphered by it in accordance with the procedures proposed by the British cryptographers for its use. Friedman was able to solve these messages in record time, with the result that the Wheatstone system, as exemplified in Pletts's modification, was rejected as a field cipher system by both the U.K. and the U.S.

Friedman enjoyed relating the story of how he recovered the keys for the set of test messages. According to his story, he was able to recover one of the two alphabetic sequences used for enciphering the test messages by straightforward cryptanalysis and found it to be based on the keyword CIPHER. Before starting on the recovery of the other sequence, he turned to Mrs. Friedman, who was also a Riverbank Laboratories employee and who was working nearby, and told her that he was going to give her a word and asked her to respond with the first word that occurred to her. When he spoke the word CIPHER, she promptly responded with the word MACHINE. Friedman then immediately tested the word MACHINE as the keyword for the unknown component and found that it was actually the keyword used. This lucky approach of course eliminated the need for recovering the second alphabetic sequence by cryptanalysis, and substantially shortened the time required for the solution of the test messages.

When Friedman gave us our first set of messages prepared by the Wheatstone device to solve, he provided each of us with a copy of Riverbank Laboratories Publication Number 20, Several Machine Ciphers and Methods for their Solution, a pamphlet which he had written while employed at the Riverbank Laboratories. He suggested that we read the portion of the publication which dealt with the solution of the Wheatstone device and then, on the assumption that such a device was being used by the "enemy" as a field cipher system, try to solve the messages and recover the keywords. The problem was not very difficult for us, and we were able to read the messages and recover the keys by the application of the principles described in the publication that he had provided to us.

The Bazeries Device

Our next problem consisted of a set of messages enciphered in what Friedman called a "multiplex alphabet system." This system employed a device invented in 1891 by Commandant Bazeries, a famous French cryptologist. The operation of the device and the techniques for its solution were also described in Riverbank Publication No. 20. Again, by carefully applying the procedures given in the publication, we were able to solve the messages.

Although Friedman was not aware of it at that time, the cryptographic principles on which the Bazeries device was based were actually invented by President Thomas Jefferson almost a century before Bazeries discovered them. We first learned of Jefferson's invention some three or four years after we had worked on the Bazeries system. This interesting fact was discovered by a friend of Friedman's who was doing some research on Jefferson's unpublished papers in the Library of Congress when he encountered a description of a "wheel cipher" that Jefferson had constructed circa 1790.

The Cylindrical Cipher Device, Type M-94

Another of our training assignments was to study an Army cipher device which was at that time authorized for field use. This device, known officially as Cipher Device, Type M-94, was modeled after the Bazeries device we had studied earlier. Captain Parker Hitt, a U.S. Signal Corps officer, had some years before (circa 1914), discovered a description of the Bazeries device in a French publication and was so intrigued by its possibilities that he joined with another Signal Corps officer, Captain Joseph Mauborgne, in the design of a device which they hoped might be used in place of the small field codes then being employed as field systems by the U.S. Army. Hitt and Mauborgne were not aware that the cryptographic principles had originally been discovered by President Thomas Jefferson. The model they designed was officially adopted by the Signal Corps and several hundred were manufactured. This device had been produced too late to be of use in World War I, but shortly after the end of that war it was officially issued as a replacement for the small two-part codes which had been extensively used during the period of hostilities.

Cipher Device, M-94, was considered to offer greater security and practicability for field use than any other device known at the time it was adopted by the Army. It certainly offered greater security than the Pletts modification of the Wheatstone device which had been proposed for use as a field cipher system by the British War Office cryptographers.

We applied the same cryptanalytic techniques that we had used for solving the Bazeries device to messages enciphered by the M-94 and found that these techniques were adequately effective, although it took much longer to achieve a solution of the M-94 than the Bazeries device required. The M-94 alphabets were much more skillfully constructed to resist cryptanalysis than the alphabets of the Bazeries device.

The Kryha Cipher Machine

Another device that we studied was the Kryha Cipher Machine which was manufactured in Germany and offered for sale for commercial as well as governmental use. When Friedman presented us with our assignment for this device, he told us that the techniques for its solution had never been documented and that we would have to devise our own methods of attack on it. He did, however, give us a general idea of how the machine might be used and demonstrated its operation for us.

The Kryha device was essentially an apparatus which slid a cipher alphabet mounted on a rotatable disk against a semicircular plain alphabet which was fixed. The rotatable disk was mounted on a spindle driven by a spring motor operating through a set of gears, one of which acted as a control gear and regulated the number of steps taken by the rotating disk between successive operations of the device. The mechanism was set in motion by depressing a lever which projected from the side of the metal case enclosing the mechanism. The control gear, which had 17 active positions, allowed the rotating disk to be driven a number of steps, varying from five to eight letters, between the depressions of the lever. The letters of the alphabet were printed on small removable metal plates held in place by metal spring clips, thus permitting both the plain alphabet and the cipher alphabet to be completely rearranged by the users.

To encipher a message, users were supposed to arrange the letters of both alphabets according to the keys they had selected, align the two sequences against each other at an agreed-upon point, and set the control gear wheel to a predetermined position. The message could now be enciphered by finding its first letter on the fixed alphabet and noting the letter of the movable alphabet which corresponded to it as the first letter of the ciphertext. The control lever was now depressed, which advanced the movable disk to a new alignment point, and the second letter of the plaintext was enciphered by finding it on the fixed alphabet and noting the letter of the movable alphabet corresponding to it as the second letter of the ciphertext. The control lever was depressed after encipherment of each plaintext letter, thereby producing a new alignment of the alphabets for each letter enciphered.

For decipherment, the recipient of the message had to duplicate exactly the arrangement of the letters in each of the two sequences and to align them and the control wheel to the identical positions used by the sender. The first letter of the ciphertext was of course sought in the movable sequence, and the letter of the fixed sequence corresponding to it would be the first letter of the clear text of the message. By depressing the lever after the decipherment of each succeeding letter of the ciphertext, the plaintext equivalent of the cipher letters could be determined and the message deciphered.

The Kryha device was accompanied by a brochure, written by a German mathematician, which extolled the security afforded by the Kryha cipher machine. The thrust of this brochure was that the Kryha cipher was mathematically indecipherable because of the enormous number of possibilities afforded by the machine and that it would be humanly impossible to produce the plaintext of messages enciphered by it through trying all the possible combinations of the letters of the alphabet as a solution procedure. As I recall, it was claimed that there were more than $17 \times 26! \times 26!$ possibilities afforded by the machine. In spite of these awesome figures, we were able to solve the messages of our assignment in a reasonably short time, most of which was spent in experimenting with the machine.

I found the Kryha machine to be absolutely fascinating. Although it gave us some mechanical trouble during our first experiments with it, it could be made to operate reliably by applying a few drops of oil at the proper points in the mechanism and keeping the motor spring wound to the proper tension. It was a noisy brute of a device, giving forth an aggravating, rasping sound followed by a loud click each time the control lever was depressed. I suspect that I acted a great deal like Mr. Toad of *The Wind and the Willows* when he first saw an automobile — I made up my mind then and there that the study of cipher machines was the field of cryptography for me.

The B-211

We encountered our first electromechanical cipher machine in the B-211, a device invented by a Swedish engineer named Damm. When Friedman presented us with the device, he suggested that we first examine the device to identify the electrical and mechanical features that had been built into it and then reduce the machine to what he called a "pencil and paper" analog. After giving us these fairly meager instructions, he left the device with us.

Since there was only one device and four of us itching to get our hands on it, some arrangement had to be worked out as to which would be the first to examine the machine. Abe and Kully got the first opportunity to work with the machine, but neither was able to make it work satisfactorily and very soon turned it over to Hurt and me. Hurt, who had little interest in things mechanical, disposed of it quickly. When my turn came to examine the machine, the first thing I tried to discover was why the machine was not operating properly. In order to get to the mechanism, I removed all the protective covers from the machine and stripped it down to its chassis so that I could get a clear view of its components. I soon discovered that two faults had developed in the machine — the gears linking the pin wheels to the commutators had jammed, and one of the electrical leads from the small dry battery which provided energy for the lamps and relays was loose. When I remedied these faults, the machine began to operate satisfactorily. We were now able to trace the electrical wiring of the device and determine the interaction of the keyboard contacts with the relays and the commutators and how these in turn selected which window would be illuminated when a key was depressed. We laid out a schematic diagram of the device on a large sheet of cross-section paper and then, by inspecting the wiring, began developing the connections among the various electrical components. After the wiring had been completely reproduced on the schematic diagram, we were able to reconstruct the cryptographic action of the machine, and by using our diagram we were able to duplicate exactly all the cryptographic functions performed by the machine.

The device that we studied was an outstanding example of model making, and its mechanical components were beautifully machined. It was about the size of an ordinary portable typewriter and employed a typewriter keyboard designed for a twenty-five-letter alphabet. Instead of a type basket just back of the keyboard there was a bank of translucent windows on each of which was printed a letter of the alphabet. Directly back of the bank of windows the electromechanical components were located.

These consisted of a set of four control wheels with adjustable pins operating in tandem, two slip-ring commutators, and a bank of five relays. Around the periphery of the four wheels the letters of the alphabet were engraved for reference purposes in setting the wheels. These wheels were geared to the two slip-ring commutators and determined whether or not the commutators advanced, depending on the setting of the pins in the control wheels. Each of the commutators had five slip rings connected to a set of ten contact studs arranged in a circle on the face of an insulating plate fastened to one end of the commutator; these ten contacts were connected to the slip rings so that each ring was connected to one odd and one even contact stud of the end plate. Five spring contacts, equally spaced around a circle, were mounted in a fixed insulating block so that they made electrical contact with the brass contact studs of the commutator end plate. A small plug-board arrangement permitted each set of five leads to the slip ring collectors to be permuted. A switching arrangement was also provided which controlled the mode, either encipher or decipher, in which the machine was to operate.

When one of the keys of the keyboard was depressed, two actions took place: (1) the four control wheels advanced one position, and (2) two contacts were closed, completing a circuit through each of the commutators so that a small lamp located behind one of the windows was illuminated. The letter inscribed on the window represented the cipher letter corresponding to the letter on the key which was depressed. This relationship could be reversed by adjusting the lever controlling the switching arrangements, which in effect interchanged the electrical connections between the lamps of the lamp bank and the keys of the keyboard.

We found that there were only ten possible settings of each of the commutators and therefore the total number of alphabets for any given arrangement of the plug board was ten by ten, or one hundred. Once we had generated all the 100 possible alphabets for any given plug board wiring, it was easy to determine the effect of the pin wheels when the setting of the pins was known. At this point the machine, which at first appeared to us to offer a mysterious and impenetrable jungle of electromechanical complexities, became nothing more than a fairly simple cryptographic system which could be easily duplicated on paper by a pair of five-by-five element substitution squares, keyed by four binary streams which corresponded to the setting of the pins on the four control wheels. To satisfy ourselves that we fully understood the functioning of the device, we enciphered a short message using both the machine and our paper analog. We were delighted to find that the ciphertexts were identical.

Friedman had been carefully following our progress and, when we reached the point where he was satisfied that we fully understood the device, he congratulated us on our approach to the assignment. Then, without giving us any clues as to how we might proceed, he told us that our next assignment was to develop a cryptanalytic technique for the solution of messages prepared by the B-211 cipher machine.

Earlier in our training we had encountered and successfully dealt with systems similar to the one on which the B-211 cryptography was based, but in these cases the length of the key was relatively short, and in all the cases we had studied, the text of the message was several times the length of the key. However, in the case of the B-211, the length of the key generated by the cryptographic mechanism was approximately 160,000 characters, and much longer than the total number of letters in the cryptograms we were expected to solve. We decided that we would have to develop some technique which would take advantage of the shorter cycles of the machine, either the individual control wheels or the pairs of wheels which interacted to control the advancement of the commutators. We decided to start our attack on the recovery of the two smaller wheels which operated together on one of the commutators, rather than to attempt to recover the effect of an individual wheel.

This was our first encounter with anything like the effect of several elements, such as the four control wheels, operating together to produce a key which in turn controlled the stepping of electrical switching components such as the commutators. None of the examples we had found in our training assignments had involved such complexities, and we found ourselves baffled by the prospect of having to recover the combined influence of the four pin wheels from the relatively meager volume of ciphertext that we had been given.

Friedman observed our frustration both with interest and some amusement, for he continued regularly to visit the vault for short intervals and listen to our discussions or observe our attempts to find a point of entry in the system. We were too proud to ask for help, and I suppose that he was pleased with our persistence, although we were making no progress. Although we finally devised a method for breaking into the system, in retrospect I feel that it took us much longer that it should have.

We spent several days trying to develop an attack on the system. Friedman watched our approach with interest, often coming into the vault and listening to our discussions without providing us with any clues as to how we might proceed. Finally, we developed an approach which theoretically could lead us to a successful recovery of the texts of the messages in our assignment. Since this approach involved considerable clerical work, we had to develop a plan for dividing the effort among the four of us and later combining the results in the hope that we could recover some of the texts of the messages. When Friedman listened to this phase of our discussions, he dropped his role of being a silent observer and encouraged us to proceed. It took several days for us to complete the recovery of the texts and keys for the messages in our assignment.

Friedman seemed greatly pleased with our work on the B-211 and he asked us to prepare a paper which presented the techniques we had successfully applied. This paper was later published as a technical paper of the Signal Intelligence Service and was used as a text by the students who followed us.

The Vernam Cipher System

In our study of cipher-machine systems, Friedman put us to work on a cryptographic system which he had successfully analyzed some years earlier. This system was, for its day, a very sophisticated cryptographic concept and was probably the first fully automatic cryptographic machine system actually constructed and service tested. It was a development of the American Telephone and Telegraph Company, and it was known as the Vernam System, after its inventor, who was an engineer employed by AT&T. Only a few models had been built, and some of these were tested by the U.S. Signal Corps on land line circuits between two Signal Corps communications centers located within the United States. Although the Signal Corps was well pleased with the results of the service test, the system was not adopted by the government.

Cryptographically, the Vernam system combined two binary key streams electrically to generate a third key stream which in turn was combined with the baudot elements forming each letter of the plaintext of the message. This produced a ciphertext made up of the thirty-two combinations of the baudot alphabet instead of the twenty-six letters of the ordinary alphabet.

The greatest advantage of the Vernam system was that the ciphertext could be automatically transmitted over a printing telegraph circuit. At the receiving end an identical piece of equipment, using duplicates of the key streams employed at the transmitting end, received the ciphertext signal and automatically and simultaneously produced the plain language of the message. In the model tested by the Signal Corps, two long master keying tapes, say one of 999 characters and the other of 1001 characters in length, were combined to produce a key stream of approximately one million characters in length. The cryptographic equipment consisted essentially of two standard tape readers (tape reading heads) which fed the signals from the two master key tapes into a bank of relays where they were combined to form the enciphering key stream. This key stream was combined in a similar manner with the binary elements of the plaintext to effect its encipherment. The deciphering process involved a similar setup, where the recipient had two master key tapes identical to those used at the transmitting end and set at the same positions as those used by the sender. Thus it was possible to reproduce the key used at the transmitting site so that it could be automatically applied to the enciphered signal as each baudot element was received and the plaintext simultaneously printed by a teletypewriter as it was received.

From a communications-security standpoint, the Vernam system had one serious weakness. If two messages were enciphered by using identical key streams, it was possible to solve them by correctly guessing the plaintext represented by a few letters of the ciphertext of one of the messages, and applying the key derived from them to the corresponding cipher letters of the other message, thereby producing the plaintext represented by the cipher letters of the second message. Once such a start was made, more plain language and more cipher key could be recovered by assuming logical words and phrases to precede and to follow the portions of plaintext resulting from the initial assumption, and from that point on the process was a great deal like solving a fairly simple word puzzle, and the complete texts enciphered by the repeated key could be recovered. If the key stream had been generated by combining two basic key tapes, as was the case in the Vernam system tested by the Signal Corps, and if enough of the combined key could be recovered, i.e. a little more than one complete cycle of the shorter key tape, it was then a simple matter to recover the two master key tapes and read all the messages for which these tapes were used.

This was the type of attack Friedman had employed to break the Vernam system, and the problem he had prepared for us was designed so that we could use the same approach. As I recall, outside of the puzzle-solving aspects of recovering the composite key which had been used to encipher two different plaintext messages, there was little to the recovery of the system except for several hours of making tedious tabulations aimed at discovering which texts of the set of cryptograms we were studying had been enciphered by identical keys.

The Hebern Cipher Machine

The most important cipher machine we studied was the Hebern machine. Hebern, an American inventor, had produced a very sophisticated cipher machine which he had demonstrated to the U.S. Navy. The Navy cryptographers were so impressed by the possibilities of Hebern's invention that a contract was entered into with him to build a machine constructed according to specifications prepared by the cryptanalysts of the Navy Department.

One of the stories I heard about the development of the Hebern machine was that the Navy had very carefully spelled out the specifications for the machine design and the operational functions it was expected to perform. Hebern had been warned that he would be required to meet the specifications in the contract to the letter. Hebern accepted the contract and constructed the device according to the specifications. When the machine was delivered, the contracting and inspecting officers carefully looked it over and checked it against the contract specifications. Since, so far as they could determine, the machine was constructed according to the contract specifications, they recommended acceptance of the devices. However, when the model was tested by the Navy cryptographers, it was found that while the machine would produce an encipherment as specified in the contract, it had no capability for reversing the process, and the texts enciphered by it could not be deciphered. The Navy protested to Hebern, claiming the machine was not acceptable to the Navy. Hebern was successful in overcoming the Navy's protest by pointing out that the contract had not specified the machine would perform the deciphering process and that, accordingly, the model met the specifications as written into the contract. The Navy had to accept the machine.

The Navy had great hopes for the Hebern cipher machine and continued the contractual arrangements with Hebern until satisfactory working models were produced. These were subjected to a most thorough testing program by the Navy cryptographers and were finally judged to be suitable for use on the Navy's highest echelon communications nets. A preliminary keying system was devised and a draft of instructions for using the machine was prepared.

Before the Hebern cipher machine was officially adopted, the Navy cryptographers asked Friedman for his assessment of the security it afforded. After examining the information provided by the Navy, Friedman responded that he considered the machine to be insecure and that if it was used in accordance with the procedures envisaged by the Navy, the messages enciphered by it could be solved. Friedman was challenged to prove his claims by demonstrating that he could actually solve a set of test messages enciphered by the machine using the keying system proposed by the Navy cryptographers.

Friedman accepted the challenge, and he and the Navy cryptographers worked out the terms of a test in which the Navy would supply a set of messages prepared exactly in accordance with the procedures which they had proposed, but using a set of cipher wheels whose wiring was to be unknown to Friedman. Friedman's task was to recover the plaintexts of the messages and to recover the wirings of the cipher wheels.[1]

---

1. The two paragraphs immediately above were highlighted by NSA as containing sensitive information. The essential information contained in these paragraphs can also be found on page 68, *The Man Who Broke Purple* by Ronald W. Clark and on page 46, *Machine Cryptography and Modern Cryptanalysis* by Cipher A. Deavours and Louis Kruh.

From a cryptographic standpoint, the Hebern cipher machine consisted essentially of four components, as follows: a keyboard similar to a typewriter keyboard, a bank of twenty-six illuminated windows on each of which a letter of the alphabet was inscribed, an encipher-decipher switch, and, most important from the cryptographic viewpoint, a set of five commutators operating in cascade which provided for the enciphering-deciphering function of the device. The commutators had twenty-six equally spaced contacts arranged in a circle on each face, and each of the contacts of one face was uniquely connected to one of the contacts on the opposite face, producing twenty-six separate circuits through the wheel. The wheels were symmetrically constructed so that they could be reversed in their mountings, thus enabling each commutator to be operated in either a "direct" or "reversed" mode.

To set up the machine for a given key period, the order of the five commutators, or cipher wheels as they were called, was given in the keying instructions, and the wheels were inserted into the machine in accordance with instructions which specified the wheel order for the date. Around the periphery of each of the wheels the twenty-six letters of the alphabet were engraved in normal order so that each letter corresponded to an active position of the wheel. To encipher a message, the code clerk selected a five-letter keyword and set the first wheel to the first letter of the keyword, the second wheel to the second letter, and so on for all five wheels. The encipher-decipher switch was then set to the encipher position and the message could now be enciphered by depressing the keys of the keyboard just as if the message was being typed. When a letter of the keyboard was depressed, a mechanical linkage caused one or more of the cipher wheels to advance in an odometer-like manner, providing a new and different substitution alphabet for each depression of a key. For the state of the cryptographic art at the time the Hebern machine was produced, it was a most formidable device.

Friedman was successful in his attack on the system. He developed a statistical approach which enabled him to reconstruct the wiring of one of the five cipher wheels. By eliminating the effect of this wheel from the ciphertext, he was able to recover the wiring of a second wheel, and from this point on, the recovery of the plaintext of the messages and the wirings of the remaining wheels was merely a matter of further skillful analytic work on the messages.

Friedman had planned for us to duplicate his analysis of the Hebern system, using the messages and information originally provided to him by the Navy. He first presented us with the Hebern cipher machine and told us that our initial assignment was to study the device and determine exactly how it functioned. We were expected to produce a wiring diagram of the cryptographic circuitry and to be able to duplicate all the cryptographic functions of the machine using, as he expressed it, only "pencil and paper."

After our experience with the B-211 we were not at all apprehensive about our ability to analyze the device and we attacked the assignment with considerable vigor and with the expectation that we would have the analysis completed in short order. After a few hours study of the machine we found that the cryptography of the Hebern machine was far more complex than any we had yet encountered and that we would have to study the circuitry of the device meticulously before we could master the principles incorporated into it. In fact, it took considerable time for us to reconstruct the wiring of the machine and to comprehend fully the exact functions of its electrical and mechanical components. In due course we succeeded in constructing a pencil-and-paper model of the device which would accurately decipher messages enciphered by the machine.

Friedman seemed well pleased with the results of our initial study of the machine, and at this point he gave us copies of the test messages the Navy had prepared and explained the procedures followed for their encipherment. He then told us that our assignment was to recover the wirings of the wheels and the plaintexts of the messages.

We studied the messages for several days, looking for any phenomena which we might exploit such as repetitions between messages, unusual frequency patterns, and whatever else we could imagine as possibly giving us some clue to the wiring of the wheels. We also reviewed carefully the operation of the machine, hoping that something might develop from this which would help us in solving the messages. After several days of unfruitful work on the messages, we still had no idea of how we might solve them. When Friedman found we were getting discouraged, he must have concluded he was expecting too much from us, and he outlined an approach which he suggested we undertake. He explained the statistical procedures involved in the approach and described to us the type of phenomena we could expect to exploit. It was a very subtle concept which he presented and one that might have taken months for us to discover, if indeed we might have been clever enough to do so. We promptly started compiling the statistical information from the texts of the messages, and from this point on we were able to duplicate Friedman's solution of the system with only occasional gentle hints from him.

The IT&T Cipher Machine

Another interesting cipher machine problem we studied was presented to us by the State Department. After his retirement, Colonel Parker Hitt, one of the co-inventors of the Cipher Device, Type M-94, had been employed by the International Telephone and Telegraph Corporation to design a cipher machine system to operate directly on a teletype line, automatically enciphering the message as the plaintext was fed into the cipher machine keyboard and simultaneously transmitting the enciphered signal over a teletype line or a radio circuit. When the enciphered signal was received at the other end of the line, it would be fed directly into a duplicate cipher machine which would automatically decipher the message and simultaneously print out the plaintext on a teleprinter.

IT&T hoped to sell the device to the U.S. Government and arranged for Colonel Hitt to demonstrate its machine at the State Department in Washington. Two machines had been built, and these were installed in two separate rooms in the State Department communications center. Colonel Hitt had invited Friedman to witness the demonstration.

When Friedman returned from the demonstration he reported that the machines had performed splendidly and that the State Department communicators were greatly impressed by it.

Colonel Hitt was eager to have Friedman endorse the device as offering a high degree of cryptographic security, and he proposed that the Signal Intelligence Section undertake a study of the system, feeling, of course, that we would not be able to solve it. Friedman accepted Colonel Hitt's proposal, stipulating that one of the devices would be provided to us for study, and that for the test a series of messages would be enciphered on the device in keys unknown to us, and that our objective would be to recover the keys and the plaintexts of the messages. Colonel Hitt accepted Friedman's terms as being a fair test for evaluating the security of the system.

A few days after the demonstration, Colonel Hitt delivered one of the cipher machines to our office. He spent some time with us, demonstrating the operation of the device and explaining the keying procedure he had devised for use with it. He informed us that a set of test messages was being prepared and that he would provide us with copies of them later.

As soon as Colonel Hitt left, we started our examination of the cipher machine. We found that the cryptographic component comprised essentially ten wheels, each of a different number of effective positions, all of which were prime to each other and driven by a common shaft. The wheels operated in pairs, controlling five sets of electrical contacts, so that five streams of electrical impulses were generated by the five pairs of wheels. These impulses in turn were fed into a bank of relays where they were combined with five streams of impulses produced by the plain language as it was typed into the keyboard of a teletype machine similar to what we had found in the Vernam device we had studied earlier. Since the number of active positions on the ten wheels had been selected from prime numbers in the neighborhood of 100, the cycle of the machine was approximately ten billion characters in length. However, in the design of the wheels Colonel Hitt had provided for them to be aligned to a keyword for the initial position of each message, thus providing for only 26^{10} starting positions. In actuality, the number of starting positions was further limited, since Colonel Hitt had proposed the use of pronounceable words and phrases of ten letters in length as keywords for the messages.

In our analysis of the system, we came to the conclusion that the ninth and tenth wheels offered the most favorable point of attack on the machine, for the key stream of impulses from the last or fifth element of the baudot code provided the best statistical base for our analysis. Once we had determined the correct setting for this pair of wheels we could remove their effect from the ciphertext, thereby reducing the machine to an eight-wheel device, with only sixteen plaintext variants for each of the cipher letters. Then, by applying similar statistical tests to another pair of wheels, we could determine their starting position. We could then remove the effect of this pair of wheels and reduce the variants to eight possibilities. At this point, we felt we could select sections of plain language from the limited number of possibilities for each cipher letter, and if we had made the correct assumptions for the plain language, we could identify the starting points for the remaining six wheels and decipher the message. We discussed this approach with Friedman, who agreed and he volunteered to join us in our attack on the test messages.

At this point Friedman called Colonel Hitt at the State Department and informed him that we were ready to begin our test. He also stated that he planned to keep an accurate record of the time we spent on each of the messages. In response, Colonel Hitt informed him that the test messages were ready and that he would have them delivered within the hour.

The messages arrived shortly after lunch and we promptly started working on them. We selected the two longest messages as our first targets. Friedman and Sinkov took one while Kully and I took the other, for we felt that by working in pairs we would be able to arrive at a solution more rapidly than if we each worked individually on separate messages. Friedman noted the exact time we started our attack, for he estimated that we would be able to break the system in a matter of hours rather than days.

Kully and I were lucky in the message we selected, for the statistical tests we made indicated that the last two wheels of the machine we set to the key letters ON. Since this was a very common digraph for ending words of ten letters, we felt encouraged. Instead of running the tests for all possible positions for the seventh and eighth wheels, we assumed that the key word might have ended in the tetragraph TION or SION, and we promptly ran the statistical tests for these two assumptions. Neither gave satisfactory results. As we were getting ready to undertake an exhaustive test of all the possible alignments for the seventh and eighth wheels, one of us suggested that we ought to try the keyword WASHINGTON on the message before we continued our statistical tests.

Friedman was evidently listening to our discussion of the possibility that the keyword WASHINGTON had been used. "Colonel Hitt would never use such an obvious keyword for one of these test messages," he observed. "you will be wasting time if you try it."

"If he actually used the keyword WASHINGTON for this message, we will be able to solve the first message in record time," we countered. This argument evidently did not appeal to Friedman, for he insisted that we at least test the seventh and eighth wheels to determine if they could have been positioned at GT. In a short time we had accumulated enough statistical information to establish that this possibility showed a high probability. As soon as Kully and I announced this finding, we proposed that we proceed directly with trying to decipher the message with the keyword WASHINGTON. Friedman was still reluctant, but at our insistence he finally acceded, and he and Sinkov stopped their testing and watched as Kully and I prepared to test our assumption.

"I cannot believe that an experienced cryptanalyst like Colonel Hitt could have selected such an obvious word as a key for one of the test messages," Friedman observed. "It must be another word ending in GTON instead of Washington."

"We can either assume that WASHINGTON is the entire keyword and immediately test it, or we can reduce the ciphertext of the message to eight possibilities for each of the letters and try to select the plaintext from these," we proposed.

"By all means try WASHINGTON as the keyword," Friedman answered. "If it doesn't decipher the message we will proceed as we had planned."

Kully and I promptly started deciphering the message using the keyword WASHINGTON and Friedman and Abe watched as we applied the keying elements to each letter. It was an exciting moment for all of us.

It took the decipherment of only a few letters to establish that our guess was correct. Friedman insisted that we continue our deciphering process until we had produced about fifty letters of plaintext to ensure that there was no question about the correctness of the keyword. When he was satisfied that the message was completely decipherable, he called Colonel Hitt, who was still at the State Department, and announced to him that we had recovered the key for one of the messages. He informed Hitt of the keyword and read the beginning of the message to him.

We continued our work on the remaining messages and by the end of the day had recovered the keys for two more of them. By now we were so sure of the effectiveness of our techniques that we estimated we would be able to decipher all of the messages by noon of the next day.

By the middle of the next morning we were well on our way to completing the test. Colonel Hitt called for a further progress report and Friedman invited him to visit us.

When Colonel Hitt arrived, Friedman met with him in the outer office and presented him with the keys and partial decipherments we had produced. His reaction was both of amazement and awe at our accomplishments, and he asked Friedman that he be allowed to express his personal congratulations to us. When we had assembled, Colonel Hitt made a short and somewhat formal speech of congratulations, in which he stated that while he was disappointed that his invention did not offer the high degree of security that he had expected of it, he was personally gratified to learn that the War Department had developed a cryptanalytic capability powerful enough to solve in such a short time a cipher machine that he had considered to be impregnable. While I am sure that he must have felt a great disappointment at having his invention proved to be unsatisfactory in such a short time, he never let it show for an instant.

The Hebern Device, Mark II

Shortly after we finished work on the IT&T cipher device, the Navy asked Friedman to assess the security of an improved model of the Hebern cipher machine. This machine, which the Navy referred to as the Mark II, had been built by Hebern on a new contract which had been negotiated with him. It supposedly contained improved cryptographic principles which overcame the weaknesses discovered and exploited by Friedman in his work on the earlier Hebern device. Friedman agreed to study the device, and he and the Navy cryptographers worked out the details of what was considered to be a fair test of the security of the Mark II. The test was based on the concept that the basic machines and the rules for their use would inevitably become known to foreign cryptanalysts, and that the true security of the device rested in a proper change of keys, which it was hoped would be kept secret.

It was agreed that the Navy would provide us with the device, the general rules for using the system, simulated traffic for a day, and the rotors used for enciphering the traffic. Our task was to analyze the traffic for the day and to recover the wheel order and the settings of the wheels and of course to decipher the messages. We sailed right through the exercise and were able to produce the decipherments of the messages in something less than a month. Our successful analysis of the Mark II caused the Navy to seek further for a secure cipher machine.

Friedman's Cipher Machine (M-134A)

The only machine that seemed to us to offer anything like the degree of security required for the most secret communications of the War Department was Friedman's own brainchild. This device was still in the developmental stage and was being built by a private engineering firm under a Signal Corps Laboratory contract. Friedman described to us the principles he had chosen for his device. The combination of cryptographic processes envisaged for both the device and the procedures to be followed in using it were far superior to those of any machine which we had yet studied. While the cryptographic design was considered to be eminently satisfactory from a communications security standpoint, the device still had to be service tested and its performance under actual code room usage assessed. Also, there was the production problem of manufacturing a large quantity of specially designed keying materials that were required for the operation of the system. It was these which provided the essential security of the device, for it was considered inevitable that the machine and its associated materials would be captured or stolen and that the security of the system rested in the proper selection of keying materials combined with a frequent replacement or change of these materials.

Twelve models of the machine were being constructed. These were considered to be pilot models and would be issued to the War Department code room and to the headquarters of the three overseas departments, where they would be used for all classified messages passing between Washington and the three overseas departments. The keying materials for the service test would have to be prepared by the Signal Intelligence Section, and we started preparations for this task. Fortunately, the rotors were to be wired by the manufacturer, and we did not have to plan for this operation.

The Enigma Machine

In order to keep abreast of developments in cipher machine cryptography, Friedman had arranged with G-2 for the purchase of cipher machines which had been offered for sale in foreign countries. This arrangement had produced the B-211 and the Kryha. A third machine was procured in Germany which was known as the Enigma.

Friedman had not had the opportunity to make a thorough study of the Enigma. When we finished our training on the other machines, he suggested that we make an examination of the Enigma device to ensure that we became thoroughly familiar with its principles. He indicated that at some time in the future he would like for us to undertake a thorough research of the security provided by the device, for he felt it highly probable that, in the future the Enigma cryptographic principles would be employed by foreign governments for enciphering their official communications. He told us that he had made a limited study of the device in order to determine if it possessed any advantages over the M-134A, the machine being built for the War Department, and had concluded that, while the Enigma device offered an unusually high degree of security, it was inferior to the machine which he had designed.

We spent some time studying the Enigma and concluded that it did not offer any advantages over Friedman's machine, although, if properly used, it could provide a high degree of cryptographic security. We also spent some time in considering how we would attack a series of messages enciphered by the Enigma, but we never got beyond the speculative stage in our study of it.

Our chief objection to the Enigma machine was that a letter could never be enciphered by itself. We felt that this was a weakness which might be exploited, particularly when the plaintexts of messages enciphered in the system were available. We did however conclude that the Enigma was a formidable machine and that a thorough research into its potential ought to be undertaken as soon as we could afford the time it would require.

In retrospect, our study of cipher machines was without question the most important step in the development of a cryptanalytic capability which was so vital to the protection of our own communications in World War II and in our success with the Japanese diplomatic cipher machines which we were able to recover completely from intercepts. The knowledge of both cryptography and cryptanalysis which we gained from our studies of cipher machines in fact put the United States ahead of all the other nations of the world in the field of cryptology. And had it not been for the foresight of those officials in Military Intelligence and the Office of the Chief Signal Officer which brought the Signal Intelligence Service into being, it is most unlikely that the United States would have produced the secure cryptographic systems which successfully resisted the efforts of the most skillful cryptanalysts of Germany, Italy, and Japan throughout World War II.

CHAPTER 7

TWO CRYPTANALYTIC RESEARCH PROJECTS

Research on the ADFGVX System

One of the most important assignments in our training program was our study of the ADFGVX cipher system. This was a type of fractionating system originally employed by the German Army in World War I as a field cipher system. Friedman told us that the Germans had chosen this particular system because it had the advantage of shortening the time required for training the German Army field radio operators in the accurate transmission and reception of field communications, since the radio messages were composed of only six letters. The Germans chose the letters ADFGVX because the Morse equivalents for these letters are less likely to be confused with other Morse signals and the number of garbles in transmission was accordingly minimized.

When the system was originally introduced by the Germans on the Western Front in March 1918, only five letters — A, D, F, G, and X — were used in the messages. By the end of March the French cryptanalysts had correctly diagnosed the system as being one in which both substitution and transposition techniques were combined. The initial break into the system is described, starting on page 215, in *Precis de Cryptographie Moderne* by the French cryptographer Charles Eyraud published in 1953. According to Eyraud, this break came early in April 1918 when the French intercepted two messages, each of three parts, which they soon determined to be retransmissions of the same basic information, since there were only slight differences in the ciphertexts of the two messages. One of the French cryptanalysts, M. Painvain, was able to exploit this case of retransmission and recovered both the transposition key and the digraphic substitution employed in the messages. With the keys recovered from these two messages, the French cryptanalysts were able to read all the other messages sent in the same key period.

Although the French cryptanalysts had recovered the full details of the system from this initial break, they were unable to solve the keys for other days, except when they were fortunate enough to intercept two messages in which substantial repetitions of ciphertext occurred.

On the first of June 1918, the Germans added a sixth letter, the letter V, so that now the messages were composed of the letters ADFGVX. Evidently they had found that the substitution square which provided only for the twenty-five letters of the German alphabet needed to be improved by providing for the numbers from 1 through 0. Expanding the coordinates of the square by the addition of a sixth letter allowed them to encipher numbers directly without having to spell out each digit appearing in the plaintext of the message. The remaining cell of the substitution square was given the plaintext value for a full stop or period. Although the expansion to six letters added to the efficiency of the system, it offered no improvement in security against Painvain's techniques in those cases where the messages contained ciphertext repetitions.

Friedman had been assigned to Painvain's cryptanalytic group during the last weeks of the war, and he had worked on the intercepts of the ADFGVX system. Since the hope of successful exploitation of a day's intercepts depended entirely on the appearance of repetitions of texts between messages in the same key and since there were many days where these could not be found, one of the primary objectives of Painvain's group was to develop techniques for recovering the keys without benefit of these special circumstances. Friedman had been involved in this research during his work with Painvain's group, but the war ended before successful techniques could be developed.

When he found a large file of ADFGVX intercepts from World War I in the Black Chamber materials, he was reminded of this wartime research on the system which he had not been able to complete. He had preserved this file of intercepts in the hope that some day he would be able to do further research work on the system. He saw in the establishment of our group the opportunity to achieve this wartime aspiration by having us continue, as a part of our cryptanalytic training, the work he had started.

Our first assignment was to solve a set of messages which he had prepared as a typical example of the German Army use of the system, except that the plaintext was in English instead of German. We were able to solve these messages by using the techniques developed by Painvain. Friedman then put us to work on the intercepted German messages preserved in the Black Chamber files and encouraged us to see if we could devise improved techniques for solving the system. After sifting carefully through the German intercepts, we discovered one day's traffic which seemed to us to offer favorable prospects for a successful attack. We were able to recover the transposition key and the fractionating square by applying a modification of the Painvain technique, a special test which we devised.

Encouraged by this success on the actual intercepts from World War I, we continued our study of the system and soon developed solution techniques which did not require the special circumstances needed by the Painvain techniques. Friedman was delighted with our work and encouraged us to recover the keys for several days to prove that we had indeed developed what he termed a "general solution" to the ADFGVX system. He made a special point of reporting this accomplishment to the Chief Signal Officer, identifying our success as an important advance in cryptanalysis and emphasizing that if our team had been available in World War I all the ADFGVX intercepts would have been solved, instead of only the fraction which succumbed to Painvain's techniques.

I enjoyed this research work on the ADFGVX system as much as I did the analysis of the machine ciphers. But in the work on the actual German intercepts I found an additional element of interest — the potential intelligence value of the information which could be obtained by cryptanalysis. I felt that the information from the unsolved messages could have saved the lives of Allied soldiers and also might have shortened the war. And for the first time I began to appreciate the importance of cryptanalysis not only as a weapon to be used against the enemy's communications but also to develop a superior knowledge of the strengths and weaknesses of our own cryptographic systems so that we could devise codes and ciphers which would afford the highest possible protection for our own vital military information.

The Strip Cipher System (M138)

Our study of the Cipher Device, Type M-94, led us directly into an area of cryptanalytic research which at that time was of considerable practical importance. There was a need for a cipher system for low-echelon communications between Army and Navy units involved in joint operations. The Army proposed the use of the Cipher Device, Type M-94, to which the Navy strongly objected, claiming that it was not secure enough. The basic objection to the Cipher Device, Type M-94, was that the alphabets were permanently engraved on the disks of the device and could not be changed. Friedman arrived at the idea of using a modification of the Cipher Device, Type M-94, in which the alphabetic disks were replaced by sliding strips of paper on which the alphabets had been printed. The idea was finally accepted in principle by the Navy cryptographers, since the paper strips could easily be replaced by another set. This agreement in principle did not include agreement on the design of the device itself, which still had to be worked out. It was, however, agreed that both the Army and Navy would make a thorough study of the system before its final adoption as a joint cryptographic system.

Friedman gave us the responsibility for evaluating the system under his direct supervision. We first made a theoretical examination of the system which was aimed at identifying its strengths and weaknesses under a variety of assumed methods of use. After Friedman was satisfied that our theoretical results were sound in principle, he proposed that we make a practical test of the system and arranged to have a simulated day's traffic enciphered on which we could test our theoretical results. Our task was to read the messages and recover the alphabets used in their encipherment.

We spent several weeks studying the strip cipher system, and Kully, who was specializing in statistics and probability, developed an excellent insight into the problem. He worked out a statistical treatment which we used to establish what we call a "maximum use limit" for a set of strips, that is, the maximum number of letters which could be safely enciphered and transmitted by radio without fear that the strips could be recovered by the enemy through cryptanalysis. After Kully had calculated the maximum use limit for a set of twenty-five strips, Friedman decided to have us test the theoretical results by preparing a test problem which he challenged us to solve.

The test used a strip system composed of twenty-five different randomly mixed alphabets which were used to encipher a number of messages totaling over 15,000 letters of plaintext. Our task was to read the messages and to recover the alphabets. We worked for several weeks on this test problem without being able to break into the system, and Friedman concluded that the theoretical limits which had been calculated were valid. When the Navy cryptographers were briefed on the results of the test, formal agreement was reached to adopt the strip system for joint communications, and the Navy Yard was called in to devise a practical means for holding the strips so they could be efficiently manipulated for the enciphering and deciphering processes. Several designs were proposed, and each of these had to be tested.

The final design, which was approved by both services, consisted of two extruded magnesium-alloy plates in which dovetail-shaped channels had been formed, hinged so that they could be folded like the covers of a book, with the channels for the strips running parallel to the hinged edges. This design turned out to be fully satisfactory, and if a substantial paper stock was used for the strips, the device performed reliably. A contract was negotiated for producing a large quantity of the devices, and arrangements were made with the Government Printing Office to print a number of sets of strips, both for training purposes and to be held in reserve until there was occasion to issue the device for actual use.

I think the greatest benefit which resulted from our testing of the strip system was found in what we did not do rather than in what we did. Although we had not been able to solve the set of test messages, Friedman decided to leave the problem in the training course, feeling that it would be good from a disciplinary consideration for the future students of crypt-analysis to come up against a problem which they could not possibly solve.

When the training program for selected junior Signal Corps officers was put into effect some months later, this test problem which we had failed to solve by the application of analytic techniques was fairly easily solved by the first team of two officers who attempted it. They were successful in reading all the messages and were able to reconstruct completely all the alphabets by making clever assumptions for the plaintext represented by the considerable number of repetitions which appeared at the beginnings of the message texts. For myself, I was chagrined that we had failed to take advantage of this fairly obvious type of attack, which we had rejected without having given it proper consideration. At that time we were dedicated to the application of purely analytic techniques and considered it beneath our dignity to employ what some of us called the "by guess and by God" approach, and which Friedman designated the "probable word method."

When we found that the "maximum use limit" we had calculated for the strip system was invalid for the probable word approach, we had to reassess the system and establish new and lower limits for its use. The strip system was finally modified so that the probable word approach was less likely to compromise the system, and the new rules for its use were promulgated to all its holders, for by this time it had been distributed and had been given some limited use.

We worked for several weeks on this test problem without breaking into the system, and Friedman seemed satisfied that the system provided the desired security. When the Navy cryptographers were briefed on the results of this test, a formal agreement was reached to adopt the system, on an interim basis, for joint communications. The Navy devised a practical means for holding the strips so they could be efficiently manipulated for the enciphering and deciphering operations.

CHAPTER 8

WE START WORK ON JAPANESE INTERCEPTS

WHEN WE COMPLETED the phase of our training program that dealt with the analysis of cipher machines, Friedman announced that we were ready to undertake the first steps in response to the intelligence mission of the Signal Intelligence Service. He praised our progress in the study of cryptanalysis and noted that in our work on the ADFGVX system, the IT&T Cipher Machine, the Strip System, and the B-211 Cipher Machine we had made new and significant contributions to the state of the art of cryptanalysis.

He then informed us that some time earlier, when the Signal Corps had reported to G-2 that the intercept arm of the Signal Intelligence Service was ready to begin the interception of diplomatic messages of other governments by monitoring the international radio circuits, the Director of Military Intelligence had expressed interest in the intelligence contained in the current Japanese diplomatic messages. He had requested the Chief Signal Officer to initiate a study of Japanese diplomatic communications as the first target of our intelligence mission. The Chief Signal Officer had agreed to this proposal with the understanding that the code production program on which we were engaged would not be interfered with by the new undertaking and that we would be allowed to finish our study of cipher machines, which at that time was not complete.

Up to this point our efforts had been equally divided between work on the code production program and our cryptanalytic training. There was still a lot of work to be done in the preparation of the larger codes required for high-level War Department communications, and there were also a number of smaller codes to be used at intermediate and lower echelons (Army and Division) which had to be compiled. We would continue to spend half of our time working on the code production program and the other half on the study of Japanese diplomatic intercepts.

"In the last two years of its existence, the cryptanalysts of the Black Chamber had solved the codes used by the Japanese Foreign Office,"

Friedman reminded us. "Translations of Japanese diplomatic messages had been regularly provided to G-2 and to selected officials of the State Department. As you know, the files which G-2 received from the Black Chamber at the time it was abolished included the results of its work on the Japanese diplomatic codes. We are indeed fortunate that these files are available, for I know of no better way of introducing you to the study of Japanese codes than for you to reconstruct the work of the Black Chamber on the systems it had solved. The first step in your attack on the current Japanese diplomatic intercepts will be for you to review the Black Chamber files so that you will fully understand the techniques and processes developed by its cryptanalysts for solving the systems used by the Japanese Foreign Office cryptographers. Also it is quite possible that some of the systems recovered by the Black Chamber are still being used, and I think that the current intercepts ought to be examined to determine if any of them can be decoded by the codes recovered by the Black Chamber."

The reconstruction of the techniques employed by the Black Chamber was a most interesting and instructive task. Although we did not find any technical reports which described the methods employed for the recovery of the Japanese diplomatic codes, we did find working files which showed both the code messages and their interlinear decodements, copies of the decoding sections of the codes used for these messages, and extensive tabulations, or catalogs as they were called by the Black Chamber, which listed the occurrences of each code group, giving the work sheet number, the line in which it appeared and the preceding and following groups for each occurrence of the group. These catalogs were a most important tool for the recovery of the plaintext meanings of the code groups, for they enabled the cryptanalyst to locate each occurrence of the code group with a minimum of effort. By examining the plaintext which preceded and followed the unknown group in each of its appearances, it was often possible for a skilled linguist to identify its meaning with an astonishing degree of accuracy. Although the code recovery process was a fairly simple and straightforward procedure, it involved a tremendous amount of clerical effort in the typing of the work sheets and compilation of the catalogs. And at that time our typing the cards for the catalogs was impossible, for we did not have the clerical help needed to do this.

We soon worked out a logical and efficient division of labor as we developed our attack on the Japanese diplomatic codes. Kully and Hurt started on a program of testing each of the codes recovered by the Black Chamber cryptanalysts on the intercepts which we found in the Black Chamber files, in order to develop accurate information on the nature of the plaintext, how the codes were employed, and other communications practices followed by the Japanese code rooms. These latter included the message numbering system, classification practices, how the message addresses and signatures were handled, routing information, and other pertinent matters. As they developed this information, Abe and I kept in touch with their work and tried to organize the intercepts which were beginning to arrive in considerable volume from the Second Signal Service Company. Also, Colonel Mauborgne's personally operated intercept position, which he had set up in the basement of his quarters in the Presidio in San Francisco, was beginning to provide us with a substantial number of intercepts from the commercial radio stations in San Francisco which worked with the radio stations in Tokyo, handling a large number of Japanese diplomatic messages.

At that time we had very nebulous ideas about the Japanese intercepts, and our objective was to sort out the incoming intercepts into homogeneous groups. This turned out to be a fairly simple matter because the Japanese used a unique and easily identifiable external indication on all their messages, evidently to make it easier for the code room personnel to identify the system to be used for decoding the message, which, needless to say, also served our purposes admirably.

Among the current intercepts we found a number of messages bearing the indicator LA, which Kully and Hurt were able to equate partially to one of the codes recovered by the Black Chamber. When they tested this Black Chamber code on the current intercepts, the resulting plaintext was something less than perfect Japanese. At first this was attributed to poor intercept quality, but when it was observed that certain of the code groups consistently produced good plaintext, it became evident that the Japanese had, at some time in the three years since the Black Chamber had been abolished, modified this code without completely replacing it. Once this possibility was realized, the correct equivalents for the code groups whose meanings had been altered were determined. Hurt was now able to produce the first translations of current Japanese diplomatic messages. While this achievement did not hold much significance for us, it caused renewed interest to be taken in our efforts by the Chief Signal Officer and the Director of Military Intelligence. It gave a new stimulus to the procurement of additional staff for the Signal Intelligence Section, since Friedman very convincingly made the point that we could either compile codes or solve Japanese diplomatic systems, but such a small staff could not be expected to do both.

Encouraged by this development, we carefully tested all the other codes recovered by the Black Chamber against current intercepts, hoping that we might find that another code had been reused, but without success. Our examination did establish that while a large percentage of the current intercepts showed the same general textual characteristics we had found in the messages that the Black Chamber had solved, none of the codes recovered by the Black Chamber would produce Japanese plaintext when they were tested on the intercepted messages. We also found that the remaining intercepts could be sorted into two categories, one identified by a five-digit group which appeared as the first group of the message, with the remainder of the message text composed of five-letter groups and the other characterized by code groups of irregular length ranging from five to fifteen or more letters.

We decided to start work on the category of intercepts which most closely resembled the systems recovered by the Black Chamber. Before undertaking the analysis of these intercepts, we checked again through the Black Chamber files to ensure that we had missed nothing that might be of help to us. Among the working notes we found a number of frequency tabulations based on the actual texts of Japanese diplomatic messages processed by the Black Chamber, as well as other statistical information about the Japanese language which had been compiled for each version of the codes that had been recovered. The frequency studies were of great value to us.

In developing our plan of attack on the current intercepts, we decided to follow the general procedures employed by the Black Chamber cryptanalysts. We searched through all our intercepts for the most perfect messages, rejecting any which we suspected as being of poor quality. In the case of the Black Chamber, there was sufficient clerical help available for typing the work sheets and compiling the voluminous card catalogs required by the cryptanalysts; in our case we would have to prepare these items ourselves, since no clerical help was available except for some part-time typing by Friedman's secretary.

The first step in our procedure was to edit the messages to ensure that the cryptographic text was properly divided into the basic digraphic elements on which this type of Japanese diplomatic code was constructed. The tests of these edited intercepts were then transcribed, either by hand or typewriter, on legal-size master sheets. For this process we used a duplicating system known as "DITTO"; we called these sheets DITTO masters, with a double space between the digraphs and a triple space between lines. This produced a work sheet which allowed us to identify the location of each digraph appearing on the work sheet by its page and line coordinates. Enough copies were produced so that each of us had a complete file of work sheets.

The next step was to prepare a three-by-five-inch card for each code group, recording it and the two preceding and following groups and the page and line coordinates. These cards were sorted alphabetically on the last three code groups and stored in card files, so that when groups from additional messages were indexed, the new cards could be readily added. Since all this clerical preparatory work had to be done by Abe, Kully, Hurt, and me, with only occasional help from Larry Clark and Friedman's secretary, our actual start on the recovery of the individual code groups was delayed until we had accumulated an adequate amount of statistical data.

We also spent several hours each week studying Japanese. Hurt was the teacher and Abe, Kully, and I were the students. We used the Rose-Innes text on conversational Japanese for our study of the spoken language and the standard national Japanese elementary language textbooks (*Koku Go Toku Hon*) for our study of the written language. These latter were printed in kana and Chinese characters, and I considered them much more useful for our code recovery work than the Rose-Innes we were studying.

Just as we felt that we were beginning to make headway on the recovery in our study of the current Japanese intercepts, Hurt discovered that he was suffering from an advanced case of tuberculosis. He had made a weekend visit to his family in Wytheville, Virginia, and while on his way back to Washington had suffered from a severe lung hemorrhage. He had to be hospitalized immediately, and since he was our sole Japanese expert our effort suffered a severe setback. Although we realized that we would not be able to turn out any translations of Japanese messages, we felt that we could, in spite of our limited knowledge of the language, make further headway in our recovery of the system on which we had started work while we were awaiting Hurt's return.

It was now clearly more important than ever for us to improve our knowledge of the Japanese language. Working through G-2, Friedman made arrangements for us to be given special tutoring by a Russian who was an expert in Japanese and who was doing some work for G-2 on a part-time basis. He had, as an officer in the Czar's army, studied Japanese at the Oriental Institute in Moscow and also had spent several years in Japan as a member of the Russian military attaché's staff. He had become a full colonel in the Russian army before he was forced by the revolution to emigrate to the United States.

Unfortunately for us, his knowledge of spoken English was so atrocious that he sometimes had to resort to using the French or German equivalent of the English term for us to understand him. Lieutenant W. Preston Corderman, who had been assigned to the Signal Intelligence Service for training, was included in our class. These special lessons in Japanese continued for about four months and were terminated for lack of funds to pay the Russian for his tutoring services. By this time we had learned enough Japanese so that we were able to advance our knowledge of it without an instructor. In fact, we soon realized that our work on code recovery was much more useful for learning the language than the classes we had been attending, for by working on the message texts we were gaining experience in the grammar and vocabulary used in official Japanese correspondence, and it was this form of Japanese which was most useful to us in our work on the Japanese codes.

In spite of our limited knowledge of Japanese, we made some progress in our recovery of the system on which we had started work. We found that we could make progress by studying the new intercepts as they were received instead of concentrating solely on the messages which had been included in our catalogs. This led us to an important labor-saving discovery: We could operate more efficiently by indexing only the unrecovered groups in those messages which we selected for inclusion in our working files. This greatly improved the efficiency of our code recovery process.

While it was impossible for us to comprehend the meaning of the more intricate passages of the messages we had partially decoded, we were able to exploit certain other features which appeared in a great many of the intercepts and thereby recover the meanings of a large number of important code groups, such as numbers, dates, punctuation marks, names of cities and countries, and the like. We were also able to identify the use of auxiliary codes within the texts of the messages which were often employed for items which could not readily be expressed in Japanese, such as the names of foreign individuals, cities, and foreign expressions which could not be transliterated by using Japanese kana or Chinese ideographs.

We also kept a watchful eye on the other two categories of intercepts which we had isolated, and these were now accumulating in considerable volume. Most of these intercepts were in the category identified by the five-digit group appearing as the first group of the message. Its most noteworthy characteristic was that these messages were transmitted between Tokyo and the capitols of a few of the most important countries of the world. Messages of this category also appeared on a Japanese Foreign Office radio net in Asia which was being monitored by the U.S. Navy and which was called the Japanese Far Eastern Diplomatic Net. We made a thorough search of the Black Chamber files for any evidence that this system was known to its cryptanalysts, and, since we were not able to find anything which could possibly be associated with this category of intercepts, we decided that they were probably in a system issued by the Japanese after the Black Chamber had been closed. And neither did we find any evidence that the Black Chamber was acquainted with the other category of traffic which we had identified.

The most noteworthy feature of this latter category of intercepts was that its groups were irregular in length, and each group could contain from five to fifteen or more letters; all other Japanese diplomatic code messages were transmitted in groups of five letters. We had also noticed that the ciphertext was composed of about an equal number of vowels and consonants and that there were numerous long repetitions in the texts of the messages. When we studied the beginnings of the texts of these messages, we found that the first three letters of the messages were limited to only a small number of trigraphs which we assumed were indicators. When we isolated the messages with identical three-letter indicators, we found numerous long repetitions, both within and between messages bearing the same indicator. We found no repetitions between messages with different indicators. When we tried to separate the texts of the messages into groups of regular length, we were unable to do so, and we decided that the system was radically different from the code system on which we were working.

～　～　～

One of the long-range objectives of our training program was for each of us to take a tour of duty in one of the overseas departments. An opportunity arose in Panama for one of us to be sent for a two-year assignment, and Abe was selected. Kully and I continued our work on the Japanese diplomatic systems, until Hurt's health improved to the point that he could be released from the hospital. We were delighted to have him back with us again, and he appeared to be in much better physical condition than when he left us some months before. Friedman urged both Kully and me, and we wholeheartedly agreed, to ensure that Hurt limited his efforts to the Japanese work. This arrangement suited Hurt, for he had never really enjoyed the other cryptologic duties.

Hurt showed a great interest in the work we had done on the recovery of the code during his absence. We prepared a fresh set of work sheets for him in which we entered meanings for all the code groups that had been recovered, including those that we had added while he was absent. As he studied the work sheets, he would occasionally show amusement at the sense of the message resulting from some of the groups that we had recovered. After having a laugh at our expense, he would point out to us the groups which were in error and then patiently examine with us each appearance of the group until we found a correct meaning for it. This procedure greatly improved our ability to recover code groups, and it was also of great value in improving our knowledge of the Japanese language.

For the next several weeks, whenever we could find the time and the opportunity, Kully and I continued our examination of the two unsolved categories of intercepts. Kully became intrigued with the traffic transmitted in irregular group lengths, while I turned my attention to the messages bearing the five-digit indicators.

One afternoon, the three of us, Kully, Hurt, and I, were quietly working at our places in the vault. Suddenly, and without any warning, Kully started to beat on the top of the table at which he was working and loudly exclaimed: "That's it! That's what they've done! It's an English monoalphabetic substitution!"

I had no idea why he had become so excited. I hurriedly got out of my chair and went to look over his shoulder. He started to wave a work sheet wildly in the air.

"That's what they are doing," he continued. "They are enciphering English texts with a monoalphabetic substitution. And all along we were looking for something else, something much more difficult."

"Show us," I said, as Hurt joined us.

Kully slammed the work sheet down on the table top. "Look at that," he said, pointing to three of the ciphertext groups that he had underlined in red. "Look at the letter patterns for those three words. Can they be anything but a monoalphabetic substitution for the English words 'the Japanese government'?"

"Now look at the following words," he continued. "Decipher them by using the equivalents from the other three words, and what do you get?" I reached for the work sheet in order to do as he had suggested, but he was so excited that he refused to release it.

"I'll tell you what you will get," he said. "The rest of the line of text will decipher to give 'requests that the government of the United States'."

"Why don't you write in the equivalents on the work sheet?" I asked. "Then you can check out the remainder of the message."

Kully rapidly filled in the cipher equivalents while Hurt and I looked on. Every letter that he entered fitted accurately, and we were able to recover all the unknown equivalents so that by the time he reached the end of the message it was completely deciphered. It was indeed a monoalphabetic substitution, with vowels replacing vowels and consonants replacing consonants. There was no doubt about it: The Japanese were using the most insecure type of cipher that they could possibly have selected for enciphering the message. It was incredible to us that they would use such a simple form of cipher, for we had certainly expected them to use something much more secure.

"I can't understand it," Kully remarked. "Why would they do anything so stupid?"

"Why don't you test another message?" Hurt asked.

Kully soon located another intercept with the same indicator. As Hurt and I looked on, he deciphered the first few groups of the message using the substitution alphabet recovered from the message he had just finished deciphering.

"That's not English," I observed.

"But it's perfect Japanese!" Hurt exclaimed. "Decipher some more groups so that I can translate it."

Kully continued his decipherment of the message until Hurt interrupted him. He took the work sheet from Kully and studied it.

"Except for a few garbled letters, this is perfect Japanese," Hurt informed us. "It is apparently a news release which the Japanese Foreign Office is transmitting to its installations abroad and is for the information of Japanese nationals in foreign countries. I have seen similar examples in the plain-language messages we have been intercepting."

Kully sought out some more messages with the same indicator. All of the messages could be deciphered and they were all in Japanese. It was really a piece of good luck that Kully had selected the only intercept with English plaintext. It could have been weeks before we might have realized that this category of traffic was nothing but a monoalphabetic substitution, for we were looking for something much more sophisticated.

"Let's see what Mr. Friedman has to say," Hurt suggested.

I stepped to the vault door and opened it. Friedman was busy at his desk and looked up at me as I stood in the vault doorway.

"Excuse me," I said. "Kully has discovered something that you will find most interesting. Would you mind stepping into the vault to look at it?"

Friedman pushed his work aside and followed me into the vault. "What have you found?" he asked Kully.

"The Japanese are using a monoalphabetic system for enciphering some of their diplomatic messages," Kully answered.

Friedman looked doubtful. "Why do you think that?" he asked.

"I just solved one," Kully gleefully answered.

"Well, that's a rather convincing argument," Friedman replied. "But there must be something wrong," he continued. "No government of today with any competence whatever in cryptography would intentionally use such a patently insecure system. A code clerk must have made a mistake, or they are using a cipher machine in which a mechanical failure occurred, thereby producing a monoalphabetic encipherment which was transmitted by mistake."

"But there are several messages on different dates which use the same substitution," Kully observed. He then spread out the work sheets and demonstrated the decipherments to Friedman. Friedman picked up the message in English and read it carefully.

"This message seems to be a note which the Japanese ambassador has been instructed to deliver to the State Department," he said. "It is possible that they used a simple encipherment merely to disguise the contents of the message from the communications personnel who would be handling it. If the Japanese were planning to provide the exact text of one of their messages to another government, they certainly would not want to encipher it in one of their secret codes. To do so might result in their code being compromised, for it would take an exceptionally secure cryptographic system to resist analysis when such a long message together with its exact decipherment was available for study."

Friedman was obviously pleased with Kully's discovery. "Well done, Mr. Kullback," he said as he left the vault.

The other messages in this category of traffic were also found to be enciphered by monoalphabetic substitutions which were readily recovered. We had now diagnosed all the current categories of traffic except that which was identified by the five-digit indicator. Kully's discovery stimulated our interest in these messages, and we decided to give them another careful examination, in the hope that we might find some useful clues which would help us to identify the type of system used for their encipherment. We felt that we might be misleading ourselves by expecting the system to be difficult and that we should take another look at it.

After several days of reexamination of the system which revealed nothing new of importance about it, the pressure of other work caused us to put it aside. But I resolved that at the earliest opportunity I would get back to work on it and search through the intercepts in the hope that I would develop some new ideas about its nature and apply all the analytical tests known to us on its most promising intercepts.

CHAPTER 9

A NEW CRYPTOGRAPHIC CONCEPT

ONE OF THE MOST important compilation tasks on our agenda was the preparation of the keying materials for Friedman's cipher machine, the M-134. These keying materials, specially designed by Friedman, required electromechanical equipment for their preparation. This equipment was to be operated by the Signal Intelligence Section personnel, and it was housed in two enclosed rooms near the area in which our offices were located. Some of the equipment had been drawn from Signal Corps surplus and it had seen considerable use.

Friedman called me into his office one morning and informed me that he was making me responsible for the preparation of the M-134 keying materials. He wanted me to spend half my time on the preparation of these materials; the other half would be devoted to the continuation of my training. The other members of the group would likewise be occupied with other compilation tasks on a half-time basis, and they too were to continue with their training. He told me that he was ready for me to start immediately on the task and asked me to come with him to the area where the equipment was located.

His plan for the rest of the morning was to instruct me in the operation of the equipment and then have me make a number of test runs to ensure that I had mastered the processes involved. He showed me how each piece of the equipment was to be operated and made sure that I was able to make it function properly. As he was demonstrating the equipment, we found that one piece was operating erratically, which fortunately we were able to repair without too much loss of time. After he felt that I understood the equipment, he had me start a test run of one set of keys and he remained with me until the run was finished. He seemed pleased with my performance and suggested that I spend the rest of the morning getting familiar with the operation by making several more test runs.

After he departed, I continued as he had proposed. I decided that I would duplicate the test run I had made under his supervision to see if the keys prepared on two separate runs were identical as they should be. When I finished the second run and compared the two keys, I found several points of discrepancy. I decided that I would make another attempt to duplicate the first run. When it was finished and I compared it with the two previous runs, I found all three to be different. And when I tried two more duplicate runs, I found that I got different results for each. At this point I decided that I had better consult with Friedman.

When I showed Friedman the results I had obtained, he came with me to the equipment room. When he tried to produce a duplicate of the test run I had made, he also obtained different results. We spent until lunchtime trying to get satisfactory results, but with only moderate success.

My first day's experience with the equipment was only a preview of the succeeding days. The equipment operated erratically, and frequently I had to dismantle a piece of it in order to locate the trouble. After pursuing this course for some time, I was finally able to make several runs with identical results. By the end of the first month I had completed only a small portion of the compilation task that I had been assigned.

Friedman seemed to be disappointed with my progress. He spent hours with me, trying to determine why the results I had been obtaining were so unsatisfactory. At first he seemed to think that I was at fault, but after operating the equipment himself on a number of runs, he reluctantly admitted that the equipment was operating unreliably. Finally, in desperation, he told me to continue with the preparation of the keying materials while he undertook the procurement of more reliable equipment.

By this time I was fully fed up with the assignment. No matter how hard I tried, the equipment kept performing erratically and I had to reject over three-quarters of the keys that I had prepared. There was no relief in sight, and I soon began to feel that I would be spending at least several months on a most unrewarding assignment.

In our study of the M-134 I had become thoroughly familiar with it and fully understood the purpose of the keying materials. As I somewhat despondently followed the process of key generation directed by Friedman, I began to speculate about other keying systems which might be suitable for use with the M-134. After a while this became an obsession and from the many ideas which occurred to me I became convinced that the process designed by Friedman could be replaced by other and more satisfactory arrangements. One arrangement that I contrived especially intrigued me, for it replaced the entire keying system of the M-134 with a small electromechanical unit. It seemed to me that it would be feasible to build such a unit, and if it functioned as I visualized it there would be no need for further generation of the keying materials using the unsatisfactory process I had been following. I spent several days developing a logical design for a unit which I felt would meet the essential requirements of the M-134 system.

When I reached the point where I was satisfied with the design of the unit, I was struck with the idea that instead of building an auxiliary device to be used with the M-134, it might be possible to construct a cipher machine using the principles I had discovered. I immediately started to design such a cipher machine, and when I began to prepare sketches incorporating the new principles, it seemed that everything automatically fell into place to produce an entirely new concept in electromechanical cipher devices. I began to spend all my free time refining the design I had originally conceived, and I finally produced three variations of the basic concept which I was convinced would not only offer greater cryptographic security than the M-134 but also would completely eliminate the need for preparing the keying materials the M-134 required. I also prepared "pencil and paper" analogs for each variant, which permitted me to encipher and decipher small samples of plaintext.

As I continued my work on the keying materials, I found that Friedman was adopting a more and more distant attitude toward me. He rarely visited the room in which I was working, and when he did spend some time with me reviewing the limited progress that had been made, he made his disappointment clear by both his manner and by the way he spoke to me. Whenever I offered suggestions for improvements or reported on malfunctions of the equipment, he often ignored them. At one time when he found that I had been unable to produce usable keying materials for a period of over two days, he severely criticized me. When I somewhat irritatedly responded that if he did not like my performance he ought to give the job to someone else, he flatly informed me that it was my responsibility to prepare the keying materials for the M-134 and that he was going to hold me to it. After making this announcement he abruptly left the room.

My morale had never before been so low. On the one hand I was stuck with what I considered to be an impossible assignment, I had been given inadequate equipment and support, and my supervisor seemed anything but sympathetic. On the other hand, I wanted desperately to continue my career as a cryptanalyst, and I had just discovered what seemed to be a most revolutionary concept for a superior cipher machine. After spending several days thinking about what I should do, I decided to ask for a meeting with Friedman to discuss the production problems for the M-134 keys. If I found him to be in a receptive mood, I planned to reveal my ideas about a new cipher machine.

It was several days later before Friedman visited the room where I was working. When I told him that I would like to discuss the compilation of the keying materials in some detail, he responded that he was extremely busy and that our meeting would have to wait until he had some free time.

Some days later his secretary informed me that a meeting had been set up and that he could spare only thirty minutes with me and that he hoped what I had to discuss with him was important. Thirty minutes was better than nothing, so I set about getting my thoughts organized to be able to make the best use of the time he was scheduling for me.

When we had our meeting, instead of making a personal complaint, I stated that I had given serious thought to the procedures I had been following for the preparation of the M-134 keying materials and that I was convinced that the process we were using, although theoretically feasible, was not practical. He promptly responded by stating that he had given careful consideration to the design of the process, that it afforded greater cryptographic security than any other cipher machine system known, and that it would be continued until the scheduled requirements were met.

When he finished his remarks, I told him that I had some ideas for a cipher machine system which I felt would offer at least equivalent security to that afforded by the M-134 and that it had the advantage of eliminating the need for the unsatisfactory process of preparing the keying materials. I then stated that I was prepared to give him an explanation of my ideas.

He seemed surprised at my remarks, for evidently he was expecting something else from me. He sat quietly for a few seconds and then stated that if that was all I wanted to talk about it would have to be discussed later. I told him that I had prepared some sketches and diagrams and that it would take only a short while for me to give him an outline of my concept of a novel cipher machine system. He however insisted that he did not have any time for such a discussion and that I would have to wait until he had more time to spend with me.

I tried hard to disguise my irritation with his attitude and his treatment of me. I thanked him for his time and asked him when I might expect to be able to present my proposal to him. He told me that he would have his secretary let me know when he could meet with me again. I responded that I would wait for his call, and as a closing remark stated that I was convinced that further reliance on the process for preparing the M-134 keying materials could only give the system a most undesirable reputation.

It was several days before Miss Newkirk advised me of the time she had set for our next meeting. Again it was for only thirty minutes. Instead of asking me about my ideas for a new cipher machine, Friedman started the meeting by stating that he recognized that the equipment we had been using was not operating up to his expectations and that he was making arrangements for replacing all of it except one item with newly purchased equipment. He added that he was sure the new equipment would eliminate the difficulties I had experienced. I thanked him for the information and then told him that I was ready to describe my ideas for a cipher machine which I was sure would be of interest to him.

When I made this remark, he looked at the wall clock and answered that he had allowed only thirty minutes for the meeting and that I should be prepared to finish my description within that time.

I had prepared an overall schematic of the cipher machine and I placed this on his desk. I then identified the various components shown on the schematic and explained their functions. He kept interrupting me with questions about both the components and the circuitry which I was able to answer satisfactorily. When I finished with the first diagram, he remarked that while he was reluctant to disappoint me, he was sure that my ideas would not work and that it would not be necessary for me to provide him with a further description. When I insisted that he listen to an alternate proposal, he grudgingly acceded. Before I had a chance to finish my explanation, he interrupted me and told me that there no point in my continuing, for the concept I was presenting simply would not work. When I asked him to show me why, he somewhat testily responded that he did not have any further time to spend discussing it and that I should get back to work on the preparation of the keying materials for the M-134.

After this most unsatisfactory meeting, I reexamined my ideas, trying to find the faults in them, and became more convinced that they were valid. I also described them to Kully and to Corderman, who agreed with me that they were markedly superior to all other keying systems we had encountered. Both were reluctant to join me in a discussion of them with Friedman. Feeling that I was not being fairly treated by Friedman, I finally decided to confront him again with my proposals and to demand at least an explanation of their deficiencies.

The morning after I reached this conclusion, I came to the office early and waited for Friedman in his office. When he arrived, he seemed displeased to find me waiting for him, and asked if I was having more trouble with the equipment used for preparing the M-134 keys. I responded that I wanted another opportunity to explain my proposal for a new cipher machine. He brusquely informed me that it would be a waste of his time, that he had already given me his opinion, and that I ought to get back to the job of preparing the materials for the M-134, for I was behind schedule in my work. I became angry and responded that my ideas were sound and that he would agree with me if he would only take the time to try to understand them.

In answer he told me that he was just as certain that they were not sound, and I retorted that one of us had to be wrong and that if he was so sure that my ideas would not work, he ought to be able to show me why. I also added that if he was unable to give me a satisfactory explanation of why they would not work, I was ready to go to the Chief Signal Officer. He must have sensed that I was now resolved to make an issue of the question and reluctantly gave me an appointment to discuss the matter the next afternoon.

I carefully prepared a briefing on my proposals and made sure that the wiring diagrams and illustrations that I needed were error-free. I also prepared an outline which I felt would fairly and logically present my ideas.

When I reported for my appointment, I found Friedman quite ill at ease, and it was clear to me that he was anything but pleased at the prospects of the outcome of our discussions. When I started my presentation, he kept interrupting me, asking for me to give a detailed explanation of certain of the more novel concepts. It seemed to me that he was trying to take advantage of every opportunity to belittle my proposals, but I was able to counter each of his objections by pointing out the advantages which they offered. After about an hour of discussion, he told me that he could not spend any more time that afternoon on the matter, and that we could have to continue our discussion later. I was disappointed with this, for I wanted to get the matter settled once and for all. When I asked if we could continue, he reiterated that he could spare me no more time until the next day and that he was leaving the office immediately.

I spent a lot of time that night thinking about my next move. From Friedman's reaction, I sensed that now his feelings toward me were anything but friendly. I could also see that if he rejected my proposals, I had no choice but to follow up on my statement that I would appeal to the Chief Signal Officer. And if I did this, I was certain that my future position with respect to Friedman would be most difficult. At the same time, I was sure that I was right in insisting the keying system for the M-134 be improved.

I arrived at the office early next morning and again reviewed my charts and diagrams to make sure that I was ready to continue my discussion with Friedman. He usually did not get in until after the office had been opened, but on this day he showed up early. I was sitting at my table in the vault when I saw him hurrying into his office. He did not stop to remove his hat and topcoat as he usually did when he arrived for work, but instead he came directly into the vault and approached me. He was obviously highly emotional and my first thought was that I was going to be fired on the spot.

"Rowlett, you're right!" he exclaimed. "You've made a wonderful discovery. If we can incorporate it into a practical device, we will have developed the most secure cipher machine in the world. I want you to start immediately on drafting patent specifications, and I will work directly with you in developing these new principles into their most advantageous form."

I had expected any kind of reaction but this one. I was pleased that he confirmed my proposals and that he was willing to endorse them. The only thing which was not clear to me was what he meant when he stated that he would be working directly with me on the preparation of the patent specifications, since the novel ideas were mine. I decided not to make an issue out of it at that time, but instead to do whatever seemed reasonable to improve the security of the War Department communications.

"What about the keying materials for the M-134?" I asked. "Shall I continue working on them also?"

"We will hold further work on the M-134 keying materials in abeyance until we get the patent specifications drafted," he answered. "If you will get your papers, we can start right away. I'll cancel all my engagements for this morning and we will work together at my desk."

As soon as Friedman cleared his schedule for the day, we went to work. He had evidently absorbed most of the information I had provided on the previous day, but he had not allowed me to describe the full range of applications of the principles I had invented, so that most of the day was spent in my describing the various alternatives I had conceived.

Soon after we started, I found that the ideas I had developed were so novel that it required considerable explanation on my part for him to understand them. By the end of the day, all we had accomplished was that Friedman now had a better understanding of the principles, and it was clear to me that he was fully converted to supporting them. During our discussion his attitude toward me had changed, and I had never before found him so friendly and so agreeable to work with. He still retained his "boss–employee" attitude, but I could see that as he reached a more comprehensive grasp of the principles I had discovered, he was accepting me as a professional cryptanalyst rather than as a student.

When, a few days later, Friedman felt that we had produced the most desirable logical design for a cipher machine using the new principles, he put me to work on drafting a description of it. By this time he was so enthusiastic about the new concept that he proposed to the Chief Signal Officer that we start immediately on the development of a pilot model of a new cipher machine, using funds which had been budgeted for the development of a field cipher machine to replace the Cylindrical Cipher Device, Type M-94. We both were disappointed with the response to this proposal, which stated that the funds for the field cipher machine development had already been committed to a project now under way at the Signal Corps Laboratory and that no other funds for cipher machine development would become available in the foreseeable future.

This response also held another disappointment for Friedman, for when he made inquiries of the Signal Corps Fiscal Office about the transfer of Signal Intelligence Service funds without his knowledge, he found that a project had been under way for several months to build a cipher machine under the auspices of the Signal Corps Laboratory. When Friedman protested that all cipher machine development was the exclusive responsibility of the Signal Intelligence Service, the Chief Signal Officer ruled in his favor and indicated that the work on the cipher machine which had been started at the Signal Corps Laboratory would continue under Friedman's supervision.

I continued working on the draft patent specifications, and, when Friedman found them acceptable, we had a meeting with Charles A. Rowe, a patent attorney employed by the War Department who handled all the Signal Corps patent matters. Friedman provided Mr. Rowe with copies of the drafts and, after warning him that the information contained in the drafts was vital to the communications security of the War Department and that great damage could result if it fell into unauthorized hands, asked that Mr. Rowe take the required steps to have an application made for a secret patent. Mr. Rowe assured us that the information in the draft would be given secure handling, but stated he would have to make a study of the information we had provided him before he could judge whether or not the ideas were patentable.

I went back to work preparing the keying materials for the M-134. The problems with the faulty equipment still continued, and I found that it was necessary to deviate from the routine which Friedman had directed me to follow. Previously when I had suggested to Friedman that the routine needed to be altered, he had turned down my suggestions. His attitude was now quite different, and although he always required from me an explanation of my reasons for changing the routine, he usually agreed with my proposals. The new equipment arrived and after a few weeks I was able to work out a feasible procedure for preparing the keying materials in the desired quantities.

Friedman followed up on the field cipher device under development at the Signal Corps Laboratory in Fort Monmouth, New Jersey. He made a trip to Fort Monmouth to find out what sort of device was being built, returning with a complete description of the device under construction which he gave to me to evaluate. The device was entirely mechanical, it was to be driven by a spring motor like the ones used in phonographs at that time, and the cryptographic principles employed in it were less secure that the Pletts cipher device which had been rejected several years before. We had both hoped that enough of the budgeted funds would be left for some work to be done on the pilot model which Friedman had recommended, but since the initial amount was for only a few hundred dollars and the project had been under way for several months, only a small portion of the funds could be salvaged, completely inadequate for starting the construction of a pilot model of another device.

Some weeks later, in one of the infrequent meetings between Friedman and Captain Joseph N. Wenger of the Navy's Communications Security Group (OP-20-G), Wenger told Friedman that the Navy was abandoning the Hebern Mark II and was planning to build another cipher machine to replace it. He added that the Navy was looking for new cryptographic principles to be incorporated in the planned cipher machine and asked Friedman for his recommendations. Wenger explained that enough money was available for the construction of a pilot model but that the project was being delayed in the hope that more satisfactory cryptographic principles could be found before construction was be started. When Friedman returned from this meeting, he promptly told me about Wenger's remarks and asked me if I would have any objections to revealing the new cryptographic principles to Wenger, provided that he could obtain the permission of the Chief Signal Officer. I told him that I certainly would have no objections and that it was my hope that the Navy would consider them suitable enough to adopt them. After our discussion, Friedman requested permission of the Chief Signal Officer to disclose the invention to the Navy, which was granted without reservation.

Friedman then informed Wenger that he had been given official permission to reveal to him some revolutionary cryptographic principles that had not yet been tested by the Army and which he thought might be of interest to the Navy. Arrangements were made for a meeting in Wenger's office, where Friedman was to describe these principles. Before he attended the meeting, Friedman spent some time with me going over the diagrams and descriptions of the various forms of cipher machines which might be constructed using these principles.

After Friedman concluded his meeting with the Navy, he called me to his desk and reported that the Navy had been impressed with the novelty of the cryptographic principles which he had disclosed to them, and he generally reviewed the questions which had been asked during the briefing. He felt that the Navy cryptologists had shown a positive interest in what he had described to them, but that he had received no indication that the Navy would adopt the new principles.

A few days after the briefing, Wenger called Friedman and asked if he would repeat the briefing for the small group of Navy engineers and cryptanalysts who were responsible for the management of the Navy contracts for cipher machine construction. Friedman agreed, and a date and time was set for the meeting, which was to take place in Friedman's office.

I had hoped that I would be asked to attend the meeting with the Navy when Friedman first explained the invention and had felt some disappointment when I had not been invited. Now that the meeting was to be held in Friedman's office I expected to be included, and as the time approached I waited at my worktable in the vault, next door to Friedman's office.

When the Navy group arrived, Friedman seated them around his desk and just before he started his briefing he closed the vault door. I was now sure that I was being excluded from the discussions. When the vault door was opened by Friedman's secretary some time later, I learned that the meeting was over and that Friedman had left for the day. Next morning when I asked Friedman about the Navy's reaction to the briefing, he reported that while they had shown interest in the ideas he had presented, they had made no statements about their intentions.

About two weeks later, Wenger called Friedman and invited him to attend a meeting in his office for the purpose of further clarifying the cryptographic principles which he had disclosed to them. Friedman accepted the invitation, and when he returned from the meeting, he told me that while the Navy continued to show interest in the concepts, there was no evidence that they intended to adopt it. When several weeks later I asked Friedman, after one of his infrequent visits with Wenger, if he had learned anything further about the possible use of the concepts in the new Navy machine, he reported that he had queried Wenger on this matter at their last meeting. Wenger had told him that the Navy engineers had rejected the concept and that the Navy was continuing its search for new ideas. I was disappointed to learn that neither the Army nor the Navy seemed to want to develop a concept which I was sure would provide the United States with the most secure cipher machines known. And what disturbed me more than anything else was the realization that there was nothing further I could do about it at that time.

CHAPTER 10

WE START USING IBM ACCOUNTING MACHINES

A FTER OUR EXPERIENCE WITH the compilation of several editions of two major War Department codes, we gave a lot of thought to improving the two-part code compilation process. We had not yet started on the preparation of the field codes to be used at army and division level which had been scheduled to follow the compilation of the War Department codes. The field codes were much smaller than the codes used at departmental levels, but a larger number of editions were required. We estimated that our compilation task was only half completed.

In our evaluation of the procedures we had used in the compilation of the departmental codes, it was glaringly obvious that we needed better techniques. Although the procedures which finally emerged from our experience with the large departmental codes had produced acceptable editions, the process we had followed was almost prohibitively time-consuming and had to be done most painstakingly. We also had to check our compilation procedures continuously to ensure that they were producing acceptable results.

Friedman had for years been searching for efficient two-part code compiling procedures. He was unable to get help from sources outside the government, for there was practically no nongovernmental demand for two-part codes because commercial codes were designed for economy and not security. He had also investigated the work which had been done in the academic field in the generation of random numbers. The research in this field was of little use to him, for it had been based on relatively small sets of numbers, and the results were not applicable to code vocabularies consisting of thousands of elements.

The most promising, though yet unexplored, possibility for overall improvement was to employ machine accounting systems using punched cards. At that time there were two accounting machine systems which might be employed. One of these was the Hollerith, which used a mechanical system for sensing the data on the punched cards. The other was the

IBM, which used an electrical sensing system. The IBM system had the advantage that the accounting programs could be changed by the user to suit his needs, while the Hollerith programs could only be changed by factory-trained personnel. The IBM system also provided greater flexibility in choice of programs. Friedman had at one time requested a modest installation of IBM equipment for the Signal Intelligence Section, but had been turned down because at that time there were no funds which could be used for such purposes.

There was some urgency about our completing the compilation of the field codes, since the funds which had been allocated for their publication had to be spent within the designated fiscal year or returned to the U.S. Treasury. Also, the Chief Signal Officer and the Director of Military Intelligence wanted us to continue the work we had started on the Japanese intercepts. Since it was impossible to hire and train additional personnel to assist in the code-compilation work, Friedman's interest in the use of IBM machines was renewed. In order to develop the necessary information on which to base a formal request, he contacted the Washington IBM office to determine what currently available equipment would be suitable for our purposes.

In his discussions with the IBM representatives he learned that the Quartermaster Corps had decided to terminate its contract for the rental of a fairly large IBM accounting machine installation at its Washington headquarters, which was located only a few blocks from our offices in the Munitions Building. He also learned that the Quartermaster Corps had started phasing out its use of the equipment and that some of the machines would be standing idle for several weeks. When Friedman inquired if it would be possible to use the idle Quartermaster Corps equipment for some experimental programs, the IBM representatives assured him that IBM would have no objections. They also volunteered to provide any training in the operation of the equipment which might be required for the experiments.

When Friedman followed through on this opportunity for temporarily using the IBM equipment without cost to the Signal Corps, he received full support from the Chief Signal Officer in making the necessary official arrangements with the Quartermaster Corps. While the details of these arrangements were being resolved, we started preparing the plaintext vocabulary and permutation table for a training edition of a field code to be used at division level. The size of this code was limited to 10,000 groups, and each plaintext element was to be assigned a four-letter code group selected from a specially constructed permutation table.

We needed four types of equipment for our experiment — an alphabetical key punch, a sorter, a reproducer, and an alphabetical tabulator or printer. IBM provided us with instruction in the operation of each of these machines, and we spent several hours in the Quartermaster Corps IBM area operating each model until we were adequately familiar with it. We also designed programs for performing some of the simpler processes of cryptanalysis such as monoliteral frequency distributions for cipher messages, prints of work sheets and several other cryptanalytic tests.

While we were getting acquainted with the operation of the IBM equipment, Friedman arranged to have the plaintext vocabulary for the code which we were compiling transferred to punched cards. Using a carefully checked and edited alphabetic listing, a single IBM card was prepared for each plaintext equivalent. Remembering our fiasco with the first departmental code we compiled, we serially numbered these cards while they were still in exact alphabetic order. This process, which would have taken several hours to accomplish by hand, was achieved in a spectacularly short time by using the IBM reproducer. We could now automatically restore the plaintext vocabulary to its original alphabetic order merely by sorting on the four columns in which the digits of the serial numbers were punched.

The next step was to disarrange — or scramble — the set of 10,000 IBM cards just as we had for the three-by-five-inch cards we used in compiling the large departmental codes. By this time we were old hands at the process and when the cards were disarranged to our satisfaction, we were ready to ascribe a code group to each card. In the compilation of the departmental codes we had done this by hand, but with the punched cards this process could be accomplished automatically. A second set of 10,000 IBM cards with the code groups in sequential order was prepared, and we used the reproducer to number them serially. Again using the reproducer, we transferred the code groups with their serial numbers to the scrambled vocabulary cards, and we were delighted with the ease in which this task was performed by the machines. Using the manual techniques and working at top speed without any interruptions, we estimated that one person could apply code groups to about ten cards per minute; with the machine techniques the punched cards passed through the reproducer at greater than 100 per minute, giving an advantage of at least ten to one, probably more like twenty-five to one, allowing for interruptions and breaks.

The punched cards now carried two sets of serial numbers, so that by sorting on one set we could arrange the cards in the proper order for the encode section and by sorting on the other set we could put the cards in the correct order for the decode section if such was needed for any purpose. Since the code groups had been applied to the cards in an exact "decode" order, we were now ready to pass the set of cards through the alphabetic tabulator in order to print the manuscript for the decode section. Even though the tabulator operated at a slower speed than the reproducer, here again the advantage in time was impressive, and within a few hours the manuscript of the decode section was printed.

The next step was the preparation of the manuscript for the encode section. This was what we referred to in our manual process as the "killer" step, and it required returning the cards to their original alphabetic order. In the manual process this was a tiring and boresome operation, which could result in considerable eyestrain if done without frequent rests. With the IBM equipment it was amazingly easy to restore the 10,000 scrambled cards to their original alphabetic order. The manuscript for the encode section could now automatically be produced by passing the resorted cards through the alphabetical tabulator.

Additional editions of the code could be produced by repeating this process. Since the punched cards contained only 80 columns and about half of these were used for the plaintext meaning, we found that a set of cards could be used for the preparation of at least four separate editions. This presented no problem, for a master deck for the plaintext vocabulary was prepared and when there was no more room left on a set of cards, we discarded the set and replaced it with a fresh one by reproducing the master deck onto a set of blank cards.

As we conducted our experiments in compiling two-part codes we kept a careful record of the time required for each step of the process. At the end of our experiment Friedman prepared a short report in which he compared the actual time required for the machine compilation with an estimate of the time which would have been required for the manual process. In this report he also highlighted the potential of the machine process for the preparation of field codes in time of war. The report was so convincing that the Chief Signal Officer allocated some unused funds to the rental of a minimal IBM unit for the sole use of the Signal Intelligence Section. When we were satisfied with our procedure for the preparation of codes to be used at the division level, we started the compilation of a larger code to be used at army level. We were able to refine our procedures so that they became more efficient, and by the time the Quartermaster Corps equipment was no longer available we had worked out an effective compilation process for completing our code production program. We were able to continue it with only a short interruption, for the equipment for the Signal Intelligence Section was delivered in a remarkably short time. Evidently the IBM Washington office rentals were being seriously affected by the depression, and management was pleased to be able to relocate some of its surplus by making prompt deliveries to new customers.

After we got into the swing of using the accounting machines, we developed a technique for using the IBM sorter for scrambling the plaintext elements for each successive edition. I do not recall which of us was responsible for the original idea, but we soon started to use the sorter to scramble the vocabulary cards. The concept behind this technique was to "unsort" the cards, and it was so effective that the production of the field codes developed into a routine procedure which offered little interference with our more interesting work on the Japanese diplomatic intercepts.

In retrospect, the acquisition of our own dedicated IBM unit was probably the most significant development we experienced. Not only did it provide us with a means for more effectively meeting our day-to-day requirements, both cryptanalytic and cryptographic, but also it opened the door for the invention of more sophisticated processing techniques which eventually led to the development of modern computers. Friedman's foresight and action in introducing the IBM accounting machines into the cryptologic processes could well be the greatest single technical contribution of his career.

ᔕ ᔕ ᔕ

The IBM accounting machines enabled us to catch up with the more pressing code compilation requirements and to bring our recovery of the Japanese diplomatic code system to the point where Hurt could occasionally produce fairly complete translations of selected code messages. We limited our output of translations to those messages which were almost completely recovered, for we were reluctant to submit translations in which there were missing passages because of unknown code groups. These translations were provided to Colonel Rufus Bratton, who at that time was chief of the division of Military Intelligence responsible for intelligence on Japan. Colonel Bratton was considered to be exceptionally well qualified for this position, since he had spent several years in Tokyo as a military attaché and he was also very proficient in Japanese. As the number of translations increased, Colonel Bratton became more and more interested in their contents, and he began to press us for fuller exploitation of the messages passing between Tokyo and Washington.

There was one instance of Colonel Bratton's interest in a translation which had a far-reaching effect on our work. Hurt had found a rather unusual message in the intercepts he was studying for code recovery purposes, the contents of which seemed to represent a broad review of Japanese foreign policy. One noteworthy feature of this message was that the decoded text began with the Japanese words "GOKU HI KAN CHOO FU GOO ATSUKAI" which Hurt translated as "National Secret. To Be Given Special Handling." This phrase had only rarely been encountered in the messages we had decoded, and when it did appear, the contents of the message always dealt with matters which were evidently of great importance to the Japanese Foreign Office.

From the portions of the message which had been recovered, Hurt concluded that its contents were of exceptional importance and that G-2 might find even a partial translation of interest. The best he could achieve was a sketchy translation in which certain key words and phrases were missing because they were represented by unrecoverable code groups. He prepared a translation in which the known groups were carefully translated, but where an unknown group, or series of groups, occurred, he inserted a parenthetical note indicating that translation was not possible because the plaintext equivalents of the code groups were unrecovered. This version was delivered to Colonel Bratton's office late one afternoon.

I was usually the first of the Signal Intelligence Service staff to arrive at the office, and, on the morning after the translation had been delivered to Colonel Bratton's office, I found him standing in the hallway just outside our area, evidently waiting for one of us to arrive. I unlocked the outer door, and, as soon as we stepped inside the office where there was no danger of being overheard, he took the translation out of his inner coat pocket and asked me if I was familiar with it. When I told him that I was, he responded that he was most anxious to discuss the translation with Hurt and demanded to know when Hurt would be available. I told him that Hurt was due at any moment and suggested that he make himself comfortable until Hurt arrived. Colonel Bratton took a chair alongside Friedman's desk, where he sat impatiently drumming his finger tips on its top while I unlocked to door to the vault and opened its windows.

As soon as Hurt arrived, Colonel Bratton pounced on him and in whispers started to discuss the possible interpretations of the portions of the message which had not been translated. Hurt invited Colonel Bratton to his desk inside the vault and brought out the file of work sheets from which he had made the incomplete translation. Meanwhile, the other members of the staff arrived, and we went about our regular duties, quite naturally curious about what had aroused Colonel Bratton's interest.

After spending more than an hour with Hurt working on the unrecovered groups, Colonel Bratton seemed to realize that it would be impossible to produce a complete translation of the message without a great deal more research. He then suggested that we give highest priority to the further recovery of the system used for encoding the message which he and Hurt had been studying. He explained to us that from the incomplete text of the message he was led to believe that Japan, Germany, and Italy were in the process of formulating a secret codicil to the tripartite arrangement which was at that time being negotiated by these three nations. He emphasized that if there was such a secret understanding, its details would be of the highest importance to the United States Government. He then suggested that we search through all our Japanese intercepts for any messages that might have a bearing on the tripartite negotiations and requested that we immediately bring any that we might discover to his attention. When he left the vault, he stopped at Friedman's desk and repeated his requirements.

〜　〜　〜

We promptly started to work on Colonel Bratton's requirement. We searched through all the decoded texts of the messages that we thought might provide information on the tripartite negotiations, but we found no reference to them in any of the messages we could partially decode. We soon concluded that if the information in which Colonel Bratton was interested appeared in the Japanese intercepts, it had to be in the messages we had not broken. And there were hundreds of unsolved diplomatic messages which had accumulated in our files and which we had not been able to study.

We took a close look at the message which had aroused Colonel Bratton's interest. It was a circular message, originating in Tokyo and addressed to all major Japanese Foreign Office installations throughout the world. Evidently its contents were intended for the personal information of senior Japanese diplomatic officials abroad, and its purpose was to bring these officials generally up to date on important developments in Japan's foreign policy. The mention of the tripartite negotiations in this context led us to believe that there must have been considerable correspondence on the subject between Tokyo and the other two Axis capitols and that all the messages relating to this subject had been encoded in a system not yet solved by us. If we were to respond to Colonel Bratton's requirement for additional information on the tripartite negotiations, we would have to solve all the Japanese Foreign Office cryptographic systems used between Tokyo and the capitols of Germany and Italy.

While Hurt continued his recovery work on the code system, Kully and I started a comprehensive review of all the other unsolved Japanese diplomatic intercepts. We found that the bulk of these intercepts was composed of messages transmitted in five-letter groups with a single five-digit group appearing as the first group of the cryptographic text of the message. This was the category of intercepts which had stimulated my interest earlier in our work on the Japanese diplomatic systems and which had so far resisted the few rather feeble attacks we had made on it. Over and above this category of intercepts, there was only a small number of nondescript messages many of which might not really have been originated by the Japanese diplomatic service.

As we dug more deeply into the mass of unsolved intercepts, we soon established that the ciphertext of the bulk of the messages started with a five-digit group. We also discovered another piece of evidence which seemed significant: the external characteristics of the cryptographic texts of the traffic bearing the five-digit group as the first textual group had undergone an identifiable change several months after it had first appeared on the radio networks. Friedman, who was now taking a strong interest in our examination of the unsolved intercepts, proposed that the Japanese might be using a cipher machine and made the suggestion that the five-digit group appearing as the first group of the message not only served as an identification symbol for the system but also indicated the specific keys employed for enciphering the message.

↪   ↪   ↪

Working under Friedman's general direction, Kully and I started our study of the five-digit traffic by applying the cryptanalytic tests we had success-fully employed in our work on the cipher machine systems which we had solved in our training course. Our application of these tests were greatly facilitated because we were able to use the IBM accounting equipment, which had not been available to us at the time we were studying cipher machines. In many cases, before we could utilize the accounting machines, we had to devise new techniques for employing them, for most of our experience with the machines had been in support of our code compilation effort. We both found this a satisfying experience, not only because the results we obtained were much more accurate and less time-consuming, but because we also gained a better understanding of the accounting machines themselves and their capabilities. Although the majority of the analytic tests we applied did not provide us with dramatic information, we did establish that for the earlier intercepts in the system the keys remained in effect for a period of ten days, while the keys for the current intercepts changed daily. This discovery enabled us to direct our further studies of the intercepts to messages which were prepared in the same key.

As our first cryptanalytic test, we decided to make an extensive search for ciphertext repetitions, for if we could establish that portions of the ciphertexts were repeated either within a message or between two different messages, we would have a basis for making other tests which could pro-vide us with important information about the cryptographic principles employed in the system. For this test we selected a number of long mes-sages from our most recent intercepts and had their texts transferred to punched cards. By processing these cards through the IBM accounting machines we could automatically produce listings of the intercepts in whatever form we desired for work sheets. By further manipulation of the same punched cards, other listings could also be prepared which would identify all repetitions of five or more letters in the ciphertexts. In the set of long messages we first processed, we found no repetitions of cipher letters which seemed to have any significance. But we did discover an important phenomenon from the monoliteral frequency counts of certain of the messages: six of the cipher letters stood out clearly, because they were either significantly higher or lower in frequency than the remaining twenty letters of the alphabet.

This discovery was so interesting to us that we stopped our search for repetitions and began to make monoliteral frequency counts of all the long messages we had received during the past few months. We soon established that the frequency characteristics remained constant for a period of ten days, and that all messages originating within that period showed the same high- or low-frequency letters. For example, all messages dated between the first and tenth, inclusive, of a given month had identical frequency patterns; messages dated between the eleventh and twentieth showed a different pattern; and messages between the twenty-first and thirtieth (the thirty-first also for months with thirty-one days) showed still another pattern. Likewise, each of the three ten-day periods of the preceding and succeeding months had its own unique frequency pattern, and, in every ten-day period we tested, we could identify six letters with frequency characteristics markedly different from those of the other twenty letters. This evidence led us to the conclusion that we could deal with all the messages originating within a ten-day period as a homogeneous unit.

When we found that the ten-day period was meaningful, we selected for study the period that had the largest number of intercepts and concentrated on it. One of the tests we applied was to search for ciphertext repetitions by lumping all intercepts of the ten-day period into one massive accounting machine run. The results of this search was disappointing, for all the repetitions of ciphertexts we found could be attributed to chance. Another test we applied was to examine the beginnings of all the messages in the ten-day period, hoping to find some evidence which would clarify the role of the five-digit group which appeared at the beginning of each message. Luckily, we discovered some cases where messages of considerable length had identical five-digit groups, and our statistical tests confirmed that for each such case the messages were enciphered by related keys. It took several days for us to complete this study, and while it did not provide us with a full insight into the cryptographic principles employed in the system, it was extremely useful in confirming our earlier conclusions about the role of the five-digit indicator. Since it seemed to us unlikely that further study of this period might develop additional useful information, we decided to make a similar examination of another key period.

The next step in our study of the system was directed at comparing messages in each key period to exploit them for any information which might help us to identify the nature of the cryptographic system used by the Japanese. We selected several key periods for study and again employed the various cryptanalytic tests to each key period. From the results of these studies we were able to confirm that messages of each key period which carried identical five-digit groups were enciphered in the same key. While this conclusion did not provide us with an insight into the cryptographic principles employed in the system, it was most useful in clarifying the role of the five-digit indicator.

As we dug more deeply into the mass of unsolved intercepts, we soon established that the messages bearing the five-digit group as the first group of the message text were transmitted over two different Japanese diplomatic networks. One of these was located in the Far East and included Tokyo and the major headquarters of the Japanese forces in Asia. The other network was really only a subnet of the world-wide Japan Foreign Office communications system, and it included Tokyo, Washington, London, Rome, Paris, Berlin, Moscow, Warsaw, and Ankara. We also discovered another piece of evidence which seemed significant, the fact that the external characteristics of the cryptographic texts of the traffic bearing the five-digit group as the first textual group had undergone an identifiable change several months after it had first appeared. In the cryptographic texts of the earliest intercepts the six vowels accounted for almost exactly half of the ciphertext letters; in the later intercepts this striking parity between the frequency of vowels and consonants was lost, and the six vowels accounted for a little less than one-fourth of the cipher letters or just about what would normally be expected for machine ciphertext.

CHAPTER 11

THE NAVY INADVERTENTLY SPURS US ON

WHILE AT THAT TIME there was a complete exchange of intercepted Japanese diplomatic traffic between the Signal Intelligence Service and the Navy cryptanalytic group, there was no direct contact between the personnel of the two units except for an occasional meeting between Friedman and Lieutenant Joseph N. Wenger, who was the head of the Navy cryptanalytic unit. One of these meetings occurred just after we had reached our conclusions about the keying periods and the role of the five-digit indicators. Friedman informed Wenger that we had started a serious study of the unsolved Japanese diplomatic intercepts and reviewed the studies we had made and the conclusions we had reached. When Friedman stated that he believed the system was based on a cipher machine, Wenger told him that some months earlier the Navy had recovered a Japanese naval cipher system which used an electromechanical cipher machine employing Japanese kana instead of the Roman alphabet. Friedman naturally pressed Wenger for more information about the system, but Wenger declined to provide it.

When Friedman returned from this meeting, he reported his conversation with Wenger to us. At first he seemed to be very excited about the information, but after discussing Wenger's remarks with us, he concluded that they were too general and indefinite to be of any significant technical value, for all along we had assumed that a cipher machine was involved in the system. However, it was encouraging to learn that the Japanese Navy was using a cipher machine, for this information tended to confirm our assumption that a cipher machine was involved in the system on which we were working.

We continued our study of the key periods we had selected for analysis, looking for other evidence which might support the premise that a cipher machine was involved in the system on which we were working. Friedman followed our efforts closely and at times would join us and take part in the analytical tests we were applying. It was evident that he was as much intrigued by the implications of the remarks that Wenger had made regarding the Navy's successful recovery of a Japanese naval cipher machine as he was by the cryptanalytic problem we were trying to solve. He felt very strongly that there might be a relation between the type of cipher machine used by the Japanese Navy and the one on which we were working. He often referred to Wenger's remarks during this period of unproductive research, implying that if the Japanese naval cipher machine had indeed been solved by the Navy cryptanalysts, a full knowledge of the techniques and principles involved in the device would be of inestimable value to us. Although he never directly expressed his feelings, I sensed that he felt he was being unfairly treated, because in his dealings with the Navy cryptanalytic group he had never withheld any technical information that might possibly have been of use to the Navy. At the end of one of our frequent assessments of our progress, he told us that he had made an appointment with Wenger for the next day and stated that he intended to confront Wenger with a direct request for complete information about the Japanese naval cipher machine and how it was used.

Next day, when Friedman returned from a meeting with Wenger, he reported to us that he had brought up the subject of our work on the Japanese diplomatic system and that he had emphasized the importance to us of information about the cipher machine used by the Japanese Navy, pointing out that the same cryptographic principles could well be employed in a cipher machine used by the Japanese diplomatic service. Wenger still declined to provide any further information about the Japanese naval device. Friedman then itemized for Wenger the conclusions we had reached about the principles employed in the Japanese diplomatic system we were studying and specifically asked Wenger to confirm or deny whether similar phenomena had been found in the Japanese naval device. Wenger had reluctantly confirmed that the kana sequence employed in the Japanese navy device had likewise been separated into two subsets. When Friedman pressed for further details, Wenger finally suggested that a search be made for a basic cycle of "more than forty and less than fifty." And that was all that Friedman could get out of him.

When Friedman discussed with us Wenger's statement that the alphabet was divided into two subsets, it was very clear that this was really of no use to us, for we had already developed enough evidence to be convinced of the correctness of our assumptions regarding the alphabet's being divided into two subsequences. However, his suggestions regarding a basic cycle puzzled us, for we had found no external evidence in any of our studies which even remotely suggested the existence of such a phenomenon. Although Friedman could not offer a precise explanation of what Wenger was trying to describe, he proposed that we undertake a search which he hoped would confirm or reject the validity of Wenger's suggestion regarding the cycle. After spending about three weeks analyzing a number of key periods without finding anything which supported Wenger's suggestion, we came to the conclusion that we had not developed the proper techniques for detecting it.

By this time we were rather discouraged. In our work on the cipher machines we had studied, we had sailed right through the exercises without experiencing the feeling of frustration which by now we had developed in our analysis of the Japanese system. It was a rather dejected crew that set about contemplating the next step that should be taken. We finally concluded that for the time being we had run out of useful ideas and that we should now concentrate on consolidating our working materials and getting our files and research records into order. Friedman announced that he would be absent from the office for a few days in order to meet with the engineers at the Signal Corps Laboratory at Fort Monmouth, to resolve some problems which had arisen in the construction of the M-134 which was being built by a private contractor.

ᔕ ᔕ ᔕ

As I drove home that night, I kept thinking about what other tests we might make to improve our understanding of the cryptographic principles employed in the system. So far, all our work had been based on an examination of a mass of intercepted messages, utilizing techniques which we had found successful in our work on the cipher systems we had encountered in our training course. The results of this analysis had been rewarding, but not sufficiently enlightening to provide us with the information we required. We needed to develop other tests which would give us a different perspective of the problem by examining it from another point of view. This was a possibility which I could not put out of my thoughts for the rest of the evening, and when I finally concluded that I would set it aside and try to get a good night's rest, I had no trouble in falling asleep.

Sometime after midnight I found myself wide awake. Instead of feeling tired, I felt refreshed and alert, and I decided to review mentally each of the machine systems that we had studied to see if we had taken advantage of all the techniques we had successfully applied in our attacks on them. It soon became clear to me that in all the systems we had mastered, we had been given full knowledge of the system and how it functioned, and the analytic techniques that we had used had been based on a complete understanding of the cryptographic principles involved. In the critiques which we had conducted for each of these systems, we had discussed how we might attack the system if its cryptography was completely unknown to us. In all cases we had concluded that if we had a sufficient amount of ciphertext with its matching plaintext, we could recover all the principles involved in the machine. For the simpler systems such as the Kryha and the B-211 only a relatively small amount of matched plain and ciphertext would be required, but for the more secure cipher machines such as the Hebern and the Enigma, hundreds, and possibly thousands, of exactly matched plain and cipher letters would be needed. Unfortunately, we had no cases of matched plain and ciphertexts for the Japanese diplomatic system on which we were working.

At this point I recalled the earlier work I had done on the five-digit indicator traffic. In searching through the intercepts from the Far Eastern Diplomatic Net, I had come across an exceptionally long message, much longer than any other message we had found in the more recent Japanese diplomatic intercepts. There were also two other very long messages which had been transmitted over the same net and which bore the same date as the unusually long message. If our theories about the system were correct, all three of these messages would have to be enciphered in the same key period.

Another favorable consideration was that they had been intercepted early in the use of the system when the six vowels comprised roughly fifty percent of the ciphertext, and we had theorized that if each vowel in the ciphertext represented a vowel in the plaintext, the vowel-consonant patterns of the ciphertext would exactly reflect the vowel-consonant patterns of the underlying plaintext. I recalled that I had tried to take advantage of this feature by formulating assumptions for the plain-language equivalents of distinctive vowel-consonant patterns appearing in the ciphertext of the long message, but at that time I was not able to prove or disprove my assumptions. Now, with a better knowledge of Japanese, and in the light of our latest concept of the system, it might be possible to develop enough assumed plaintext for portions of these earlier intercepts to produce matched pairs of plaintext and ciphertext letters and thus determine the type of cryptography being used in the system. This represented a distinct change in strategy in our attack, which had up to this point been directed at a statistical analysis of the texts of the intercepts. Before I went back to sleep, I resolved to reexamine my earlier work on these three messages as the first item of business for the next day.

Next morning I arrived at the office well ahead of the regular opening time. I soon located the work sheets on which I had based my earlier studies; they were in good order and included the data sheets and tabulations I had prepared. When I examined the copies of the intercepts, I found them to be of excellent quality, and in fact there were several duplicate copies of all three of the messages which had been taken by separate intercept stations. This latter was important, for error-free copies of the ciphertexts would greatly facilitate our analysis; by comparing the duplicates, we could identify any errors which might have been introduced as the messages were being intercepted. I was now convinced that these three messages offered a more promising point of attack than the more recent intercepts we had been examining.

When Kully arrived he found me at work editing the three messages and preparing them for processing by the IBM unit. He too had been considering the next step in our attack on the system and had come to the conclusion that we ought to continue our statistical investigations by examining another key period in the hope that we would find one more favorable for our purposes. I outlined for him the conclusions I had reached regarding the course we ought to follow, showed him the three long messages I had selected for study, and reviewed for him the data sheets and the tabulations I had prepared for them. He listened with interest to my proposals for modifying our strategy, but expressed his doubts that we would be able to develop enough new information to provide us with the advantage we needed. As we exchanged our views on the next steps to be taken, it became clear that we were in agreement that additional key periods needed to be examined. Kully proposed to select a current period containing a large number of intercepts and subject it to the analytic processes we had used for the other key periods. I wanted to investigate the possibilities of the three long messages that I had selected, by subjecting them to our testing program. We finally agreed that both proposals had merit and that we should give precedence to the study of the three earlier messages, since they were almost ready to be processed by the IBM unit.

While Kully searched through the files of recent intercepts for another favorable key period, I completed the editing of the three messages and took them to the IBM unit for processing. I then joined Kully to assist him in the editing of the intercepts he had selected. The key period he had chosen seemed very promising, for it contained a large number of intercepts, some of which were very long.

While we were waiting for the results of the IBM machine processing of the three messages, I continued to review the notes and work sheets prepared in my earlier studies of the messages. The results were consistent with the ideas we had developed from our latest researches on the more recent intercepts. The most interesting items I found in my notes were the studies I had made for the vowels in each of the three messages. I had developed three arrangements of the vowels, one for each message, based on certain statistical tabulations, and the remarkable feature of these three arrangements was that two of them were identical while the third was the exact reverse of the two identical ones.

When I pointed out this phenomenon to Kully, his interest immediately heightened. He carefully examined the work sheets and the process which I had used to produce them. When he verified the results, he began to look at the three messages with greater interest. I repeated my conviction that if we could accurately develop a few phrases of plaintext for some of the ciphertext passages we certainly would be in a better position to evaluate the statistical findings. I showed him some of the earlier assumptions I had made for bits and pieces of plaintext based on the vowel-consonant patterns appearing in the longest message, and after a short examination of these he started to suggest further possibilities. By this time he seemed to be as enthusiastic about working on the three messages as I, and together we continued our search through the text of the longest intercept, using my working copy, looking for other patterns for which we could make plaintext assumptions.

The orthographic structure of the Romanized Japanese used by the Japanese Foreign Office in its telegraphic communications worked to our advantage at this point in our attack. In this form of Japanese certain limitations applied to the letter Y; it was always followed by one of the other vowels, most frequently by O or U, very infrequently by A, and almost never by E or I. Pairs of vowels frequently occurred, and the most common were the combinations OO, UU, AI and EI in about that order of frequency. YUU and YOO often occurred, preceded by a consonant, in combinations such as RYOO, RYUU, KYOO, and KYUU. It was our hope that we could use these characteristics of the Japanese language to make accurate assumptions for plaintext which, when analyzed, would reveal to us how the encipherment process was performed. We had no definite concept at that time of the nature of the substitution system employed, and so we had no idea of what sort of evidence we might discover. Also, we had no assurance that our attack along these lines would produce the desired results. When the message prints were delivered from the IBM unit, we transferred what we considered to be the best of our assumptions to them in order to have the most favorable base for our further work.

As in the case of many cryptanalytic situations where the analyst is feeling his way into an unknown system, we did a considerable amount of experimentation with the data developed from the assumptions we had made. We worked carefully, painstakingly evaluating each bit of information as we developed it. It took us several hours of deliberation before we began to find consistent relationships between the plain and ciphertexts of certain of our assumptions. When we finally consolidated our data, we found that we could produce a logical arrangement of the six vowels. And the most significant aspect of the vowel arrangement we developed was that it exactly duplicated the one I had produced months before from a statistical study of the same message.

This development not only encouraged us but also spurred us on to reexamine the most favorable assumptions we had made. We began to develop a technique for applying the vowel arrangement to each of our assumptions so that we could confirm those which were correct and eliminate those which we felt were questionable. We found that we could also use the vowel arrangement to make tentative decipherments of the pairs and triplets of vowels in the ciphertext for which we had made no assumptions, and we were delighted to find that in almost all of these cases our decipherment produced acceptable plaintext.

At this point we began to feel certain that we were on the right track. We had examined enough of our assumptions to ensure that the vowel arrangement was correct and that our techniques for applying it were producing valid bits and pieces of the message plaintext. What we had to do now was to discover how we could apply the vowel arrangement, following a consistent pattern, so that we could correctly decipher all the vowels in a long passage of ciphertext. In most of the cases where we had found valid plain language, the decipherment had been effected by a regular displacement of the vowel arrangement one position for each letter of the ciphertext, regardless of whether the ciphertext letter was a vowel or a consonant. After several letters had been deciphered, the resulting plaintext would lose all its resemblance to proper Japanese, and additional displacements had to be introduced before the deciphered letters again assumed the appearance of good Japanese. When we recognized the effect of the additional displacement and took it into account, we were able to convert the vowels of long passages of ciphertext into acceptable plain language by a judicious insertion of an additional shift of one or two positions at the point where the decipherment lost its plaintext qualities.

As we continued to apply this process to the ciphertext of the message we were studying, we came across a combination of cipher letters which when deciphered produced OYOBI, which is the Japanese word for English AND. Its frequency in Japanese approximates the frequency of AND in English.

It did not take us much longer to establish the pattern followed in the displacement of the vowel arrangement. Once this had been determined, we were able to decipher accurately all the vowels of the message. It was now midafternoon. We had been working steadily since early morning, and we found ourselves in need of a break. We decided we had better have lunch before we continued with our work on the message.

While we ate lunch, we reviewed what we had learned about the system. There seemed to be two subsequences, one for the vowels and one for the consonants. Apparently these subsequences provided for independent encipherment of the vowels and consonants; a vowel would always be replaced by a vowel and a consonant by a consonant. Evidently the two subsequences operated in synchronism, both advancing with the encipherment of each letter of the message whether it was a vowel or a consonant. There also appeared to be a motion pattern which controlled the advancement of the two subsequences, introducing additional steps at certain points. We had recovered the vowel arrangement and the stepping pattern used for it. If our assumptions regarding the synchronous operation of the two subsequences were correct and if the same stepping pattern was used also for the consonant subsequence, all that was left for us to recover was the arrangement of the consonants. We felt this could be easily accomplished, for the vowels which we had already deciphered accounted for approximately half of the plaintext of the message.

The stepping pattern which we had recovered for deciphering the vowels repeated itself at cycles of exactly forty-two positions. When we noted this, Kully and I agreed that possibly Wenger was referring to the stepping pattern in the Japanese naval machine when he used the expression "greater that forty and less than fifty" in his conversation with Friedman.

It took us a little over an hour to get a good start on the recovery of the other subsequence, and we soon had completely identified an arrangement of the consonants which could be used for the decipherment consonants in exactly the same way as the vowel arrangement had been used. By the time we had finished the recovery of the consonant sequence and had confirmed the operation of the stepping pattern, it was well after our regular closing time.

We found that all the other members of the office staff had departed, and that we were the only ones left in the area. We had been so engrossed in our work that we had lost all track of the passage of time. We decided that instead of testing the principles we had recovered on the other two messages, we should lock up the office and go home.

"What do you think our boss will have to say about our day's work?" I asked Kully as we walked down the stairs leading to the front entrance of the Munitions Building.

Kully's eyes lit up and he grinned broadly. "We'll know when he gets back from Fort Monmouth," he answered.

As we left the Munitions Building, Kully heading up 21st Street toward his apartment and I walking down Constitution Avenue to my car, which was parked near Lincoln Memorial, I am sure we were both experiencing the same emotions — a great elation over what we had accomplished and a considerable amount of awe at the amount of work which would have to be done as a result of our achievement. There were hundreds and hundreds of Japanese diplomatic messages which we would have to solve, decipher, and translate before the U.S. could reap the full benefits of our recovery of what evidently was the most important Japanese diplomatic cryptographic system then in use. I was also certain that we would find in those messages the information about the tripartite negotiations that was of such great interest to Colonel Bratton. And I was sure that when we found this information, the Director of Military Intelligence would bring great pressure on the Chief Signal Officer for rapid and full exploitation of all Japanese diplomatic intercepts.

∽　∽　∽

Next morning, Kully and I got an early start on the other two messages. Within less than an hour, we had made an entry into one of the messages, using the vowel and consonant arrangements we had recovered the day before. We were able to decipher long passages of the ciphertext and to determine the stepping pattern. Since the message bore a different indicator from the one we had solved, we were not surprised to find that the stepping pattern was different from the one we had recovered, nor that the starting points of the vowel and consonant sequences were also different. This led us to the conclusion that the indicator served to identify the starting points of the vowel and consonant sequences and the stepping pattern used for the message on which it appeared. We also noted with interest that the length of the stepping pattern was forty-one, within the range of "more than forty and less than fifty" suggested by Wenger.

Our next task was to decipher the third message. We applied the techniques we had used for the second message, but without success. When we recalled that one of the vowel arrangements I had recovered from my earlier work on the three messages was the exact reverse of the arrangements developed for the other two messages, we checked to determine which of the three messages produced the reversed arrangement. When we found that the reversed sequence applied to the message we were studying, we promptly reversed the vowel and consonant sequences and applied them to the text of the third message. When we did this, it required only a little manipulation of the starting points of the sequences to produce valid plaintext Japanese. After deciphering a fairly long passage of ciphertext, we found that a third stepping pattern of forty-three elements had been employed. It was also within the range suggested by Wenger.

We now felt that we understood the cryptography of the early use of the system well enough to solve any message enciphered by it. Because of the continued use of the five-digit indicator, together with the separation of the cipher letters into two subsets of six and twenty elements, we believed that the basic device employed for enciphering the earlier messages we had solved would still be used for the current traffic bearing the five-digit indicators. The immediate question was whether to continue our examination of the earlier intercepts for which we had developed a successful method of attack or to start work on the current intercepts. We decided to attack the current intercepts, for if we found we were not able to make an entry into them, we could always return to the earlier messages and work our way up to the current period through attacking the backlog of intercepts, on a key period by key period basis if necessary.

For our first attack on the current intercepts we chose one of the recent ten-day periods which had already been processed by the IBM unit. Our general plan of attack was first to determine the order of the letters in the shorter (or vowel) subsequence and, if we were successful in this, to decipher each of their occurrences until we found passages for which we could assume possible Japanese plaintext. We would then use these plaintext assumptions to recover the arrangement of letters in the longer (or consonant) subsequence. At this point we were not concerned about the effect of the stepping pattern, for we believed it could readily be recovered after the order of the letters in the two subsequences had been established.

Our first step was to organize the intercepts into a format which would enable us to develop the statistical data we needed for recovering the shorter subsequences. This took some time, since it required a complete new set of message prints designed to take full advantage of the information we had developed from the messages we had solved. While these were being prepared we studied each of the intercepts in the key period, selecting only the ones we felt would be best suited for our studies. It was almost closing time before we had our materials in suitable form for starting our attack.

↜ ↜ ↜

Next morning Kully and I arrived at the office well in advance of the regular starting time, for we were both eager to get our attack on the more recent intercepts under way. We had barely finished organizing our materials for starting our studies when Friedman arrived. Evidently he had finished his business in Fort Monmouth sooner that he had expected.

We wasted no time in acquainting him with our success. He was elated, and he followed with intense interest our description of how we had broken into each of the three messages we had solved. When we summed up our concept of the cipher machine, he agreed with our findings. We then outlined for him our proposal to attack one of the current ten-day periods and he expressed his approval.

"Have you informed anyone of your success?" he asked. We replied that we had not, explaining that we thought it might be premature to claim that the system was broken until we had deciphered some current intercepts.

"I fully agree," he remarked. "From what you have accomplished, I believe it will be only a few days until we are able to produce translations of current messages in this system. I would like to present Colonel Bratton with several up-to-date translations at the time I inform him that we have broken the cipher machine system used for the most secret communications of the Japanese Foreign Office."

He then asked us to explain in detail how we planned to attack the current intercepts. While he did not discourage us, he seemed to feel skeptical about our chances of success in employing the methods we proposed to use and observed that we might have to resort to other techniques. When we explained that we expected to get a solution in a much shorter time and with less effort by following the approach we had chosen, he encouraged us to go ahead with our attack as we had planned it. At that point he congratulated us on our work, expressing his personal gratification that we had been able to recover an unknown cipher machine system by working only from intercepts without previous knowledge of the principles used in it and without help from any outside source. When he started to leave the vault and just before he stepped through door, he turned to us and said: "I am now glad that Wenger did not disclose to me the details of the Japanese naval cipher machine and how it was recovered. You have clearly demonstrated that the Signal Intelligence Service does not need cryptanalytic assistance from anyone."

Encouraged by our discussions with Friedman, Kully and I enthusiastically returned to our attack on the messages we had prepared for study. Our first aim was to recover the six-element subsequence by a statistical analysis of the relationships of the six letters we had identified as belonging to it. Our first results were disappointing, for after applying the tests to at least half a dozen of the longest messages we found it impossible to develop any arrangement of the six letters which met our requirements. At this point we began to speculate that changes might have been made in the system subsequent to the date of the messages we had solved and that we might have to resort to an attack on the earlier key periods and work our way through the backlog of messages to find when the changes were introduced. Fortunately, before giving into this suspicion we decided to use a modification of the procedure by which we had recovered the order of the six vowels in the first message we had solved. The results were most gratifying, and from this point on it was all downhill sledding. Almost every test we applied worked beautifully, and by the middle of the afternoon we had reconstructed both subsequences and had successfully deciphered long passages of several of the intercepts. Evidently the only change the Japanese Foreign Office cryptographers had made in the system was to remove the earlier limitation on the vowel-consonant composition of the two subsequences.

Friedman kept in close touch with our progress, showing great interest in each step in our attack as we applied it. When we were satisfied that we could decipher any intercept of the key period at will, he suggested that we decipher all the messages belonging to it before starting an attack on another key period.

Friedman explained to us his reasons for this requirement. He had for some time felt that the staff of the Signal Intelligence Service needed to be increased, but he had been reluctant to press for more personnel because of the extremely tight budget under which the War Department was being forced to operate as a result of the Depression. He expected G-2 to insist on full exploitation of the system we had just solved, and he wanted to be able to provide the Chief Signal Officer with accurate information about the magnitude of the additional workload if G-2's requirements were to be satisfied. For these purposes he wanted us to compile certain data about the exploitation of the Japanese diplomatic systems, such as the number of intercepts received each day, the number of man-hours required for each step of the exploitation process — cryptanalysis, decipherment, translation and clerical — and the time spent on the recovery of the Japanese diplomatic codes. Kully and I were pleased to hear these remarks, for we had already concluded that it would be impossible for our small staff to cope with the processing and translation of the machine-system intercepts, even if we were relieved of all other duties.

We had been so preoccupied with the solution of the system that we had given no thought as to how we would decipher the intercepts after we had recovered the keys used for them. The first practical scheme that occurred to us was to produce a "pencil and paper" analog of the device with which we could somewhat laboriously determine the plaintext equivalents of the cipher letters, taking into account the stepping pattern which controlled the movement of the two subsequences. Friedman expressed his opinion that the Japanese were using an electromechanical device, which automatically performed the enciphering and deciphering operations. He noted that he had been giving some thought to having a special apparatus constructed that would duplicate the operations of the Japanese device. He added that since there were no funds available to the Signal Corps for such purposes, it might be impossible to produce a satisfactory device in less than two or three years and that for the time being we would have to use the "pencil and paper" approach or whatever other makeshift arrangement we could devise.

It was with something less than enthusiasm that we started to organize for the task of deciphering the solved messages. In the process of recovering the keys we had partially deciphered portions of several of the intercepts, and we elected to start with these, using whatever deciphering technique that seemed most suitable. I found the decipherment of the messages to be a tedious job. If the plaintext had been in English, or if my Japanese had been better, the job might not have been so boring. I could determine that the stream of letters I was producing formed acceptable Japanese only from the regular distributions of vowels and consonants and the occasional occurrence of a familiar word or phrase. Hurt, who was impatiently waiting for the full texts of the messages to be deciphered so that he could translate the most important, hovered over both Kully and me, assisting us by verifying the correctness of our decipherments and at the same time satisfying his curiosity about the subject matter of the messages.

While we were occupied with the deciphering process, Friedman regularly came into the vault to observe our progress. Hurt would excitedly report to him the interesting items he had noted in the messages we had deciphered, and he remarked that their contents seemed to be much more important than he had found in any other system we had solved. He also noted that the translations of the cipher messages would be more accurate than the ones produced from the code systems.

"Except for an occasional single-letter garble, the texts are wonderfully clear and unambiguous," he told Friedman. "Colonel Bratton will not be able to complain about portions of these messages being missing because of unrecovered code groups," he added.

After watching us laboriously develop the clear text from the cipher messages for a while, Friedman began to appreciate the full dimensions of the deciphering task. He spent some time with us discussing ways for speeding it up, short of building a special device as he had earlier mentioned. We also speculated about using the IBM accounting machines, but rejected this as being more time-consuming than the simpler pencil and paper approach we were using. We finally reached the conclusion that the decipherment would have to be done by some modification of the methods we were using and that the only relief for Kully and me was to assign other personnel to the task, even if only on a part-time basis. It was quite clear to all of us that Hurt would not be able to assist us, for he would be fully occupied with the translation of the deciphered texts.

In the days that followed, Kully and I completed the decipherment of the messages in the key period that we had solved. We then continued our analytical work on the system, recovering the sequences for the more recent ten-day periods and concentrating on the development of information about the stepping patterns and the starting points of the subsequences associated with each of the five-digit indicators. One practical benefit of our work on the indicators was that we found that the stepping pattern associated with each indicator was invariant, and we were able to use this feature to advantage in deciphering the solved messages. Larry Clark and Sammy Snyder, who at that time were operating the accounting machines, and Miss Louise Newkirk, Friedman's secretary, were assigned part-time to assist in the decipherment of the messages for which the keys had been recovered. After considerable experimentation with a variety of techniques, we finally concluded that the most efficient deciphering procedure was to use a sixty-point disk, with the two subsequences continuously inscribed at different levels around its periphery. We made the first models of these disks from heavy white drawing paper, which soon disintegrated under use. Later on we constructed several devices from white plastic-like material about one-eighth-inch thick, and these models were found to be more durable. These homemade cipher disks remained in service until an electromechanical analog of the Japanese diplomatic machine was constructed by the U.S. Navy Yard model shop over two years later.

CHAPTER 12

THE IMPACT OF THE RED MACHINE RECOVERY

WHEN FRIEDMAN FELT THAT the last shred of doubt about our ability to recover the keys for current intercepts in the cipher machine had been removed, he briefed the small number of officers of the Signal Corps and G-2 who, by the nature of their assigned duties, were authorized to have access to information about our activities. Hurt had found some highly interesting intelligence items among the messages we had deciphered, and Friedman proudly exhibited translations of these as examples of the type of information we would now be able to produce. Some of these translations dealt with the tripartite negotiations in which Colonel Bratton had expressed an interest and which had set us on the course that led to the solution of the system.

Both the Chief Signal Officer and the Officer-in-Charge, War Plans and Training Division, made personal visits to the vault to express their congratulations. I am sure that up to this point neither of these two officers had felt that the Signal Intelligence Service could achieve such a startling success so early in its life, and they looked on that attainment with a great deal of organizational pride. The officers in G-2 likewise were liberal in their praise of our accomplishment, but the best news of all was that the Director of Military Intelligence had pledged his support for the employment of additional personnel to assist in the exploitation of the Japanese diplomatic intercepts.

The impact of our success on the few War Department officials who were fully familiar with our duties was considerable. From this point on, the members of the Signal Intelligence Service were visibly accorded greater respect. Before we had broken the Japanese diplomatic cipher machine, the normal attitude toward us was that while we represented an activity highly essential from a war-planning concept, we were still in training status; we were preparing for a wartime situation, and our effectiveness still had to be proved. When they learned that we had broken a Japanese diplomatic cipher machine, using only the information we had developed from intercepted Japanese messages, almost overnight their attitude of polite tolerance turned to one of visible respect. Needless to say, Friedman's requests for additional personnel for the Signal Intelligence Service received full support from all responsible officials.

When Hurt began turning out translations of current intercepts on a regular basis, both the Chief Signal Officer and the Director of Military Intelligence became concerned about the lack of formal regulations governing the dissemination of information about the work on the Japanese diplomatic intercepts and the disposition of the translations made from them. Friedman was asked to draft a set of regulations for controlling all information on the Japanese diplomatic effort, including the handling of the translations which were turned over to G-2. The final version of the rules approved by the Chief Signal Officer and the Director of Military Intelligence stipulated that no technical information on the Japanese effort would be released without the specific written authorization of the Chief Signal Officer, and only specially designated Signal Corps officers whose duties required it would be authorized to receive information about our work on the Japanese intercepts. G-2 would be provided with all translations, but no information about the technical aspects of our work, such as the details of cryptanalysis and the nature of the Japanese system involved, would be released to G-2. Only those officers in G-2 who were specifically authorized in writing by the Director of Military Intelligence would be permitted access to translations of the Japanese diplomatic messages, and any such translations retained by G-2 would be kept in a designated area, safeguarded by combination locks, except when the translations were in actual use.

During the preparation of these regulations the suggestion was made that a cover name ought to be assigned to the Japanese diplomatic cipher machine system. We had been referring to it simply as "The Japanese Cipher Machine," and it was felt that our continued use of so descriptive a term might result in an inadvertent security breach. Friedman consulted with Kully, Hurt, and me, asking for our recommendations for cover names not only for the Japanese device, but also for other machines we might encounter in our future work, for he was convinced that cipher machines would in time replace the conventional code systems. The ideas developed in our discussions on this subject led to the adoption of the colors of the spectrum as cover names for cipher machines. All of us were in agreement that the first color of the spectrum was an excellent choice as a cover name for the first cipher machine that we had solved which was actually used for enciphering official messages of a foreign power. And from this moment on, the Japanese diplomatic cipher machine was always referred to as the "Red Machine." It was not until some time later that we learned from intercepts that the Japanese referred to it as "ANGOOKI TAIPU A," which, when freely translated into English becomes "Cipher Machine, Type A."

↜ ↜ ↜

Since the full exploitation of both the current intercepts and the backlog of RED machine messages was not possible with our limited capabilities, we had to be selective in choosing the messages which would be processed. In collaboration with G-2, we developed priorities for sampling both the backlog and the current intercepts so that the G-2 analysts could determine which circuits would be the most profitable to exploit. At first, G-2 was very desirous of identifying the messages dealing with the tripartite negotiations, and we gave first priority to deciphering messages between Tokyo and the other two Axis capitals. As a second priority, Colonel Bratton requested that we make a sampling of current intercepts on all other circuits so that G-2 could assess the information being transmitted over each circuit. This arrangement suited us perfectly, for we still had to complete our recovery of the indicator list.

As Hurt had predicted, translation of the cipher machine intercepts was a great deal easier than translation of the partially recovered code messages. He was literally in a state of perpetual linguistic euphoria. Through his work on code recovery he had mastered the linguistic style used by the Japanese in their diplomatic communications and was able to produce a number of translations each day. Kully and I, being mindful of his health, tried in every way possible to assist him, but our help was limited to performing the clerical and other routine tasks associated with his translation work. While our knowledge of Japanese was sufficient for us to solve the keys for the RED machine messages and to assist in the code recovery work, it was not good enough for us to translate the specialized prose used by the Japanese diplomats.

The translations produced by Hurt were typed in final form by Friedman's secretary, Miss Louise Newkirk. Hurt soon started the practice of dictating the translations directly from the deciphered texts which we had prepared for him, which substantially increased his output. There was one disadvantage to this arrangement: when Hurt was dictating, the rest of us who were working in the vault had to avoid all activities which might create interference. Sometimes, it was rather amusing to listen to his dictation for he would get so involved in expressing the meaning of the message he was translating that he would stride up and down the rather crowded vault area, rendering the Japanese into English as if he were giving an oration.

One consequence of the solution of the RED machine was that our work on the recovery of the Japanese diplomatic codes had to be given a lower priority, and only enough attention was paid to the intercepts in the other Japanese diplomatic systems to determine if any significant cryptographic changes were being introduced. Friedman defined this monitoring process as "maintaining cryptanalytic continuity." Fortunately for us, the Japanese evidently felt that their diplomatic code systems were adequately secure, and they complacently continued to use them without introducing any significant modifications.

~ ~ ~

Shortly after we had established that our recovery of the RED machine was complete, Friedman prepared a memorandum to the Chief Signal Officer in which he recommended that the Navy cryptanalytic group be provided with full information on the RED machine system. In this memorandum he emphasized the importance of a complete exchange of cryptanalytic information between the Army and the Navy, pointing out that technical collaboration between the two services in both cryptographic and cryptanalytic matters was necessary to ensure that the U.S. military cryptographic systems were of the highest security possible. The Chief Signal Officer felt that this proposal needed the concurrence of the Director of Military Intelligence "before affirmative action could be taken." The Director of Military Intelligence concurred with this recommendation and further proposed that G-2 would arrange to provide ONI with selected translations of the RED machine intercepts.

In due course agreement was reached on Friedman's proposal, and he was authorized to provide the Navy with full technical details of the RED machine and the cryptanalytic techniques employed in its recovery. At the same time, and in a parallel action, G-2 was authorized to apprise ONI of the recovery of the cipher machine system used by the Japanese Foreign Office and to provide ONI with selected translations of the RED machine intercepts.

When G-2 started providing ONI with translations of the RED machine intercepts, the reaction of the ONI intelligence analysts at first was more of curiosity than of interest in their usefulness, since the messages contained practically no information on Japanese naval matters. As the number of translations increased, it became evident to the ONI analysts that the Japanese diplomatic intercepts contained information of great value to the State Department and to the White House. When one of the more important translations was shown to the Secretary of Navy by ONI, he directed that it be brought to the attention of the Secretary of State. The ONI representative who presented that translation to the Secretary of State was somewhat embarrassed to find that the Army had already provided the State Department with the same information. Soon a spirit of rivalry developed between G-2 and ONI as each tried to "scoop" the other in servicing the State Department with information from the RED machine intercepts. A feeling of resentment began to develop among the G-2 analysts who felt that ONI was being presumptuous in passing on the State Department intelligence information which had been produced by the Army. The Navy countered with the argument that its action was not improper, since some of the translations had been made from intercepts provided by the Navy to the Army.

When this developing controversy came to the attention of the upper levels of the War and Navy Departments, ONI and G-2 received orders to the effect that the Army and Navy would share equally in providing Japanese diplomatic intelligence to the State Department, but the parameters governing the division of effort were not specified. The Navy, which up to this time had shown no interest in working on Japanese diplomatic systems, accepted these orders as a mandate to participate equally with the Army in the analysis and translation of the Japanese intercepts. This interpretation was welcomed by the Army, since it offered an immediate solution to the provision of the required additional resources.

As the first step in the sharing of effort, Friedman and Wenger arranged for a series of meetings in which we provided the Navy cryptanalytic group with all the technical information we had developed on the cryptographic systems used by the Japanese Foreign Office. We explained how we had solved the RED machine system and the procedures we were following in the recovery of the Japanese codes. When we found that the Navy cryptanalysts were especially interested in our use of the IBM accounting machines, we prepared a special briefing in which we presented in detail the procedures we had developed to assist us in our cryptanalytic work. Since that was the first time the cryptanalysts of the two services had directly collaborated, the meeting were conducted in an atmosphere of quiet, although friendly, reserve. When the series of meetings had ended, Wenger advised Friedman that it would take some time for the Navy to realign its effort, and that when this had been accomplished, the Navy would begin work on the Japanese diplomatic intercepts.

〜 〜 〜

While the meetings between the cryptanalytic groups were being conducted, G-2 and ONI similarly undertook to develop practical working arrangements for providing the State Department with Japanese diplomatic intelligence. Since both intelligence services previously had been unhampered by any limitations on the manner in which they exchanged intelligence with the State Department, it took considerable negotiation between ONI and G-2 to devise mutually satisfactory guidelines which would provide for the equal participation they had been instructed to achieve. These discussions culminated in an agreement that the Navy would provide the State Department with translations on odd days and the Army would be responsible for the even days. While this arrangement seemed simple enough, unexpected complications immediately developed when it was put into practice.

At that time the copies of translations which the SIS provided to G-2 and ONI carried two dates, namely, the date on which the message was intercepted and the date on which the translation was made. Both these dates could be variable. For example, a message originating in Tokyo on an odd date might bear an even date if the station which intercepted it was located on the other side of the international date line. Also, the translation day could vary over a range of three days to three months, depending on a variety of factors, such as the time required to forward the intercept, the difficulty of translating the message, the time needed for solving the key used for its encipherment and the like. As a result of these variables, after the Navy group started the processing and translation of diplomatic intercepts, quite often an important message would be translated and distributed by both services. In order to eliminate this undesired duplication, the discussions between G-2 and ONI were resumed. When the participants in the discussions were unable to arrive at a satisfactory arrangement for equally dividing their responsibilities, they finally consulted with the cryptanalytic groups. The solution we recommended was a simple one, and that was to continue the "odd-even" day concept and to use the date the Japanese officially applied to the message when it was originated. This practice was also adopted by the cryptanalytic groups and it remained in effect until the Navy turned over the full responsibility for work on the Japanese diplomatic systems to the Army shortly after the Pearl Harbor attack.

In the early plans for building up a staff of skilled cryptanalysts, provision was made for each individual selected to take a two-year field assignment in one of the three overseas departments. Sinkov was the first of us to be selected for such an assignment, while Kully and I remained in Washington. Just about the time Kully and I recovered the RED machine, Friedman learned that circumstances were favorable for one of us to be assigned to the headquarters of the Hawaiian Department for a period of two years. When Friedman informed Kully and me of the assignment, he indicated that one of us would be selected. Since my wife was expecting our first child, I told Friedman that I would prefer to remain in Washington. Kully accepted the assignment, and several weeks later left for Hawaii.

The additional personnel requested by Friedman soon began to materialize. Friedman personally interviewed all the candidates who were considered eligible by the Civil Service Commission. Two of the individuals he selected turned out to be exceptionally well suited for cryptanalytic work. These were Robert O. Ferner and Albert W. Small. Ferner, whose academic background included mathematics and physics, was a very quiet individual with a pleasant personality. Small also had studied mathematics and physics and was a most outgoing person. The two of them soon formed a team, and their contrasting personalities combined in a way that they represented a most effective addition to our cryptanalytic potential. Two others selected by Friedman also developed into able cryptanalysts. These were Genevieve Grotjan and Mary Jo Dunning, both of whom had a capability for meticulous work and who could be depended on to perform cryptanalytic tasks expeditiously and accurately. We were also provided additional clerical staff to assist in the sorting, handling, and registration of the intercepts and to perform the typing of the translations and other clerical tasks associated with our work. A most important addition to our staff was the acquisition of IBM key punch operators. By this time we had established the value of the accounting machines in our work, and we were using them extensively in code compilation as well as for performing a variety of statistical studies and for indexing the appearances of unknown code groups in our code recovery work.

Although there was a pressing need for additional Japanese language experts to assist Hurt, Friedman was unable to find anyone who was sufficiently qualified until some weeks after we had solved the RED machine system. For a time the only relief was provided by the temporary assignment of language officers from G-2. Unfortunately, these officers were able to spend only a few months with us, and although they were considered qualified in spoken and written Japanese, they were at a loss in dealing with the Romanized texts and the unusual linguistic style found in the Japanese diplomatic intercepts. By the time they became sufficiently acquainted with our work for them to make a useful contribution, their temporary duty assignments ended. Their replacements likewise spent most of their assignment becoming familiar with the specialized form of the language, and consequently this arrangement proved to be of little help to Hurt.

Fortunately for us, and also for the Navy, two brothers who had spent most of their earlier life in Japan and who were exceptionally well qualified in Japanese were discovered by the Navy. One of the brothers, Phillip Cate, was employed by the Navy, and the other, Paul Cate, was hired by the Signal Intelligence Service. Paul soon mastered the form of language used in the Japanese diplomatic intercepts and was able to augment appreciably the output of translations. He also became very proficient in code recovery.

CHAPTER 13

DELVING INTO THE RED MACHINE

F ROM A CRYPTANALYTIC VIEWPOINT, the Japanese diplomatic cipher machine system was composed of three distinct subsystems. One of these was the machine itself, which automatically performed the enciphering and deciphering processes. It consisted of a typewriter keyboard, a cryptographic mechanism, and a printing apparatus. Although we never saw a model of the RED machine, we suspected that the Japanese had constructed the keyboard and printing mechanism from commercially produced typewriters which they modified to perform the input and output functions of the device.

The little evidence that we developed from the few intercepts that discussed the operation of the device, and from our observations based on our analysis of it as well as the practices followed by the Japanese code room personnel in using it, led us to believe that the cryptographic mechanism was uniquely developed and constructed by the Japanese. As we visualized it, the cryptographic mechanism consisted of a pair of electrical commutators which were geared together and which stepped either forward (direct mode) or backward (reverse mode) with the encipherment of each letter of the message. The movement of these two commutators was controlled by a mechanism which at intervals introduced additional steps into the movement pattern of the commutators.

The cryptographic component was also provided with a plugboard and plug arrangement from which twenty-six pairs of wires led to the keyboard and printing components. This plugboard arrangement allowed the connections between the keyboard and printer to be changed manually by the code-room personnel and was an important keying element in the security of the device. A means was also provided for switching the device from the enciphering mode to the deciphering mode and vice versa.

In the procedure followed by the Japanese when they first began using the RED machine system, the plugboard arrangement remained in effect for a period of ten days, starting at midnight Tokyo time on the first, eleventh and twenty-first of the calendar month. The date-time group on the message identified the time of origin of the message and the plugboard arrangement to be used for it. Each message carried a five-digit indicator which identified the initial settings of the commutators, the stepping pattern used in the message, and its starting point, and whether the message was prepared in the direct or reverse mode. When these components were set to the positions given in the list from which the indicator was chosen, the machine was ready to be used for enciphering the message.

With the machine set in the enciphering mode, the first letter of the message was enciphered by depressing the key on the keyboard corresponding to it. This sent an electrical impulse through the plugboard into the commutating mechanism, from which it returned through the plugboard to the printing mechanism. There it caused the appropriate solenoid to operate, automatically recording the cipher equivalent. On release of the key, the cryptographic mechanism would automatically advance so that a new wiring arrangement would connect the keyboard contacts with the solenoids of the printing mechanism. To encipher the second letter of the message, the key corresponding to it was depressed and its equivalent was automatically recorded; when the key was released, the commutators again advanced to a new position. This process was continued until all the letters of the message were enciphered. To decipher the message, the plugboard sequence and the settings of the commutators and the stepping mechanism had to be exactly the same as those used for its encipherment, except that the machine had to be operated in the decipherment mode.

The most mysterious aspect of the RED machine was the plug and plugboard arrangement used by it. We had no idea at all as to its physical form and appearance. The only clues we had found in the intercepts which might apply were the occasional uses of the Japanese term "INJIBU" in translations of intercepts which discussed the operation of the machine. They were used in a context which led us to believe that "INJIBU" applied to the part of the cipher machine which the Japanese code room personnel used for changing the ten-day keying elements of the system. Although Hurt searched through all his dictionaries for this term and queried all the Japanese language experts in G-2, he was unable to arrive at a satisfactory translation for it.

Even before Kully and I solved the first RED machine message, I had started to keep a record of all the significant information we had developed on the "five-digit indicator system" as we called it then. One section of this record was devoted to the "ten-day sequences" in which the sequences were listed in the order of their recovery, rather than in the chronological order of their use. By the end of April 1937 the space I had originally allocated for tabulating the ten-day sequences was filled and I decided to retabulate the sequences in a more convenient form. As I did this, I became curious about the manner in which the Japanese might have listed the sequences in the instructions they had issued with the machine.

I spent some time studying the sequences we had recovered, hoping to find some characteristics which would enable me to tabulate the sequences exactly as they were given in the Japanese instructions. My first efforts were unsuccessful in providing any insight into the manner in which the sequences were listed, but as I continued to enter each new sequence in my notebook when it was recovered, I compared it with each of the other sequences I had recorded. I began to notice that certain of the letters contained in the six-letter component of one ten-day sequence sometimes occupied similar relative positions in the six-letter component of another ten-day sequence. This observation led me to a reexamination of all the sequences we had recovered to determine if this or a similar relationship could be identified in the other sequences. As I pursued this line of investigation a logical pattern soon began to appear, and I discovered that by appropriately shifting the sequences against each other, I could fit certain of the sequences into a consistent pattern. When I had placed a number of the sequences into what seemed to be their proper relationship with each other, it took only a little further experimentation to discover what appeared to be a logical pattern which controlled the location of certain letters in the two sequences. By applying this pattern to other sequences, I was able to generate a family of sequences all of which possessed the same attributes. While I was generating this family of sequences, imagine my surprise and delight when I recognized one of the sequences as being identical to a sequence we had recovered in one of the earliest key periods that we had solved.

This startling discovery led me to examine each of the other sequences which I had not yet been able to fit into the logical pattern, and I was soon able to establish that after a certain date all the recent ten-day sequences which had been recovered could be found among the sequences which I had generated. Obviously the Japanese had either followed a regular procedure for generating the sequences as they were required or had incorporated a special commutating element in the RED machine for automatically providing a different sequence for each ten-day period.

Friedman, who had been deeply interested in the RED machine analysis before Kully and I first broke into it, had recently been leaving the management of the daily effort on the Japanese diplomatic intercepts to me, seemed truly puzzled by this discovery when I reported it to him. When he asked me for my assessment of its implications, I told him that it would no longer be necessary for us to recover the ten-day sequences by cryptanalysis, since I expected that the new sequences would be found among those I had generated. His response was that we would have to wait for the intercepts in the next key period to arrive to check my observations and also that it would take some time and effort to search out the sequence which was being used. From his remarks and his attitude, I received the impression that he was minimizing the importance of my discovery, and I found this to be very disappointing.

After my discussion with Friedman, I worked out a simple statistical test to be applied to the ciphertext of an intercept which would lead to a rapid identification of the sequence from the family that I had generated. Without waiting for the intercepts in the next key period to arrive, I proved the validity of my conclusions by applying the test to several key periods in the backlog of unsolved intercepts. I got considerable personal pleasure out of demonstrating to Friedman that my predictions were valid. I also got additional satisfaction out of promptly identifying the sequence used in the next key period by applying the text that I had devised.

CHAPTER 14

THE PURPLE MACHINE DEBUTS

I N LATE 1938 AND EARLY 1939 we deciphered several messages in the RED cipher machine system originating in Tokyo and addressed to the Japanese embassies in Washington, London, Ankara, Paris, Berlin, Moscow, and Warsaw which excited us from a cryptanalytic standpoint but caused some concern on the part of our intelligence analysts in G-2 and ONI. These messages dealt with distribution of a new cipher machine identified in the messages as "ANGOOKI TAIPU B", which could be expressed in English as "Cipher Machine, Type B." They also announced that a cryptographic expert was making an official tour of the embassies to which the messages were addressed in order to install the new cipher machine. He was expected to ensure that the new cipher machine was in good working order and to instruct the code room personnel in its proper operation and maintenance. Needless to say, we followed the movements of this expert with great interest.

Except for the name given to the new cipher machine by the Japanese, there was nothing in the messages which gave us any information about the cryptographic nature of the new machine. The significance attributed to the name was based on the consideration that the machine currently in use, the RED machine, was referred to as "ANGOOKI TAIPU A," or, in English, "Cipher Machine, Type A." We felt it likely that since the new cipher machine was called the "B" machine, it could be an improved model of the RED machine. Whether the "B" represented only a mechanical or electrical updating of the RED machine or whether it employed entirely new cryptographic principles were questions that gave rise to considerable discussion in the Army and Navy cryptanalytic groups.

We were not really surprised to learn that the Japanese were distributing a new diplomatic cipher machine system. For a long time we had been expecting the Japanese diplomatic cryptographers to recognize the weaknesses of their code and cipher systems and to take steps to improve them. We had now reached the point where we were promptly solving each new diplomatic code system as it was introduced. For several months we had been in the unique position of being able to decipher every diplomatic message that we intercepted and in many cases could provide translated texts of the intercepted messages to G-2 and ONI before the Japanese code rooms could process and deliver the texts of these messages to their intended recipients. In the light of this situation we felt it was inevitable that the Japanese would in time realize that the security of their codes and ciphers needed to be improved and that they might well indeed overhaul their entire cryptographic security arrangements.

Over and above this security consideration there was considerable evidence that several of the RED machines, most of which had been in use since the early 1930s, were becoming more and more unreliable in operation. In the messages we had deciphered, there were numerous reports of electrical and mechanical troubles with the RED machine. It was our estimate that in about half of the embassies holding the RED machine only one of the two machines originally issued to each embassy could be relied on to function properly. In one embassy both cipher machines were in poor condition, and we had to exercise special care in the decipherment of messages prepared on the faulty machines. We had also noted with great interest several messages from Tokyo to this embassy requesting retransmission of parts of certain messages for which the faulty machine had been used, possibly because Tokyo was also having difficulty in deciphering these messages.

The distribution of the new machine system generated considerable speculation about the effect it might have on our intelligence-producing capability. If the new machine turned out to be nothing more than a mechanical updating of the RED cipher machine, we felt that we would be able to solve it without difficulty. However, if the Japanese had gone so far as to incorporate new cryptographic principles which were unknown to us, several months might be required for its recovery, if indeed it would be at all possible for us to solve it. Our speculation about what sort of cryptographic principles the Japanese cryptographers might select for their new machine led us to review carefully each of the cipher machine systems known to us, in the light of our understanding of the Japanese cryptographic philosophy. We hoped we might develop some ideas from this review that would facilitate our break into the new system when it was put into effect.

Among the cipher machines known to us there were three foreign devices that we thought might be considered by the Japanese. One of these was the Kryha Cipher Machine, which cryptographically was closely related to the Japanese RED machine. The model of the Kryha we had studied was a noisy and clumsy apparatus powered by a clockwork type of mechanism that performed a Vigenère type of encipherment by erratically sliding one mixed alphabetic sequence against another mixed sequence.

The second was a Swedish cipher device call the B-211. This was a most unreliable electromechanical contraption which was very difficult to operate without error. The B-211 had been invented by a Swedish engineer named Damm, and we at times referred to it as the "Damm Machine."

The third possibility was a rotor device offered for sale by its German manufacturer under the trade name "Enigma." In addition to these three foreign cipher devices there was the Hebern cipher machine, which had been invented by an American who developed two models under contracts with the U.S. Navy. One of these was the machine which Friedman had broken on a challenge from the Navy, and the other was the one which had been tested by us in 1932, which had been rejected because we were able to demonstrate that it lacked the desired cryptographic security. The Hebern had been fully disclosed to the public since Hebern had been issued a patent on it by the U.S. Patent Office. Like the Enigma, the Hebern machine employed wired rotors, and in our judgment might be readily modified to satisfy the general operating concepts we had discovered in the Japanese usage of the RED machine.

In our evaluation of these prospects, we thought that the Japanese would favor the use of some form of wired rotor device and would most likely adopt either the Enigma or the Hebern cryptographic principles, since we could visualize the ready adaption of each into the form of a successor to the RED machine. Also, the Enigma and Hebern systems offered much greater cryptographic security than that afforded by the Kryha and Damm devices, and we expected the Japanese to recognize this advantage. We also felt that we could not discount the possibility of their using entirely new principles, significantly different from any with which we were familiar.

Our thoughts on what cryptographic principles the Japanese might adopt for the "B" machine were purely speculative, but these speculations were useful for they persuaded us that we should devote some of our effort to training our newer cryptanalysts in all the techniques known to us that could be applied in the solution of these cipher machine systems. We also included some instruction in the theory and application of statistical methods in their training. Outside of these adjustments, business went on as usual.

We kept a close watch on the RED machine intercepts, looking for some indication as to when the new system would be put into use. We followed the itinerary of the cryptographic expert who was installing the new system, hoping that at some point in his travels he would make a report that would provide us with some useful information about the nature of the new cipher machine. Finally messages dealing with his activities disappeared from our intercepts, and we concluded that the installations had been completed.

∽   ∽   ∽

It was not until late March 1939 that we found any evidence that the new system might be in use. When we received the intercepts for March 20, 1939, we found three diplomatic messages from Warsaw to Tokyo bearing the date of March 20 which did not fully conform to the normal pattern of Japanese diplomatic traffic. These intercepts were thought to be bona-fide Japanese diplomatic messages since each was addressed to GAIMUDAIJIN TOKYO and each bore the signature of the Japanese ambassador to Poland. They had all the outward appearances of normal RED cipher machine system messages except for one significant characteristic — the numerical indicator appearing as the first group of the ciphertext of each message did not conform to the pattern of indicators normally used with the RED machine messages.

Since Warsaw was one of the last cities visited by the Japanese cryptographic expert, we promptly concluded that these three Warsaw messages represented the first intercepts in the new cipher machine system. We searched through all the intercepts of March 20 from the other embassies visited by the cryptographic expert, hoping to find other examples like the Warsaw messages. We did find a number of intercepts with five-digit indicator groups, but all of these turned out to be regular RED cipher machine system messages which were readily decipherable in accordance with the normal RED machine system procedures. There were no other intercepts with indicators which resembled those we had found on the three Warsaw messages.

Our immediate reaction was to test the three Warsaw messages to determine if they had been enciphered in the RED machine system, possibly by using modified keying procedures. The first step in this test was to make a monoliteral frequency distribution of the ciphertext of the three messages. In each of the three messages, six letters stood out clearly above the other twenty. This led us to believe that we were possibly confronted with a modified use of the RED machine and that the messages would succumb to the straightforward cryptanalytic procedures we had developed for solving the RED machine messages.

Once the identity of the sixes was known, we could usually determine the sequential order of the letters forming the sixes by examining the patterns of their appearances in the cipher messages. Almost always when the order of the sixes was determined, the recovery of the order of the twenties and the effect of the motor key on both sequences could be achieved without much difficulty. But when we applied this procedure to the three Warsaw messages, it failed to produce the desired plaintext.

For the first few days in April there was a sharp decline in the number of RED machine messages intercepted. At the same time the new type of traffic increased in volume, providing further evidence that the RED machine system was gradually being replaced. By late April we were certain that the new system was being used almost exclusively for information which had previously been transmitted in the RED machine system. A small number of messages in the RED machine system continued to be intercepted, and when these messages were deciphered they exhibited the normal characteristics of RED machine traffic, including the use of the predicted daily keys. This led us to believe that the RED machine system was independent of the new system.

In the group working on the Japanese diplomatic intercepts the interest and excitement was intense. Everyone, whether typist, translator, cryptanalyst, traffic sorter, stenographer, or clerk, was eager to see a break into the new system. Major William O. Reeder, who at that time was the Officer-in-Charge, War Plans and Training Division, and who was responsible for the Signal Intelligence Service, visited our working area regularly. He was often accompanied by the Chief Signal Officer, who expressed a great personal interest in our progress on the new system. The liaison officers from G-2 and ONI who daily visited our offices to collect the translations of the Japanese diplomatic intercepts we had processed never failed to inquire about our progress. We maintained close contact with the Navy cryptanalysts working on the new system, kept each other advised of all new developments, and organized our files and technical records so that both units would automatically be informed of all new cryptanalytic data produced on the new system. Special instructions were issued to both the Army and Navy intercept stations to ensure that the radio circuits on which the messages in the new system were transmitted were fully covered. The work on the new system was given highest priority in our IBM accounting equipment section, and orders were placed for additional IBM equipment to ensure that the fullest possible machine support was available.

For the first few weeks of our work on the new machine, we referred to it in our conversations and our working notes as the "B" machine, the term the Japanese had employed for it in the messages we had deciphered which dealt with its distribution. The first occasion for official mention of the new Japanese cipher machine arose when Friedman told me that our progress on it should be noted in the regular monthly report on the Signal Intelligence Service activities required by the Chief Signal Officer. He asked me to prepare a draft report summarizing what we had learned about the system up to that time. In my draft, I referred to the new machine as the "B Machine," and my use of this term caused Friedman to suggest that we assign a cover name to the device since he considered it a poor security practice to use the Japanese term. After a short discussion, we concluded that we should continue the practice inaugurated when we selected a cover name for the RED machine. We had already assigned to other cipher machines all the common terms for colors except for two, namely, purple and violet. For reasons which I do not now recall, we both felt that purple was more appropriate than violet as a name for the new Japanese diplomatic cipher machine. From that time on it was identified as the PURPLE machine in all written references, as well as in our discussions. We even referred to the group working on the system as the "Purple Section."

 ᕤ   ᕤ   ᕤ

While we were getting acquainted with the nature of the new Japanese cipher-machine traffic and working on the recovery of the encipherment used for the sixes, we were also busy in preparing for the distribution of the M-134 to the three overseas departments. It was to be used for the encipherment of all secret communications between Washington and the headquarters of the three departments. This was considered a most important cryptographic milestone, since the War Department had never before used a cipher machine at this level. Our objective was to determine the practicability of using a cipher machine in the upper echelons of the War Department and to identify any deficiencies in the design of the M-134 so that these could be avoided in the next generation of War Department cipher machines.

For some months Friedman had been preparing to make a special trip on one of the U.S. Army transports to the three overseas departments. The purpose of the trip was for him to distribute the new machines and to train the code room personnel at the headquarters of each of the three departments in its use. He was also to inspect the physical security arrangements provided for its physical protection.

As I recall, the cipher machines were loaded on the military transport at Baltimore, where they were to be kept under twenty-four hour guard until each had been delivered to its destination. Arrangements had been made for Friedman to travel on the same transport so that he could personally supervise the physical security arrangements both on the transport and when the machines were delivered. The first two machines were to be installed in the code room of the Panama Canal Department. The transport would then proceed to the Hawaiian Department, where two more machines would be delivered. Finally the last two machines would be delivered to the Philippine Department. Friedman was to remain on the transport until it made its first port call in the United States on its return trip, at which point he would leave the transport and return to Washington by rail. The transport schedule allowed enough time at each headquarters for

Friedman to train the code room personnel in the operation of the machine and to ensure that adequate physical security arrangements had been made for safeguarding the machines and their associated keying materials. We expected that he would be absent from the office for at least two months.

At that time the Navy was also intensively working on the new Japanese diplomatic system, and I had developed a very close working relationship with the Navy cryptanalysts. I soon discovered that none of the cryptanalysts assigned by the Navy to the solution of the Japanese diplomatic systems had either the depth of experience in Japanese diplomatic communications practices or adequate training in cipher-machine analysis for them to be able to make substantial contributions to our work on the new machine system. As a consequence, I found myself spending considerable time in sharing our knowledge in these fields with certain of their cryptanalysts.

One of the Navy officers assigned to the Japanese diplomatic effort, Lt. Comdr. Wesley A. Wright, better known to his friends as Ham Wright, had shown considerable interest in our recovery of the sixes. One day, as I was working with him on the recovery of the sixes, we were speculating about what type of cryptographic mechanism the Japanese might have used to produce such an unconventional substitution system.

"Maybe they're using something like what we're planning to use in our new Navy cipher machine," Wright remarked. "Let me explain it to you, and you can give me your opinion of it." He then started to sketch out for me the cryptographic circuitry of for the new Navy cipher machine.

It did not take very long for me to recognize the exact principles which I had explained to Friedman some two years earlier and which he in turn had revealed to Wenger some months later. This came as a surprise to me, for I had understood from Friedman that Wenger had told him the Navy considered the principles to be impractical and had decided against using them. I did not reveal to Wright that I was already familiar with these principles but let him continue his description. I was able to demonstrate to Wright that for technical reasons it would be impossible for these principles to have been used in the Japanese PURPLE machine system. When I asked him who had invented these principles, he told me that he believed that Wenger had discovered them, for Wenger had provided them to Safford, who was now sponsoring their use. I am sure that he did not suspect that I was already familiar with the principles he had just described to me.

As soon as Wright left my office, I went to see Major Reeder to report to him what I had learned from Wright. Major Reeder listened to my account, and when I had finished he asked me how I personally felt about the Navy's using these principles in its new cipher machine. I told him that I was glad to learn that the Navy had decided to use them for I considered them to be superior to any other principles known to us and that I was sure that they would provide the Navy with a most secure cipher device.

"I am pleased that you feel that way," Major Reeder told me. "A few days after Friedman left," he continued, "I was told by Wenger that the Navy had decided to use the principles Friedman had revealed to him. Within a few weeks a working model of the cipher machine in which they are being used will be delivered, and we have been invited to attend a demonstration of it. By that time Friedman will have returned, and I have arranged for you and Kullback and Sinkov with Friedman and me to be present at the demonstration. From what I have learned in my discussions, the Navy is convinced that these principles will provide far better cryptographic security than any others they have considered."

CHAPTER 15

THE SIXES VS. THE "SIX-BUSTER"

A T THIS POINT IN our work on the new machine there was only one concept of which we were certain: the twenty-six letters forming the ciphertext were treated as two separate components, one of six and the other of twenty, similar to the concept found in the RED machine. While we had other speculative ideas about the nature of its cryptography, there was no convincing evidence that any of these were valid. On the basis of our experience with the breaking of the RED machine, where we first attacked the sixes and successfully recovered the method of their encipherment, we felt we might well follow the same approach in our attack on the new machine. We decided to concentrate at first on the analysis of the six-letter component. We hoped we would be able to recover the cryptographic principles employed in it, and, if we were successful, we could then undertake the recovery of the system used for enciphering the twenty-letter component.

The procedures we designed for recovering the cryptography of the sixes was straightforward. We had already established that in practically all cases we could determine the identity of the six letters forming the shorter component from a monoliteral frequency distribution of the ciphertext of the new-machine intercepts. We now had to devise a technique for determining the cryptographic relationship between each appearance of these letters in the ciphertext and its plaintext equivalent, but this determination was possible only when the identity of the plaintext letter was known.

Again we drew on our experience with the RED machine. After we had fully recovered its principles and before we had been fortunate enough to predict the sequences prior to their use, we had developed a most effective procedure for recovering an unknown sequence when it was put into use. This procedure took advantage of the Japanese practice of enciphering the message number at the beginning of each message for which the RED machine was used. By keeping careful logs of the messages numbers for each holder of the system, we could predict with a fair degree of accuracy the underlying plaintext for the first few groups of each RED machine intercept. If the Japanese were following the same message-numbering practice with the new machine, we would be able to make accurate identifications of a great many plaintext equivalents just as we had in our experience with recovering the RED machine sequences.

This technique turned out to be eminently satisfactory when we applied it to the new-machine intercepts. It led us to a complete recovery of the method used for the encipherment of the six-letter component. While we had no idea of what sort of enciphering mechanism the Japanese cryptographers were using, we were able to design a "pencil and paper" analog which enabled us to decipher the sixes wherever they appeared in the intercepts. This analog was essentially a deciphering chart six columns wide by twenty-five rows deep representing a polyalphabetic substitution system of twenty-five differently mixed alphabets composed of the same six letters. Although we were unable to discover a systematic relationship among the alphabets of the deciphering chart, it was evident that it had been carefully designed, since the six basic elements were evenly distributed with each of its columns. Recovery of this chart enabled us to decipher the sixes of any key period by the straightforward process of relating each of the six letters to its proper position in the chart. When we reached this point we felt we were ready to start work on the recovery of the twenties.

While we were recovering the cryptography used for the sixes, we had superficially examined the messages we studied for any clues which might help us in the recovery of the twenties, but we had not noticed anything which we considered significant. This led us to the suspicion that the recovery of the twenties could be a difficult task. Accordingly, we decided to make carefully designed plans for our attack on the twenties before we plunged into an attempt to recover them.

One of the most disappointing developments during the summer was the Navy's decision to reassign its personnel working on the PURPLE machine systems in order to reinforce its effort on Japanese naval intercepts. This action on the part of the Navy left us with the full responsibility for the recovery of the PURPLE system. Fortunately, the Navy's decision did not adversely affect the interception of Japanese diplomatic traffic. The Navy continued its coverage of radio circuits carrying diplomatic traffic, including the Japanese Far Eastern Diplomatic Net, which provided us with some of our most important intercepts.

The loss of the Navy cryptanalytic effort was more than compensated for by the increase in staff which was authorized for the Signal Intelligence Service. When new employees were assigned to the Japanese diplomatic section, we arranged for them to devote part of each day in a special training course we had prepared for them. The remainder of their time was spent in assisting in a variety of tasks associated with the processing of the Japanese diplomatic intercepts, for we wanted them to become as familiar as possible with this effort.

During the summer a situation developed which interfered for a time with all of the work of the Signal Intelligence Service. Owing to the increase in staff, the offices originally assigned to us became overcrowded. This problem was solved by obtaining new office space for the Signal Intelligence Service in another wing of the Munitions Building. Although we tried to keep the interference with our technical work to a minimum, it took more than a month for us to settle down in our new location.

In the strategy which we developed for attacking the twenties there were two distinct steps. The first was the production of the maximum amount of information from each day's intercepts. This involved the recovery of the sixes for each key period, and, if they looked favorable, we would then decipher each appearance of them in the messages which we considered most suitable for making plaintext assumptions for the text represented by the letters forming the twenty-letter sequence. These partially deciphered messages texts would then be studied by the Japanese linguist with the object of reconstructing as much of the underlying plaintext as possible. The second step was directed at the analysis of the relationships between the plain and ciphertext letters of the reconstructed plaintext passages in the hope that clues could be developed which would lead us into the recovery of the cryptography used for the twenties. By this time we had completely ruled out the Enigma principles as a possibility, and, while none of the evidence indicated that the Hebern type of circuitry might have been used for the twenties, we still considered it to be a long-shot possibility. The more we worked with the intercepts, the more we became convinced that we were confronted with a type of machine encipherment that was significantly different from any that we had yet encountered.

In meeting the requirements for the first of the two steps of our strategy, we found that the decipherment of the sixes using our "pencil and paper" analog was a time-consuming process and almost a hopeless task. We tried to devise several schemes for speeding up the deciphering process, hoping that we would be able to discover some method of using the IBM accounting machine equipment. The IBM procedures that we worked out not only were more expensive, but also took much longer to apply than our manual techniques. We finally decided that the most effective method of deciphering the sixes was to build a deciphering machine, designed especially to recognize the appearance of the six letters in the intercepts and to replace each with its proper plaintext equivalent. Our design for such a device included a keyboard of twenty-six keys, a solenoid-operated typewriter, a twenty-six-position plugboard, and a cryptographic mechanism which would duplicate the substitution process we had recovered. Everything we needed was already available to us except for the cryptographic mechanism, which would have to be specially designed and built.

Friedman returned from his overseas trip during August, but before he became involved in the regular work of the Signal Intelligence Service, he isolated himself in his new office in order to complete a written report on his trip to the three overseas department headquarters.

~   ~   ~

When Friedman completed his trip report, he scheduled a series of briefings in order to bring himself up to date on the developments during his absence. When I briefed him on the Japanese diplomatic effort, I told him of our need for a special device for deciphering the sixes and described to him the design we had produced. His reaction to my proposal was most enthusiastic, and he suggested that Leo Rosen, a reserve officer who had reported for duty while Friedman was absent, might be of help to us in designing and building such a piece of equipment. Rosen had joined the ROTC while he was studying to become an electronics engineer at MIT and had been recently called to active duty with the Signal Intelligence Service. At this time he had almost completed his cryptanalytic training, and all of us who had been associated with his instruction had been most favorable impressed with his performance. I was especially pleased with Friedman's suggestion, for I felt that Rosen would be a genuine asset in our work on the Japanese diplomatic cipher machine.

Friedman sent for Rosen and when he arrived told him that his help was needed on a very important project. We spent some time giving Rosen a general briefing on our work on the Japanese diplomatic cipher machine. Friedman then asked me to describe in detail the device that we needed. We then emphasized the novelty of the method used by the Japanese diplomatic code rooms for enciphering the sixes, pointing out that it represented a type of cipher-machine substitution that we had never before encountered. Friedman then asked Rosen if he would like to undertake the design and construction of a mechanism to perform the deciphering operation. Rosen enthusiastically agreed. I then took Rosen into the area where the work on the PURPLE machine was being conducted and arranged for him to become fully acquainted with the deciphering operation which we were performing on the recovered sixes.

Just a few days later — as I recall, it was the day after Labor Day — Rosen brought to my office a brochure from a manufacturer of telephone equipment which contained a description of telephone stepping switches of twenty-five positions. One of the models described was designed to handle six separate circuits, and Rosen pointed out that this was exactly what he needed for building the cryptographic mechanism for deciphering the sixes. He also noted that the stepping switches could be built to operate from a power supply of 110 volts DC, which was ideal for our requirements, for this was the type of power normally supplied throughout the Munitions Building. What delighted me most was that one model of the stepping switches met all the requirements for constructing the substitution component of our device without any modification being required.

Friedman promptly went to see Colonel Akin and explained to him our need for a supply of the stepping switches described in the brochure. Colonel Akin told Friedman that he had a personal friend who was an official of the company manufacturing the stepping switches and promptly placed a telephone call to his friend to determine the availability of the particular switch requested by Rosen. When he was advised that the switches could be provided without delay, Colonel Akin asked that two be shipped personally to him by air and that the remainder of the order be shipped to the Signal Procurement Office. We were delighted with the prospects of being able to produce the special deciphering equipment without having to follow the seemingly endless process of official procurement actions.

In order to be prepared for the arrival of the stepping switches, Rosen and I looked over the supply of cipher machines which were available to us, and we decided to cannibalize one of the earlier models of the M-134 which had been damaged during shipment. The solenoid-operated IBM electric typewriter was in excellent condition, but the remainder of the device, including the keyboard, was damaged beyond repair. When we searched further for a suitable keyboard, Rosen spotted the first pilot model of the M-134, which had been built by the Signal Corps Laboratory some years earlier. When he closely examined this device, he found its keyboard was ideally suited for his purposes. I told him that this particular item was very dear to Friedman's heart and that before we removed the keyboard we would have to obtain Friedman's permission. When we asked Friedman for his consent, he agreed with considerable reluctance.

Rosen went ahead with the assembly of all the parts except the stepping switches required for the deciphering mechanism. Colonel Akin showed a great personal interest in the construction of the device, and when he found that Rosen needed materials not available in our store room made arrangements for the local Signal Corps Procurement Office to make special purchases of the required items. Within a few days two stepping switches arrived by air mail, and, after some experimentation with their operation, Rosen wired one of them so that it duplicated the operation of the component of the Japanese diplomatic cipher machine which enciphered the sixes. It took just about two weeks for him to complete the device. For want of a better name, we called it the "Six Buster."

When we started using the Six Buster we found that we were able to transfer the cryptanalysts who had been spending a great deal of their time on the manual decipherment of the sixes to other tasks much more important to our analysis of the new system. It also improved the quality of our work sheets by producing cleanly typewritten copies, far superior to the hand-printed decipherments resulting from our previous "paper and pencil" techniques. In fact, it proved to be such a useful device that we decided to build two more.

When the remainder of the stepping switches arrived, Rosen started work on assembling two additional devices. Everything needed for their construction was on hand except for satisfactory keyboards. Fortunately, IBM had just produced an improved keypunch machine which used an alphabetic keyboard, and this machine was just them being demonstrated in the Washington, D. C., area. Rosen had an opportunity to examine one of these keyboards and found it to be ideally suited for the additional devices. We contacted our old friend Mr. Lamont, who at that time was in charge of the IBM Washington office, with a view to procuring some of these keyboards. We were disappointed to learn that purchase of such items was not possible under IBM's business policy, but when it was impressed upon Mr. Lamont that these were intended for a special Signal Corps research project, he graciously provided us with two keyboards on an indefinite loan basis.

From the moment we found that a conventional telephone stepping switch provided a completely satisfactory basis for building a cryptographic mechanism for deciphering the six-letter component, all of us who were working on the Japanese diplomatic cipher machine speculated that the Japanese might have utilized these switches as a basis for the PURPLE machine. Those of us who were of an inventive inclination produced numerous concepts of cipher machines built around a bank of telephone stepping switches.

We soon developed a logical design for a hypothetical cipher machine using stepping switches for the substitution or commutating component. This design envisaged a set of four twenty-five point, six-level stepping switches, operating in tandem as a basic cryptographic unit for enciphering the twenties. Our concept did not limit the mechanism for the twenties to a single unit of four stepping switches, but rather envisaged a mechanism in which several such units would operate in cascade, thereby providing a total cycle of sufficient length to suppress the occurrence of repetitions in the ciphertext. But we also kept in mind that instead of using stepping switches, the Japanese might have used another form of cryptographic mechanism for enciphering the twenties. This latter possibility was somewhat supported by our finding evidence that the cryptographic means for enciphering the twenties was much more complicated than the one used for the sixes.

One of the most important items of information we developed in our early analysis of the twenties was that, when two messages of the same date carried the same indicator, our statistical tests confirmed that they were enciphered by identical keys. This evidence suggested to us that the code-room procedures for the new machine were patterned after the ones used for the RED machine. In the case of the RED machine the date determined the sequence, i.e., the plugging arrangement, while the settings of the other keying elements for each message were obtained from a list. Although the use of the same indicator on the same day occurred infrequently, we soon found enough cases so that this theory was completely validated.

When we were satisfied that this observation was correct, it reinforced our earlier conclusion that our best prospects for recovering the enciphering for the twenties lay in the recovery of a large number of plaintext equivalents for the twenties. Now that the sixes could be efficiently deciphered, our ability to make accurate assumptions for passages of plaintext in the partially deciphered messages was greatly enhanced. We worked out a systematic approach to analyzing each day's intercepts in order to select the most favorable cases for reconstructing plaintext. Since the language normally used in the intercepts was Romanized Japanese, the Japanese linguists were the most prolific contributors. Occasionally we found messages in which English was used, and these were subjected to intensive study by the entire staff. We soon realized that it could take several months for us to produce enough of the plain and cipher equivalents to provide us with an adequate base for the recovery of the twenties; however, at this point we could imagine no other course of attack that seemed to offer us comparable prospects.

Almost a year to a day after Rosen produced the brochure describing the stepping switches, we got the big break we were looking for. We had been searching through the special work sheets for several days when one midafternoon shortly before Labor Day, Genevieve Grotjan, one of our most skilled cryptanalysts, make the discovery of the first case of positive evidence that we were on the proper course to a full recovery of the PURPLE machine.

Bob Ferner, Albert Small, and I were in my office reviewing the results of our search and discussing possible ways and means of improving our techniques. Miss Grotjan entered the room, obviously excited, and asked if she could show us what she had found in the work sheets she had been assigned to study. We could see from her attitude that she must have discovered something extraordinary and promptly accepted her invitation. She led us to her desk in the adjacent room, where her work sheets had been displayed, so that she could readily point out her discovery. She stepped up to the desk and indicated an area on the work sheets where she had drawn circles around selected plaintext and ciphertext equivalents. She called our attention to certain relationships between the equivalents in this area and then pointed to a second area where there were also circled equivalents. She then indicated a third and a fourth area where the relationships found in the first two areas were again exhibited. After she pointed to the last example, she stepped back from her desk, with her eyes beaming through her rimless glasses, obviously thrilled by her discovery. It took only a glance for us to realize the full significance of what she had found — it was a beautiful example of what we had hoped our search would uncover.

Small promptly started dancing around her desk, raising his arms like a victorious prize fighter, and yelled "Whoopee." Ferner, who was usually very quiet and not very much inclined to show enthusiasm, clapped his hands, shouting "Hurrah! Hurrah!" I could not resist jumping up and down and waving my arms above my head and exclaiming "That's it! That's it! Gene has found what we've been looking for!"

We made so much noise that the others in the section crowded into the room to learn what was causing the excitement. Within minutes everyone in the section had gathered around Gene's desk. The noise was so great that Friedman came in and asked "What's this all about?"

I beckoned for him to approach Miss Grotjan's desk. "Mr. Friedman, please take a look at what Miss Grotjan has just discovered," I said.

Gene, still excited, took off her glasses and started wiping the tears out of her eyes, trying to regain her composure. Since she seemed unable to express herself, I moved over to her desk and pointed to the work sheets, identifying the areas of evidence she had discovered.

I explained to Friedman the relationships of the circled letters in each area and the significance of her discovery. He carefully examined each of the areas and it was obvious that he grasped their implications. Suddenly he looked tired and placed his hands on the edge of the desk and leaned forward, resting his weight on them. I pulled a chair forward and offered it to him. He sat down and after a few seconds turned and looked directly at me and asked: "What are you going to do now?"

Small, Ferner, and I answered his question as with one voice: "Look for more!"

"We will continue until we locate enough examples to determine the nature of the commutating units," I added.

At this point Friedman turned and, addressing everyone in the room, remarked: "The recovery of this machine will go down as a milestone in cryptanalytic history. Without a doubt we are now experiencing one of the greatest moments of the Signal Intelligence Service."

Small, who was still showing excitement, exclaimed: "I think we ought to celebrate. Why don't we take a break and send for some Cokes?" I looked at Friedman, who nodded his head in assent. He then excused himself and returned to his office.

We gathered around Gene's desk while she gave us a detailed account of how she had made her discovery and then spent some time discussing its implications on our further work on the system. From the attitude of all those present it was obvious that each person was relishing the experience. I was delighted with this development, for I felt that such a spontaneous reaction on the part of the staff was food for the morale of the group, and I made sure that each person present was somehow involved. When the discussion lost its momentum, I suggested that we ought to make sure that the last-minute chores of the day were completed and that we should go home and be ready for starting the final push on the recovery of the PURPLE cipher machine system early the next morning.

After the group broke up, I went into Friedman's office to learn his reaction to the day's developments. He was sitting at his desk, studying some notes he had made on a pad. When I entered the room, he sat quietly, merely looking questioningly at me.

"Do you have any suggestions about what we should do now?" I asked.

"Are you sure that you will find other examples like the one I saw this afternoon?" he answered.

"It may take some time, but I am sure that with all the indicators for which we have prepared work sheets there will be other cases," I responded.

Instead of making any further remarks, he sat quietly, evidently waiting for me to make additional observations.

"Have you seen Colonel Akin yet?" I asked.

"Not yet," he answered. "Do you think I should?"

"I am sure that he will want to know about this development," I answered. "While it would be better to wait until we have found other corroborative examples, he has shown so much personal interest in the PURPLE system that I believe it would be advisable to tell him."

"Maybe you are right," he answered. "Anyway, I cannot see him today, for he left his office about two hours ago and will not return until late tomorrow morning."

"We will get started early tomorrow morning, and maybe by the time you can see him we will have another case like the one Miss Grotjan discovered today," I answered. "What we have learned from her discovery will greatly simplify our procedures and should expedite our examination of the additional work sheets."

He did not seem to be in a mood to continue the conversation, and I wished him good night and went back to my office. Ferner and Small were still waiting for me, and I told them that Friedman was planning to see Colonel Akin next morning and that we hoped we could find a corroborative example before Friedman met with Colonel Akin.

Both Ferner and Small expressed their willingness to continue the search right then. I advised against this, pointing out that it would be much better for us to get a good night's rest and start our search early next morning. I also suggested that since we had now precisely identified the type of phenomenon we could expect to find, it might be more efficient for two persons to be assigned to the examination of each indicator instead of one. Both agreed with this suggestion. By this time everyone else had left, and we decided to close up the office and call it a day.

Next day we started out by realigning the effort and redistributing the indicator work sheets, so that from this point on two individuals would work together on an indicator. We also arranged for Ferner and Small to act as a focal point to which all new discoveries would be reported. Now that we knew exactly what to look for, the search through the work sheets for each indicator went rapidly, and by the end of the day we had found several more cases like the one discovered by Miss Grotjan. As soon as the second was discovered, I reported it to Friedman so that he could inform Colonel Akin. When he returned from Colonel Akin's office, he told us that Colonel Akin had been pleased to learn of the development and had sent his congratulations.

During the next few days, more and more information was developed from the indicator work sheets, and we were soon able to establish the relationships between certain of the indicators. As this phase of the recovery developed, the wiring of the commutating mechanism began to take form, and we were able to use it to decipher portions of the messages for which we had not been able to assume plaintext. For me, this marked the peak of the most difficult portion of our analysis of the machine, and from this point on our task became easier and easier. It was a most exciting and rewarding experience for all of us.

The partial recovery of the wiring confirmed to us that the Japanese had indeed used the stepping switches as a basis for the construction of the enciphering mechanism for the twenties. Rosen promptly started to prepare the layout of a complete cipher machine to duplicate the cryptographic functions of the PURPLE machine. Colonel Akin again made a telephone call to his friend in Chicago and brought back the news that there would be some delay in the delivery of enough of the stepping switches for Rosen to build even one machine. This development led us to consider the construction of a manually operated analog which would duplicate the enciphering and deciphering processes of the Japanese machine. Although it would facilitate the deciphering process, it would still not operate as rapidly or as efficiently as we desired.

We had now established that the Japanese machine was using three commutating units in cascade, and we believed that each unit was made up of four twenty-five point, six-level stepping switches. Rosen's design of the manual analog replaced each of these units with a bakelite panel approximately fifteen by twenty inches in dimensions. On each panel he laid out a pattern of twenty-five rows and columns. At the intersection of each row and column, he drilled a small hole to accommodate an 8/32 brass machine screw. A round-headed screw was fitted into each hole and secured with a brass nut. Enough of the screw projected beyond the nut so that a wire could be soldered directly to the screw. On the upper side of each panel he mounted two one-half-inch metal rods at the right- and left-hand edges, and fashioned bars from one-inch square bakelite to slide up and down the two rods. On one side of each slide he mounted a set of twenty phosphor-bronze spring contacts to match the spacing of the screw heads, so that as the slide moved up and down the panel these springs made contact with the successive rows of screw heads, thereby duplicating the action of the wipers in the stepping switches. Each panel was then wired to correspond to the charts which were being prepared from the indicator work sheets. Input switches were connected to the contacts on the sliding bar of the first panel, and its output was connected to sliding bar of the second panel. Likewise, the output of the second panel was connected to the sliding bar of the third panel. The output of the third panel was finally connected to a bank of twenty small light bulbs mounted behind small opal glass windows, on each of which would be printed one of the letters of the twenties.

While this apparatus was clumsy and awkward to use, it appreciably speeded up the deciphering process and greatly facilitated the recovery of the unknown twenties. Its greatest drawback was that it required considerable strength to slide the contact bars up and down the panels, which made it impossible for any but the strongest of our staff to operate it.

It took about three weeks of hard and driving work for us to recover the wiring of the three commutating units used for the twenties. Each unit consisted of twenty by twenty-five individual connections, and each connection had to be identified by determining the ciphertext and plaintext relationships between two letters of an intercept and confirming the relationship by finding at least two other cases.

In essence, the instructions to each member of the team working on the recovery of the wiring were as follows: "Record all findings, identify the source of data for each recovery, keep each member of the section informed of your results, and, above all, make no mistakes."

Our work was not made easier by circumstances over which we had no control. A fourth floor was added to the Munitions Building during the late summer of 1940. Construction of this addition started with the east end of the building and progressed a wing at a time to the west end. During most of the time we were recovering the wiring of the commutating units for the twenties, the construction of this addition was started directly over the area in which our offices were located. I can vividly recall the distraction created by the building operation in progress just over our offices while we were searching through the indicator work sheets for clues leading to the location of connection after connection in the wiring diagrams of the commutating units. Our ears and minds were filled with the distracting sounds of hammering, banging, and shouting; when the construction cranes hoisted heavy materials to the workmen above us, we could feel the building shake as the loads were dropped on the roof; and worst of all was the incessant vibration from the jackhammers overhead, which started early in the morning and continued all day long. And this took place while the heat of the late summer was still with us, long before the days of air-conditioning. When we closed the windows to cut down on the noise, we sweltered. When we opened them to get relief from the heat, the racket was unendurable. At times, especially when the jackhammers were being used, it was impossible to communicate. In spite of this handicap, we continued our recovery effort and finally succeeded in filling the last positions on our wiring charts so that the panels of the analog device Rosen was constructing could be wired to duplicate the functions of the commutating units used in the Japanese PURPLE machine.

When the airmail shipment of stepping switches arrived, Rosen started assembling three commutating units. Since all of the connections of the commutating units had been recovered by that time, we were ready to start wiring the three units Rosen was fabricating so that they would exactly duplicate the cryptographic functions of the corresponding units of the PURPLE machine. Rosen had planned to convert one of the Six Busters into a complete replica of the Japanese machine. This would be much easier and faster to accomplish than to attempt to construct an entirely new machine, since all that was necessary was to add a unit for handling the twenties.

The most difficult part of the construction of the cipher machine was the actual wiring of the commutating units. Only one person could work on a unit at time. Fortunately, the Second Signal Service Company had some enlisted men skilled in radio and telephone repair work, and a few of these were detailed to the Japanese diplomatic section to do the wiring. Our experience with the construction of the commutating unit for the sixes enabled us to prepare appropriate wiring charts for each of the three commutating units. The enlisted men selected for this assignment rapidly mastered the techniques of transferring the information on the charts to actual connection on the commutating units. Frank Bearce, Rosen, and I were sufficiently skilled in this electrical-wiring techniques so that we were able to continue when the enlisted men were off duty or took a break for lunch. We also spent some time in the evenings on this effort, since we were all extremely eager to have a working duplicate of the Japanese PURPLE machine at the earliest possible moment.

When the wiring of the commutating units was completed, Rosen mounted them on a rack which he had fabricated out of one-inch angle iron, and we were now ready to interconnect the three units and add the control circuits so that they would duplicate the action of the Japanese machine. He also had to provide for connecting the units into the plug-board so that the daily key sequences could be set up for deciphering each day's intercepts. At this point the only unrecovered element of the Japanese machine was the wiring of the control switch which governed the order of movement of the three commutating units for the twenties. While we could easily duplicate the movement of the commutating units on the analog merely by operating the sliding bars in the proper order, this function had to be performed automatically in the cipher machine under construction, and appropriate switching circuitry had to be provided.

With the exception of the wiring of the motion-control switch, the assembly of the reconstructed machine was completed one afternoon about four o'clock. Rosen and I then started work on the determination of the control-switch wiring. Up to this point we had not given much thought to how the contacts of the control switch would have to be interconnected in order to duplicate the exact movement pattern of the commutating units. In fact, in the little time I had spent on it, I had incorrectly assumed that it was a trivial item which could be promptly solved when we were ready to make the connections to the switch.

The more we studied the control-switch wiring problem, the more difficult its solution appeared. We carefully went over the routine we had developed for manually deciphering the intercepts to ensure that we had actually duplicated the sequence of operation of the commutating units in the Japanese cipher machine. We finally narrowed the problem down to the point where only the wiring of a six-position, multi-level switch remained unknown. Possibly because it was at the end of a long and strenuous day for both of us, we just did not seem to be able to arrive at a wiring arrangement for the control switch which would produce the desired results. Finally, in the hope that we might learn from experimentation, we actually wired up two or three promising arrangements and tested them out by actually operating the machine. None of the wiring arrangements we tried produced the desired action of the commutating units.

It was now about eight o'clock in the evening, and we were not only tired but also frustrated and provoked by the unexpected difficulties we had encountered. I examined the control wiring, curiously wondering if there was anything we had overlooked in our assessment of the motion pattern or if we could possibly be making some sort of stupid mistake in our interpretation of its function. As I studied the exposed control switch, I attempted to assume the role of the Japanese designer of the cipher machine and toyed with the idea of how I would arrange the wiring of the switch had I been building the Japanese machine. While I was playing this game with myself, I visualized a wiring arrangement for the control switch, mentally picturing a logical wiring pattern for the switch connections and exploring its effect on the motion pattern of the three commutating units. I was happily surprised to find that my assumed wiring seemed to satisfy all the requirements for the motion patterns we had found in the PURPLE machine. When I started to sketch the wiring pattern on a work sheet, it occurred to me that I could actually perform the wiring on the switch more easily that I could reproduce it on paper, and I reached for the soldering iron and changed the connections on the control switch to the wiring arrangement I had assumed. Rosen began watching my actions with interest. When I had soldered the last connection and checked my work, I asked him what he thought of the arrangement.

"The easiest thing to do is to try it," he said. "I just hope it works." With these remarks, he plugged the machine into the power outlet and threw the master switch.

I watched his experiment with growing excitement. He set the control switch at each of the six possible movement patterns, and for each one the results were just exactly what we desired. When he completed that last test, we agreed that we were ready to attempt our first decipherment of one of the intercepts.

Earlier in the day I had made a selection of three messages to be used for testing the cipher machine when it was completed. Two were in the same indicator, one fairly short and the other of about two hundred groups. The third message was in another indicator, and all messages used the same key sequence. All we now had to do to test the machine was to insert the plugs into the plugboard in the correct order for the sequence to be used and to set the stepping switches of the commutating units to the proper starting points.

When we had arranged the plugs for the daily sequence, Rosen set the stepping switches to the proper positions for deciphering the short message. I sat down at the keyboard, and as soon as he finished adjusting the stepping switches, I started typing the ciphertext of the message. For the first few groups I typed, the machine performed beautifully, producing letter-perfect plaintext. Just before I got to the end of the first line of the message, the machine stopped and refused to operate further.

I got up from the keyboard so that Rosen could have full access to the machine. He carefully checked over the power-supply circuits and soon discovered that the master relay contacts were fused together. He asked me if we had a spare relay, and I checked the supply cabinet and found that there was only one relay suitable for replacing the one which had just gone bad. Before installing it, Rosen did some fast arithmetical calculations and selected a condenser from our supply cabinet. He wired it across the contacts of the replacement relay, which he then installed in place of the faulty one. He then reset the commutating units to the starting point of the short message.

"Now try it," he suggested, as he stepped back from the machine. I sat down at the keyboard and started typing the ciphertext of the short intercept. The machine performed just as we had hoped.

We decided then to decipher the other two examples I had selected, since we felt that if we could process the two longer messages, we could be reasonably certain that the machine was operating satisfactorily. We were delighted to find that the machine deciphered both messages perfectly.

It was now after nine o'clock. We had both become so wrapped up in the testing of the machine that we had lost all track of time. We both agreed it was time to secure the area, and go to our homes for a good night's rest.

CHAPTER 16

WE DEMONSTRATE THE NEW MACHINE

NEXT MORNING I HURRIED to the office so that I could outline the change in the work pattern which would result from the building of the new machine. An operator would have to be selected and trained so that we could get started on deciphering the intercepts as soon as possible. Also, a system of priorities would have to be established for selecting the messages which would be processed, for with only one machine we could only hope to keep current with the more important circuits, and we would have to ascertain from G-2 which intercepts were of highest intelligence interest. A great deal of work still remained to be done in recovering the machine settings for the unsolved indicators, and a cryptanalytic team would have to be organized to continue this work. These were only a few of the tasks ahead of us.

Ferner and Small soon arrived, and I reported to them that Rosen and I had checked out the machine he had built and that it was operating satisfactorily. Soon others in the Japanese diplomatic section started to arrive, and all were curious to learn if the new machine was finished. When Rosen arrived, we all assembled in the room where the machine was located, and Rosen and I prepared to demonstrate its operation.

It was a very special event for all of us. Some of us had been working on the recovery of the PURPLE machine since it first appeared in March of the previous year. All of the others in the room had been involved in the recovery of the twenties, and they were also intensely interested in seeing in operation the device they had helped reconstruct.

Just as I finished typing the last groups of the first message we were using for the demonstration, Friedman came into the room. The group which had gathered around the machine stepped aside so that he could fully observe what was happening. I removed the page of Japanese plaintext from the typewriter component of the machine and handed it to him. He looked at it carefully and smiled.

"Beautiful!" he exclaimed. "Lieutenant Rosen, you are to be congratulated.

Without your help, it would have taken months to produce this device. We can now start deciphering the intercepts in this system as soon as they are received."

"I think Rosen should promptly start the construction of another device," I remarked. "It will take more than a single machine to decipher the current intercepts. And if we have to decipher any of the accumulated backlog of intercepts, we will probably need a third machine."

"I have all the materials needed for at least two more machines," Rosen stated. "If I can get some help in wiring the commutating units, I can convert two more of the 'Six Busters.' I can have another machine ready in a few days."

"Excellent," Friedman remarked. He then turned to me and asked if I had informed Colonel Akin that the first machine had been completed. I answered that I had not and told him that we could put on a demonstration for Colonel Akin whenever it was convenient for him. Friedman then left the room, remarking that he would see Colonel Akin right away and invite him to a demonstration.

When Friedman left the room, I asked Mrs. Jerome, who had been doing an excellent job of deciphering the sixes for us, to try her hand at deciphering a message. I selected another message, using the sequence which we had plugged into the machine, and Rosen explained to her how the commutating units could be adjusted for the starting points given by the message indicator. Just as she was ready to start typing, Friedman arrived with Colonel Akin.

There was no need to give Colonel Akin a detailed explanation of the machine, since he had been following our work very closely during its construction. I merely told him that Mrs. Jerome was ready to decipher a message and suggested that he observe the operation of the machine as she typed the ciphertext of the message and that we would explain the functions of its various parts after she had finished. He agreed.

Mrs. Jerome somewhat nervously started typing the ciphertext of the message we had selected, while Colonel Akin and Friedman watched the operation of the commutating units and the printing out of the deciphered plaintext. When she finished typing the last group of the ciphertext, I removed the sheet of paper on which the decipherment had been printed and handed it to Colonel Akin. For a few seconds he looked at it curiously, and then he shook hands with each of us, expressing his personal thanks and his congratulations for our "magnificent achievement." He then asked if we were ready to show the reconstructed machine to the Chief Signal Officer. We told him we were ready.

"I will see if he is available," he said as he left the room.

In only a few minutes he returned with General Mauborgne. Colonel

Akin stopped just inside the door of the machine room, and with his face beaming, addressed General Mauborgne.

"Last night your magicians completed the reconstruction of the new Japanese cipher machine," he explained proudly. "They wanted you to see it in operation."

General Mauborgne stepped up to the table on which the components of the cipher machine had been assembled. We described the functioning of each of the components and then deciphered an intercept. He closely followed the operation of the cipher machine as the ciphertext of the message was typed. When the decipherment was finished, he bent over the typewriter component of the machine and closely examined the plaintext which had been produced.

"By God, it really works beautifully!" he exclaimed. "But what does it say in English?" He seemed to be as thrilled with the operation of the machine as if he had personally participated in its reconstruction.

At the end of the demonstration, General Mauborgne, Colonel Akin, Friedman, and I retired to Friedman's office for an informal discussion of the implications of our success. General Mauborgne's first question was simple and direct.

"If we can do this to the Japanese intercepts, what can other nations do to our codes and ciphers?"

Our answer was as simple and direct as his question. "Until improved systems are prepared and issued, the foreign intelligence services of any nation with a comparable cryptanalytic competence can exploit our communications," we responded.

"What about our new Army–Navy cipher machine? How good is it?" General Mauborgne asked. Friedman and I then explained to him the weaknesses which had enabled us to recover the Japanese machine and emphasized that we had avoided these weaknesses in our design of the new Army–Navy cipher machine under development. His knowledge of cryptanalysis was sufficient for him to appreciate the advantages and strengths of our new machine.

General Mauborgne then remarked that he felt that knowledge of the recovery of the PURPLE machine was a highly sensitive matter and that appropriate measures should be taken to ensure that it was not compromised. Colonel Akin responded that at this point the only person outside of the members of the Signal Intelligence Service who was aware of our success was General Mauborgne himself, adding that for the past several months we had not kept the Navy cryptanalysts informed of our work on the system. General Mauborgne responded that he was not concerned about the security practices of the Signal Intelligence Service, but that he felt we should employ special handling procedures for the translations of messages which were distributed outside the Signal Corps, and that he would have to discuss this subject with the Director of Military Intelligence as a matter of urgency.

At the end of this discussion, using Friedman's telephone, General Mauborgne personally called the Director of Military Intelligence, informing him that he had an important matter to discuss. He left immediately for the G-2 area where the office of the Director of Military Intelligence was located.

After about an hour he returned unannounced and reported on his discussion with the Director of Military Intelligence. The Director had sent his congratulations to all who had participated in the recovery of the new system. He was in full agreement with General Mauborgne that the strict compartmentation measures we had developed for controlling information about the PURPLE system would be continued in effect and reinforced, if necessary. Formal orders would be issued by the Chief Signal Officer reaffirming these security measures, and an addendum to these orders would specify by name the officers from G-2 who would be authorized to have access to the translations of the PURPLE messages. These orders would forbid any further expansion of the already established compartmentation without the written approval of either the Chief Signal Officer or the Director of Military Intelligence.

It is interesting to note that General Mauborgne insisted that these orders were to be typed by one of the women in the typing pool which prepared the translations of the Japanese diplomatic messages for distribution to the intelligence recipients authorized to receive what was then being called "MAGIC."

As I look back on these arrangements and how they came into being, I realize that here was the first formal compartmentation of intelligence, and possibly of any sensitive information, that I had witnessed. Up to this time, particularly in the War Department, any special regulations for the restrictive handling of sensitive classified information were usually passed along by word of month. Since the PURPLE translations would become the most important element of MAGIC, the strict compartmentation applied in PURPLE would in due course be extended to cover the dissemination of MAGIC. In the following years I watched with interest as these compartmentation rules were adopted as a model for limiting the distribution of other types of sensitive information throughout the United States intelligence community.

꒰ ꒰ ꒰

The recovery and reconstruction of the cipher machine had set the stage for the exploitation of the intercepts in the PURPLE system. A tremendous amount of work still had to be done before the benefits from it could be realized. During the eighteen months which had passed since the Japanese had started to use the PURPLE machine, hundreds of Japanese diplomatic messages bearing the PURPLE indicators had been intercepted. All these had to be exploited. The cryptanalytic task ahead was substantial, for many keys corresponding to the indicators still had to be solved and the sequences for each day had to be recovered.

Just like the RED machine, the PURPLE machine used a daily sequence which, for any given date, was applied to all messages enciphered on that day between 12:01 a.m. and midnight, Tokyo time. Once this daily key had been recovered, any intercept using it could be immediately deciphered if the machine settings corresponding to the message indicator had been solved. The indicator identified the settings of the commutating units and the motion control switch. In our recovery of the PURPLE machine, we had determined the settings for only a small number of the indicators, and clearly one of our priority projects was to recover the full list of message keys. Fortunately, no new cryptanalytic techniques had to be developed, for in our recovery of the PURPLE machine we had devised procedures which could be applied successfully to messages sent on any day for which the primary key had been recovered. But these procedures had to be applied mainly by skilled cryptanalysts, and, while straightforward in nature, their application was a time-consuming task.

There was also the problem of how to deal with the mass of intercepts being received daily which had to be processed promptly. Dealing with this daily input was a full-time task for the analysts working on the Japanese diplomatic messages. The situation was further complicated by the fact that during the last weeks of the actual recovery of the PURPLE machine, all other work for which they were responsible had suffered because we had transferred to the PURPLE effort every individual who could make any contribution to the cryptanalytic work on the PURPLE machine.

There was also a clearly defined and pressing intelligence requirement for processing the backlog of PURPLE messages. In the months before the PURPLE system was introduced, Japanese messages enciphered in the RED machine system passing between Tokyo and Berlin and Tokyo and Rome had discussed the secret details of the implementation of the tripartite pact that was being negotiated by Japan, Germany, and Italy. When the PURPLE system was put into effect, messages dealing with the tripartite arrangements had disappeared from our exploitable traffic; obviously this information was being enciphered in the PURPLE system. Only by processing the accumulation of unbroken PURPLE messages could we discover what had developed in the negotiations among the Axis Powers on this high-priority intelligence item. This requirement in itself was enough to justify processing the backlog of PURPLE messages, and pressure was immediately put on us by G-2 for the full exploitation of the backlog of Tokyo–Rome and Tokyo–Berlin messages in the PURPLE system.

Another important matter had to be resolved in that a decision had to be reached about the role of the Navy in the further exploitation of the PURPLE intercepts. A friendly and mutually profitable collaboration had developed between the Army and Navy cryptanalytic units in the exploitation of the RED machine intercepts. This collaboration had embraced all work on the Japanese diplomatic systems, with a full and free exchange of information about all exploitable systems. However, since the time that the Navy had some months earlier announced to us that it was dropping its PURPLE effort, the interest of the Navy cryptanalysts in our progress had become reduced until there was only incidental discussion of the work on the PURPLE system between the Army and Navy cryptanalysts. This was a natural development since all the Navy cryptanalysts who had been working on the PURPLE system had been assigned to the study of Japanese Naval intercepts. Also, on the part of the Army cryptanalysts, as soon as we began to sense the first glimmer of success, we felt it to be a prudent course to limit the knowledge of our progress to the small circle of individuals who were actually involved in the analysis of the PURPLE system. Since the Navy was not working on the system and for some time had shown no interest in our efforts, discussion of our prospects with the Navy cryptanalysts would naturally be avoided.

As soon as we began to emerge from the euphoria of our success, we realized that it was imperative that the Navy intelligence and cryptanalytic organizations be informed in full detail regarding both the intelligence and the technical aspects of the PURPLE cipher-machine system recovery. There were two overriding reasons: (1) The intelligence from our initial sampling of the PURPLE intercepts clearly established that ONI would have a high interest in the information they contained, and (2) the cryptographic principles employed in the PURPLE machine and the cryptanalytic techniques developed for their solution were of utmost importance to the Navy cryptanalysts, since the Japanese Navy might well adopt a similar machine for enciphering its communications. In this latter respect, to say the least, the Navy cryptanalysts would not have to undertake the time-consuming and extremely difficult task of reinventing these principles as we had been required to do in our solution and reconstruction of the PURPLE cipher machine system.

꒰ ꒱ ꒰

When Friedman and I presented to Colonel Akin our views regarding the disclosure to the Navy of our success on the PURPLE machine system, we found him in full agreement. He promptly discussed the matter with General Mauborgne, who insisted that before any disclosure was made to the Navy cryptanalytic and intelligence organizations, the Navy would be required to give full assurances that the security arrangements he had ordered for the protection of the PURPLE information would be met. In turn, General Mauborgne approached the Director of Military Intelligence with the proposal, who concurred with General Mauborgne's views. They were both also in agreement that providing the information to the Navy was a matter of urgency.

When Colonel Akin informed us that approval had been given for us to make a full disclosure of the technical information to the Navy cryptanalysts, he told us that as the first step the Director of Military Intelligence and General Mauborgne would meet with the head of ONI. They would announce that the solution of the new diplomatic cipher-machine system had been achieved and that the Army was ready to make a full disclosure of the cryptanalytic techniques employed and that Naval Intelligence would be provided with copies of all translations produced from the system. In return, the Navy would be required to give assurances that the extraordinary security arrangements which had been established for the handling of this information would be followed. If the Navy accepted this proposition, the Army would then invite the Navy to participate in the exploitation of the new machine system. Colonel Akin specifically directed that neither Friedman nor I give any indication of our success to the Navy cryptanalytic group until General Mauborgne and the Director of Military Intelligence had met with ONI.

Shortly after the meeting with ONI, Colonel Akin informed Friedman that the Navy had accepted the security requirements proposed by General Mauborgne and had agreed to participate in the exploitation of the PURPLE machine system intercepts. He also told Friedman that Captain Safford, who at that time was in charge of the Navy cryptanalytic group, had been designated by the Navy as the individual who would initially be briefed on the recovery and that arrangements could be worked out with him for the briefing of other Navy cryptanalytic personnel. Colonel Akin emphasized that no technical information would be withheld from Captain Safford and that the security requirements for handling the PURPLE information would be fully explained to Captain Safford.

Evidently the Navy had also acted promptly after the meeting with General Mauborgne and the Director of Military Intelligence, for when Friedman called Safford to suggest an appointment, Safford told him that he had just been instructed that he would be briefed by Friedman on an important matter. Friedman suggested that Safford meet with him in Friedman's office next morning.

In June 1965, Frank B. Rowlett received the Distinguished Civilian Service Award from President Johnson. Pictures taken near the Rose Garden of the White House.

Frank B. Rowlett and Colonel Harold Hayes guide General Omar Bradley on the latter's visit to Arlington Hall Station.

Frank B. Rowlett at his desk in 1948.

Back row: Major Hamil D. Jones, Lynn Spurling, unidentified, Frank B. Rowlett, Dr. Solomon Kullback, unidentified, Dr. Abraham Sinkov. *Front row:* Colonel George A. Bicher, Colonel Harold Hayes, William F. Friedman.

General Dwight D. Eisenhower visits Arlington Hall Station after the war to meet the people who broke the Japanese codes and who provided him with information concerning German defenses in France prior to the invasion.

Arlington Hall days. *Front row, left to right:* Colonel A.J. McGrail, Colonel Corderman, William Friedman. *Back row, left to right:* Mark Rhodes, Solomon Kullback, John Hurt, Colonel Vogel, Frank B. Rowlett, Abraham Sinkov.

Arlington Hall "B" Branch staff, 1943. *Left to right, back row:* unidentified, Maurice Collens, Dorothy MacCarthy, William Smith, Dale Marsten. *Middle row:* Robert Packard, C.P. Collins, Albert Howard Carter III, William Hazlep, Maurice "Mo" Klein. *Front row:* Mary Louise Prather, Robert O. Ferner, Frank B. Rowlett, Franklin Bearce, William F. Edgerton.

Frank B. Rowlett with his son, Thomas M. Rowlett (pointing), viewing the SIGABA on exhibit at the Smithsonian Museum in Washington, DC in March 1981.

Picture taken in June 1966 in the Oval Office of the White House, during the presentation by President Johnson of the National Security Medal to Frank B. Rowlett. *Left to right:* Vince Wilson, Major Glenn Lanier (White House Police), Dr. Louis Tordella, unidentified, Allan Dulles, Herb Connelly, Mrs. Frank B. Rowlett, Mary Dunwittie (Frank B. Rowlett's secretary), Frank B. Rowlett, Frank B. Rowlett, Jr., President Johnson, Mrs. Frank B. Rowlett, Jr., Mrs. Tom M. Rowlett, Admiral Rayburn (Ret.), Tom M. Rowlett, Richard Helms (Deputy Director, CIA).

In February
1946, Frank B.
Rowlett received
the Legion of
Merit from
Gen. William P.
Corderman.

The Frank B. Rowlett family at the presentation
of the Legion of Merit. *Left to right:* General
Corderman, Colonel Rowlett, Thomas M.
Rowlett (age 4), Frank B. Rowlett, Jr. (age 8),
and Mrs. Edith Irene King Rowlett.

CHAPTER 17

OUR ACHIEVEMENTS ARE RECOGNIZED

E ARLY NEXT MORNING I completed the preparations for Safford's briefing. Although there was an enormous amount of intercepts to be deciphered, we felt that this task could be delayed long enough to demonstrate the reconstructed PURPLE machine to the Navy for the first time. I selected the materials which I thought would be most suitable for the cipher machine demonstration and I asked Mrs. Jerome, who was responsible for operating the machine, to work at another task for the morning. I selected a set of the wiring charts and other technical materials which I felt would be useful for briefing Safford and took them to Friedman's office, where we had temporarily installed the PURPLE machine. While we waited for Safford to arrive, I verbally outlined for Friedman the ideas I had developed for the briefing.

We did not have to wait long for Safford's arrival. He was escorted into Friedman's office by our receptionist, and after the usual personal greetings were exchanged, Friedman suggested that we take our places at the conference table. Friedman opened the discussion by asking Safford if he had been told the purpose of the meeting.

"All that I have been told is that you would disclose some important cryptologic information to me," Safford responded. "I have been instructed to give you full assurances that any information provided to me will be handled in strict accordance with the procedures laid down by the Army. Other than that, I have been told nothing. Needless to say, I am consumed with curiosity."

"Mr. Rowlett will describe for you a cryptologic development which we feel is of great significance," Friedman answered. "After he has finished, we will then discuss the security arrangements we have developed for handling the information related to this development. If this is satisfactory to you, Mr. Rowlett is prepared to start his briefing."

"That will be satisfactory," Safford replied.

I was surprised that Friedman had chosen to have me make the presentation of the technical information, for he had not mentioned it to me. I had assumed the he would do this himself, since this had been his practice in all previous cases. I felt I should get right to the point of the meeting.

"We are going to show you a PURPLE machine," I announced.

Safford had a slight speech defect which often became noticeable when he was excited. It was evident that my statement took him by surprise, for in his response this defect was quite noticeable.

"Where did you find it?" he asked, stammering slightly.

Friedman could not restrain himself, and promptly answered Safford's question.

"We didn't find it," he exclaimed. "We built it."

Safford sat quietly, waiting for us to continue.

"If you will come with me," I suggested. "I will show it to you."

I went directly to the machine and removed its cover so that the full machine was exposed. Friedman and I both watched Safford as he minutely scrutinized each of the components. The assembly of telephone stepping switches seemed to stimulate his curiosity more than any other part of the machine.

"And you say you built this complicated piece of equipment?" he remarked, shaking his head in amazement.

"What are those?" he asked, pointing to the commutating units. "Did you build them?"

"We assembled them from standard telephone stepping switches which we purchased from a manufacturer of telephone equipment." I answered. "We are reasonably sure that the Japanese used similar equipment in their PURPLE machine."

"Let me operate it for you," I suggested. "Then it will be easier to explain it."

I took one of the intercepts from the samples I had selected earlier and went through the procedure of deciphering it. As I performed each step in setting the machine to the daily key and the message key, I gave an explanation of each operation. When all the keying elements had been set, I inserted a blank sheet of paper in the typewriter component and started typing the ciphertext of the intercept into the keyboard. Safford bent over the typing component and scrutinized the plaintext as it was printed. Since the message I had chosen was a fairly short one, it took only a couple of minutes to complete its decipherment.

For Friedman and me it was a most satisfying moment. Of all the individuals of the Navy cryptologic effort, Safford was the most knowledgeable about cipher machines. To witness his fascination and amazement at the operation of the reconstructed PURPLE was a rare and most gratifying experience for us. Safford's whole attitude was one of frank admiration.

When the demonstration of the cipher machine was finished, I went through the work sheets and wiring diagrams and explained the techniques we had used to recover the wiring of the commutating units. I also outlined the cryptanalytic task which was ahead of us, and projected the work load which we expected for a full exploitation of the system.

At the end of my briefing Safford was effusive in expressing his admiration of our work, stating that he believed our recovery of the PURPLE cipher machine was the "greatest cryptanalytic accomplishment of all time." He also expressed his conviction that all information about our success needed to be fully protected and asked for our suggestion as to how he and his cryptanalytic group could be of help.

"We want you to know all we have learned about the PURPLE machine system," Friedman told Safford. "The principles employed in it are entirely different from any we have heretofore encountered. As we learned in the case of the RED machine principles, we feel it is quite possible that this type of cryptography could be used by the Japanese Navy. Also, there is undoubtedly a wealth of intelligence information in the PURPLE intercepts which could be of great interest to ONI. We want the Navy to know everything the Army knows about Japanese diplomatic cryptography. All we ask from you is your help in establishing secure arrangements for handling this information so that our advantage is not lost."

Safford responded that he was in full agreement with Friedman's remarks. He added that before he could commit himself he would have to discuss the matter with ONI and that he would do so most discretely. He expressed his opinion that ONI would be equally desirous of protecting the information and would without doubt be willing to comply with the security requirements.

Friedman then outlined for him the security measures which had been established for handling the PURPLE information and showed Safford a copy of the written instructions which General Mauborgne and the Director of Military Intelligence had signed. He extended an invitation to the Navy to share in the exploitation of the PURPLE intercepts, suggesting that the pattern which we had adopted for the RED machine intercepts might again be followed. Safford responded that he would recommend that that offer be accepted, pointing out that some adjustment of personnel assignments of his staff would be required and that as soon as these could be effected the Navy would join in the exploitation effort. Friedman added that we were ready to reveal to his cryptanalysts the cryptanalytic techniques we had developed and that we would be glad to assist in training them in the exploitation procedures. Friedman finally offered our apologies for holding the secret so tightly that the Navy had not been informed earlier. Safford, openly sincere in his response, answered that under the same circumstances the Navy might have acted similarly and that he was happy the we had been successful. He also expressed his appreciation for the Navy's being informed so promptly of such an important development.

When Safford was ready to leave, I accompanied him to the hallway just outside the entrance to our area. As we shook hands, he again expressed his admiration for our work and his thanks for sharing it with him. He then turned and started down the corridor leading to the Navy Building, where his offices were located. I watched him as he walked slowly away from me, his head bowed as if in deep thought, and I could not help but wonder if he was pondering over what he would say to his superiors when he briefed them on what he had learned that day.

〜 〜 〜

The requirements of our code production program and the heavy work-load resulting from the need to process the Japanese diplomatic intercepts placed a heavy workload on the Signal Intelligence Service. It was clearly evident that if these requirements were to be satisfied, additional trained personnel would have to be procured. General Mauborgne and Colonel Akin emphasized the high interest of the White House and the State Department in their requests for increased personnel authorizations. When the Army Chief of Staff, General George C. Marshall, was briefed on our requirements for additional personnel, he showed such an interest in the work on the Japanese intercepts that a special demonstration was arranged for him. Colonel Akin personally directed the preparations for this demonstration.

Without giving me any indication of what he was planning, Colonel Akin had me prepare a full display of the Japanese diplomatic systems in an unoccupied room in our secure area. In this display we included samples of each type of cryptographic system the Japanese were currently using, including a working model of the PURPLE machine. When the display was completed, Colonel Akin told me that he planned to bring an important official of the War Department to view the display. He added that I was to be present to answer technical questions and to be prepared to demon-strate the operation of the PURPLE machine by deciphering a typical inter-cepted Japanese diplomatic message.

Colonel Akin spent several hours familiarizing himself with the materi-als I had provided for the display, asking questions about the various items and their purpose. When he was satisfied with the selections and their arrangement in the display, he told me that the display was to be left in the locked room until he gave me further instructions. About a week later he called me to his office and informed me that we should be ready for our visitor the next afternoon and that only he and I would be present.

By this time I was not only mystified and curious about the identity of the visitor, but I also had become somewhat nervous about the demonstration. Shortly after lunch on the day he was expecting the visitor, Colonel Akin called and asked that I meet with him in the demonstration room for a final inspection of the display. When he had assured himself that everything was to his satisfaction, he asked me to wait in the room until he returned with the expected visitor, and told me that we should be prepared to complete the demonstration in approximately thirty minutes. With these instructions he left me alone in the room until he returned with the expected visitor.

I had been waiting for almost an hour when I heard a light knock on the door and Colonel Akin opened it and ushered a most distinguished looking individual into the room. I did not realize that our visitor was General Marshall until Colonel Akin introduced me to him. I was so surprised and awestruck with the identity of our visitor that for a few seconds I was absolutely speechless. General Marshall graciously shook my hand and with a few remarks about his interest in our activities put me at ease. In a short while I got over my stage fright, and when I started to describe the various Japanese code and cipher systems, I found myself perfectly at ease.

Colonel Akin had cautioned me to be sure to cover the exhibit in less than thirty minutes, but I soon found that this would be impossible because of General Marshall's questions. As the time approached for the planned termination of the demonstration, Colonel Akin suggested that I omit some of the materials we had planned to discuss and go ahead with the demonstration of the PURPLE machine so that General Marshall would not be detained beyond the thirty minutes we had planned. General Marshall indicated that he was finding the Japanese cryptographic materials so interesting that if it would not inconvenience us he would like to spend whatever time was necessary to cover the entire exhibit. I continued with the demonstration, taking almost another hour to complete the presentation and answer General Marshall's questions about our effort on the Japanese diplomatic systems.

The item which impressed him most was our reconstruction of the Japanese PURPLE machine. In demonstrating the PURPLE machine, I had deciphered a short message and used this as a basis for explaining the operation of the machine. General Marshall was so fascinated by the device that Colonel Akin had me remove the protective covers for the cryptographic mechanism so that General Marshall could get a better view of the action of the stepping switches as I deciphered another short intercept.

When we finally finished with the PURPLE machine explanation,

General Marshall noted that if we could, through an analysis of intercepted messages, recover a complex cipher machine such as the PURPLE device, might we not expect foreign intelligence services to be as successful in reading our diplomatic and military messages. Colonel Akin responded that while we at that time were not aware of any foreign success against our current cryptographic systems, it was possible that they were being exploited. He then told General Marshall of the new cipher machine that was being produced jointly by the Army and Navy for securing our highest level military communications and asked me to compare its security with that afforded by the Japanese PURPLE machine.

I then gave a short explanation of the advantages of our proposed machine over the PURPLE and the other foreign cipher systems known to us, pointing out that we had applied the cryptanalytic knowledge and experience we had developed in our successful recovery of both the RED and PURPLE machines we had solved to select the principles used in our new machine. This last point seemed to impress General Marshall, for he then made the comment that it appeared to him that the best way to ensure the security of our own communications was to be able the solve the most secure communications of other world powers and to use the knowledge so gained to improve our own systems. After spending almost two hours with us, General Marshall graciously thanked us for "the most informative and interesting briefing on codes and ciphers" he had ever received.

When Colonel Akin returned from escorting General Marshall to the front entrance of our wing, he returned to the display room. When he opened the door of the room, I could tell by the look on his face that he was well pleased with the results of the demonstration. His only adverse criticism was that the briefing could have been most unsatisfactory if General Marshall had not been able to spend the additional time with us. He instructed me to store the materials of the exhibit so that we could repeat the demonstration at a later date for other War Department officials.

About two weeks after General Marshall's visit Colonel Akin called me and told me that General Marshall wanted to schedule a similar briefing for the Secretary of War and his two top assistants. He instructed me to reassemble the materials we had used for General Marshall's demonstration and indicated that we should be prepared to give the demonstration on a very short notice. I promptly reassembled the exhibit, and Colonel Akin, after reviewing the materials and streamlining the presentation, informed General Marshall that we were ready to brief the Secretary and his assistants.

When Mr. Stimson, who was then Secretary of War, arrived he was accompanied by Mr. John J. McCloy and Colonel William P. Bundy. The demonstration moved along on schedule until Mr. Stimson came to an exhibit containing some of the more interesting translations of the PURPLE machine messages. When these caught his attention, he casually sifted through them until he came to a fairly long message from the Japanese Ambassador in Washington to the Japanese Foreign Office in Tokyo which reported on a conversation between Mr. Hull, our Secretary of State, and the Japanese Ambassador. After scanning the first few words of the translation, Mr. Stimson turned to Mr. McCloy and Colonel Bundy and called their attention to the message. He then adjusted his eyeglasses and, striking an erect stance with the fingers of his left hand inserted in the openings in his vest, held the translation in his right hand and read the entire text in an oratorical voice as if he were giving an address. When he finished reading the message, he remarked that "our nation is indeed fortunate to have access to such important information, vital to the success of our diplomatic endeavors." When he made this statement, I recalled the allegation that he had closed down Yardley's Black Chamber when he was Secretary of State in 1929, and I could not help but wonder if that story was true.

Aside from this unexpected diversion by the Secretary's interest in the PURPLE translation, the briefing went very smoothly, and ran only a few minutes over schedule. It was abruptly terminated when Mr. Stimson's office called to remind him of another meeting that had been scheduled.

The strategy developed by General Mauborgne and Colonel Akin in impressing the Secretary of War and the Army Chief of Staff with the achievements of the Signal Intelligence paid great dividends. Our personnel allotment was increased, and approval was given for the procurement of additional personnel to be trained in cryptanalysis and cryptography. A number of ROTC students were called to active duty, and they reported in the early summer shortly after their graduation. Only those with outstanding scholastic records were assigned to the Signal Intelligence Service, and we found them without exception to be valuable additions to our technical work force.

Another most important source for our new civilian cryptanalysts was the American Cryptogram Association. A number of its members were interviewed and some of them were offered positions. The American Cryptogram Association members who were assigned to the Japanese diplomatic work and trained in its technical operations proved to be a real asset.

CHAPTER 18

A NEW DIPLOMATIC CODE APPEARS

A T JUST ABOUT THE time we got the processing of the PURPLE Machine intercepts to the point where it was a routine procedure, a circular message was intercepted which notified the major Japanese diplomatic installations that a new code was to be put into effect. The message stated that this new code was to replace the system which supplemented the RED and PURPLE machine systems and which was an important component of the Japanese foreign office cryptographic-security arrangements. There were only ten holders of the RED and PURPLE machine systems, and this supplementary system was intended to be used for the most secret communications exchanged with installations not holding the machine ciphers. As an example of its importance, when a Tokyo circular message was intended only for the holders of the machine systems, then either the RED or PURPLE system was used for its encipherment, but if the circular message was intended also for an installation which did not possess a cipher machine system, the circular message was always encoded in the most secret code system held by all addressees. Evidently the Japanese cryptographers were fully aware of the dangers of sending the same message text in two different cryptographic systems.

We were not particularly concerned about the introduction of a new code system. We were fresh from the successful recovery of what we considered to be a truly sophisticated cipher machine, and we felt that we could solve any code or cipher system that the Japanese cryptographers were capable of producing. Our reaction to the introduction of the new system was more one of curiosity about its nature rather than concern that we would not be able to solve it.

In due course acknowledgments from all the holders of the new system were intercepted. At the appointed date the new code was put into effect and the first examples appeared in our incoming intercepts. It was easy for us to identify the messages prepared in the new code by the form of the indicator on each message. Somewhat nonchalantly we set the first intercepts aside until enough material was accumulated for a proper attack on the new system to be undertaken. We complacently anticipated that the new code would be nothing more than another variation of the type of codes which the Japanese Foreign Office had been using for the past few years and that no significantly different cryptographic measures would be introduced.

It took only a few weeks to collect enough intercepts in the new system for us to make an initial attempt at its recovery. Our interest heightened when the first careful examination of the new traffic showed that the characteristics of the new system differed greatly from all the Japanese diplomatic code systems we had previously encountered. At this point that we began to sense that breaking the new system might after all be more difficult than we had at first estimated.

We discussed the new system with the Navy cryptanalysts who were working on the Japanese diplomatic systems. They, too, had made preliminary studies and had come to the conclusion that the new system was more formidable than the ones previously used by the Japanese diplomatic service. The Japanese were evidently using an unusual type of cryptographic system, which showed none of the external characteristics of their previous code systems, and, as the first step in our attack on it, we would have to undertake a full diagnosis to determine the general nature of the cryptography involved.

Over the years we had been exploiting the Japanese diplomatic systems, we had developed a good understanding of the Japanese foreign office cryptographic-security philosophy. We felt that the Japanese Foreign Office cryptographers would not completely throw out all their old concepts. In the improvements they had introduced in their systems, they had tenaciously adhered to a form of syllabary code for converting the written Japanese plaintext into code groups made up of letters of the English alphabet, and in rare instances where unusual secrecy was required had applied a form of transposition to the resulting code text as the final step in preparing the message for transmission. The earlier forms of transposition had been relatively simple and consequently easy to recover, but they became more and more complicated as newer forms were introduced. Accordingly, we assumed that the new system would fit into the established pattern, except that in the latest system, it appeared that a more complex form of transposition might have been chosen.

With this general concept in mind, we searched through the intercepts looking for any evidence which would either confirm or deny this assumption. Our approach was to sort all the intercepts in the new system by date and then make a careful comparison of the messages within each date in the hope that we would be able to develop more definitive clues about the nature of the underlying cryptography. As we conducted our search, we were led more and more to the conviction that the new system was indeed a form of transposed code. Although after several days of work we had not been able to establish the validity of this assumption, we had developed a good body of evidence to support and none to contradict it.

The most intriguing aspect of our assumptions regarding the nature of the new system was its similarity to a system employed by the German Army during World War I for field communications. This system, known as the ADFGVX Cipher, had been only partially exploited by the Allied cryptanalysts, and their solutions had been limited to the key periods in which they found messages where portions of the plaintext had been repeated. The Allied cryptanalysts had done some research work on the system in the hope of finding a general solution which would enable them to exploit a greater volume of the intercepts, but they had been unsuccessful in their efforts. Friedman had been a member of the Allied cryptanalytic group and had become convinced that such a solution was possible. At the end of the war he had arranged for copies of the unsolved ADFGVX intercepts to be sent to Washington, where they finally were merged with the Black Chamber materials. He had assigned Kullback, Sinkov, Hurt, and me the task of developing a general solution to the ADFGVX system as a part of our training program. As a result of this assignment, we had developed a technique for breaking the ADFGVX system which did not require the special case of messages with repeated passages of plain language. In fact, by using this technique we recovered several of the ADFGVX keys actually used by the Germans which the wartime cryptanalytic organization had not been able to solve.

The cryptanalytic relationship between the ADFGVX system and our assumptions regarding the new Japanese diplomatic system led us to the belief that the techniques we had developed for the general solution of the ADFGVX would enable us to be successful in our attack on the new Japanese system. Accordingly, we devised a cryptanalytic attack based on the ADFGVX general solution technique.

At that time only three of us — Bob Ferner, Albert Small, and me — were studying the intercepts in the new system. Our plan of attack assumed that sooner or later the Japanese would send a pair of messages in which portions of the plaintext would be repeated, and our first objective was to search through all the intercepts we received in the new system in the hope that we would be able to find two such messages. Accordingly, we divided among the three of us the task of examining the intercepts for messages in the same key with repeated texts. Although we anticipated that this phenomenon would occur infrequently, when we finished our search through the intercepts for the first month without having found a single case we began to feel discouraged.

During the first few weeks of the use of the new code system, we regularly discussed it with the Navy cryptanalysts, who were also studying it. They, too, had been examining the intercepts in the new system but had developed no plausible theories about the nature of its cryptography. When we presented our theories about the cryptographic similarity between the new Japanese diplomatic code system and the ADFGVX system, they showed little interest in pursuing them.

In spite of the lack of enthusiasm shown by the Navy cryptanalysts for our proposed attack on the new system, we continued our efforts to find the messages which we believed would provide us with the break for which we had been hoping. As each day's intercepts were examined with negative results, we naturally began to question the validity of our assumptions and, in our discussions, debated the possibility that other types of cryptography were being used in the new system. However, after each such discussion, we invariably returned to our original assumption and, though somewhat less enthusiastically, continued our searches.

The new system had been in effect for, as I recall, slightly over a month when I received a telephone call from the cryptanalyst in charge of the Navy's work on the Japanese diplomatic intercepts. He announced that he had something special to discuss and that he would immediately leave for my office if it was convenient for me. When I assured him that it was, he requested that I meet with him alone for he wanted our discussion to be private.

In a few minutes he walked into my office carrying a large manila envelope which was securely taped and sealed. He closed the door as he passed through it, came directly to my desk, and with barely a good morning placed the envelope squarely in the center of my desk.

"Before you open that envelope you will have to promise me that you will give its contents the same security treatment you asked us to apply to the PURPLE information," he stated. From his serious attitude, I surmised that he had brought something of unusual importance, for generally when he came to my office he spent several minutes engaging in small talk before getting down to business.

"How can I make such a promise if I do not know what I am letting myself in for?" I answered.

"You are not letting yourself in for anything that you would not agree to if you knew what was in that envelope. I assure you that you will not regret making such a promise when you look at its contents," he responded.

I was mighty curious about the contents of the envelope. If it was important to the work we now were doing on the Japanese diplomatic systems, it almost had to be information on the new system that the Japanese had introduced.

"That envelope contains materials relating to the new system the Japanese have introduced, and which we are now trying to break, does it not?" I asked.

"How did you know?" he asked naively.

"If that is what you have in the envelope, you have my promise," I said. "I assure you that I will do everything reasonable to meet your requirements for the security of its contents," I added.

"Agreed," he answered. "And now open the envelope."

By this time I began to feel some of the excitement of the moment and tore the seals off the envelope. Inside was a second wrapper which I broke open, revealing a pack of glossy eight-by-ten-inch photographs. I thumbed through the photographs quickly. Here was the information in detail on the new Japanese diplomatic code. It was indeed the type of system that we had expected — a basic code for converting Japanese plain language into code text and a transposition system for superenciphering the code text. Somewhere a safe had been cracked, a code-room official had been bought, or a courier's briefcase had been violated.

"I don't regret that I gave you my promise," I said. "Now tell me how you want these materials to be handled."

"You will find that when you examine the photographs you may be able to identify the Japanese installation where they were taken," he responded. "ONI insists that we hold this information to the smallest number of individuals possible. We do not think it would be wise to use the photographs for deciphering and decoding intercepts. We are now transcribing the cryptographic information, that is, the code and the transposition keys and the other relevant data into the form we have customarily been using so that it will give the general appearance of being cryptanalytically recovered. When our transcription is finished, we will provide you with copies. All we ask is that you apply the same security measures to the transcribed information that you asked us to apply to the PURPLE information. I brought the photographs to assure you that we are holding nothing back from you."

"Fair enough," I answered. "By the way, have you tested the information in the photographs against intercepted messages?"

"Yes, we have, and it works perfectly," he told me.

Together we carefully examined the photographs to ascertain how much the Japanese had deviated from the pattern they had been following. We were pleased to note that the code used in the new system in general followed the organization and vocabulary of its predecessors. However, the system employed for its superencipherment showed significant changes. It was much more complex than anything the Japanese had used previously. It was basically a columnar transposition system, using a matrix in combination with a transposition key which could vary in length from sixteen through twenty-five elements.

The most significant aspect of the superencipherment system was the introduction of the matrix concept. In the past the Japanese had used a simple columnar transposition scheme for superenciphering their codes, but in the new system they had provided a number of diagrams giving the construction of a set of matrices, each of which was twenty-five columns in width. In each of the matrices some of the cells in the upper portions of certain of the columns were blocked out, so that these cells would not be used when a message was inscribed. Each key period used a different transposition key and matrix, and a list of keys was provided which identified the transposition key and matrix to be used for each date. When the transposition key was twenty-five elements long, all the columns of the matrix would be used; in case the key was less than twenty-five elements in length, only the number of columns corresponding to the length of the key would be used. For example, if the length of the key was seventeen elements, only the first seventeen columns of the matrix reading from left to right would be used.

After I had completed my examination of the photographs, we discussed the arrangements for exploiting the intercepts in the new system. In order to limit knowledge of the photographs to a minimum, the Navy cryptanalytic group would finish the transcription of the code and its related transposition keys and provide us with copies. The established odd-even day formula would be applied for the exploitation of the intercepts, with priority being given to the processing of current intercepts. I promised that I would show the photographs only to Friedman, Colonel Akin, and General Mauborgne, and to no others unless specific approval from the Navy was obtained.

"Now that you have seen what the new system is like," my visitor asked, "do you still think you could break into it?"

"Yes," I answered. "It would take a lot of work, and we'd have to have some luck. But it would not be impossible."

"You surely can't mean that," he answered. "How would you ever get started on solving such a system?"

"Do you recall my remarks about the ADFGVX system used by the German Army during the last war?" I asked.

"Yes, but what about it?" he answered.

"Let me show you something," I answered. I went to the file cabinet where I kept some of my technical notes. I was looking for a technical paper which described the general solution to the ADFGVX system we had developed. I removed a copy of the technical paper from the file and handed it to my visitor.

"Take this back to your office and study it carefully," I suggested. "You will find that the cryptanalytic technique this paper describes will apply to the new Japanese system. The theoretical work has been done, and all we have to do is to adapt the principles to the new Japanese system."

My visitor thumbed through the paper with interest. "I have never seen this document," he observed.

"You should have, for a complete set of our technical papers was provided to your organization," I informed him.

After my visitor left, I sat for a few minutes considering how I would deal with the materials he had provided me. It was clear to me that before I did anything at all with the materials, I would have to show them to Friedman and explain the assurances that I had given in accepting them. I knew that he would also want to inform Colonel Akin and General Mauborgne that we had received full information on the new Japanese diplomatic system from the Navy, and I was sure that they would also want to examine the photographs. When I reached this conclusion, I left the photographs on my worktable and went to Friedman's office, where I found him alone.

"I have in my office some important information from the Navy that I believe you should look at immediately," I informed him.

"What is it?" he asked.

"Photographs of a copy of the newest Japanese diplomatic code," I answered.

Friedman's face showed his surprise. He promptly got out of his chair and started for my office.

"Where did they get the photographs?" he asked, after we had entered my office and I had closed the door.

"ONI made a surreptitious entry into a Japanese diplomatic code room and photographed the code book." I answered. "That is all that I know about how they obtained them."

As he examined the photographs, I described to him the arrangements that the Navy had stipulated for handling them. He readily endorsed my promise to apply the security arrangements for the PURPLE to the information from the photographs.

"Before anything further is done with these photographs," he remarked, "I must discuss this development with Colonel Akin and General Mauborgne. That should be done without delay, and I will talk to Colonel Akin immediately about arranging for a meeting with General Mauborgne."

When he left my office, I returned the photographs to the envelope and stored it in my safe. Friedman soon returned and told me that Colonel Akin had arranged to bring General Mauborgne to his office directly after lunch. He suggested that I test the photographs on current intercepts and to be prepared to demonstrate the results at the meeting.

ᔕ ᔕ ᔕ

When we met with General Mauborgne and Colonel Akin in Friedman's office after lunch, we displayed the photographs, and I demonstrated the deciphering and decoding processes, using a current intercept. Both General Mauborgne and Colonel Akin showed high interest in the materials, obviously impressed with the new complexities the Japanese cryptographers had introduced.

"Do you think we could have solved this system, Billy?" General Mauborgne asked.

Friedman's answer surprised me.

"A properly enciphered code can be one of the most difficult of all systems to break," Friedman replied, "and in this case the Japanese have selected a method of superencipherment which completely disguises the underlying code text. If we had either the code or the transposition keys, we might cryptanalytically recover the other, but if we have neither, solution is obviously impossible."

After Friedman finished, General Mauborgne turned to me, as if he expected me to express my opinion also. This I felt reluctant to do, since Friedman had categorically answered the question when it was put to him, obviously confident in the accuracy of his own conclusions. However, since only that morning I had told the Navy that I considered the system was breakable, I felt that I had no choice but to express my own views, even though they were in conflict with Friedman's.

"I was asked that same question this morning by the Navy cryptanalyst who delivered the photographs," I remarked.

Friedman quickly turned to me. "What did you tell him?" he asked.

"I said that we could break this system," I answered. "An attack on it could be based on the work we did on the ADFGVX cipher system some years ago. This new Japanese system is essentially a variation of the ADFGVX system. If the Japanese were transposing the type of plain language that they encipher with the PURPLE, we could easily break the system. Since they are using a code to convert the original text of their messages before applying the transposition superencipherment, the solution will be more difficult. The only concern that I have about our ability to break the system is that the underlying frequencies of the code text letters may not be statistically significant enough for us to make an entry through an analysis of the intercepts. In that case, we would have to wait for the Japanese to send a special type of message before we could recover the key for a day's intercepts. The special message we would need is one in which there is a substantial portion of the plaintext repeated between two messages using the same transposition key. This does not happen frequently in Japanese diplomatic messages, but I have seen a few such cases. It usually happens when Tokyo sends a message, say to Mexico City, and then repeats the same text to Washington with some explanatory remarks for Washington not included in the text of the message to Mexico City. If we find one such case, and if the repetition is long enough, it would provide us with all that we need to make an initial break into the system."

I then directed my next remark to Friedman. "The solution of the special message is just like the technique Painvain developed for the ADFGVX cipher system which you explained to Kullback, Sinkov, Hurt, and me when you introduced us to the ADFGVX system early in our training program," I reminded him.

Evidently Friedman had not equated the new Japanese system to our work on the ADFGVX system. He turned to the materials and examined the transposition keys again.

"Yes," he said, somewhat grudgingly. "These keys are indeed much like the ADFGVX keys. If the underlying code is constructed so the certain letters are favored as initials, and others as finals, it is possible that in the most favorable cases some progress could be made. But I still have my doubts that the system could be recovered just from a study of the intercepts."

"It seems to me that it is only a matter of a few weeks until you fellows will have a chance to try out your theories," Colonel Akin observed. "When this system has run its course, the Japanese will replace it. And if they use this or some other type of system, it will be your job to break it. I don't know much about cryptanalysis, but I do know our cryptanalysts, and I am confident that you will be successful."

"There is an important principle involved here that must be explored," General Mauborgne remarked. "Billy, did you or Frank know anything about ONI's plans for a clandestine entry into a Japanese diplomatic installation?"

"I first learned of it this morning when the photographs were brought to my office." I stated.

"I was also unaware of it until I saw the photographs," Friedman remarked.

"Spencer, did you have any knowledge of it?" General Mauborgne inquired of Colonel Akin.

"None at all," Colonel Akin responded.

"I do not like the manner in which this was handled by the Navy,"

General Mauborgne said. "We, at considerable effort and expense, continued on our effort to recover the PURPLE machine system after the Navy gave up on it. After we broke the system, we provided the Navy with all the results and even trained some of their cryptanalysts in the techniques of recovering the daily keys. Now, the Navy has made a clandestine entry into a Japanese diplomatic installation, without any discussion of their intentions with the Army. If this installation had held the PURPLE system, and if the Japanese discover that the Navy made a clandestine entry into it, they could be expected to replace their PURPLE system or dramatically change it. As a result of this type of action by ONI, it is reasonable to conclude that we could lose our capability for exploiting the Japanese diplomatic systems with the consequent loss of valuable intelligence."

As I listened to General Mauborgne's remarks about the risk associated with the Navy's clandestine action, I began to feel some concern. It was possible that the Japanese might still discover that one of their code rooms had been surreptitiously entered, and if they did, General Mauborgne's concern was valid. We could not be sure that we would continue to enjoy the capability that we had achieved for exploiting all the Japanese PURPLE machine system intercepts which had taken us years to develop.

"From this moment forward," General Mauborgne continued, "I want to make it clear that no clandestine operation will be undertaken by anyone, including ONI, against a Japanese diplomatic installation until it has been officially cleared with me. And I want each of you to express my feelings about this matter to your opposite numbers in the Navy. We cannot allow any action of this sort to jeopardize our ability to read Japanese diplomatic messages. You can also make it clear that I will take this matter to the White House for a decision if the Navy shows any unwillingness to cooperate."

When General Mauborgne and Colonel Akin left, Friedman and I spent some time discussing how we could most effectively achieve General Mauborgne's desires. He suggested that as soon as possible I make the Army's position clear to the head of the cryptanalytic group working on the Japanese diplomatic systems. As a parallel action, he would take the matter up with Captain Safford. He felt that it was important for us to act promptly on General Mauborgne instructions. We both anticipated that we would meet some opposition from both ONI and the Navy cryptologic organization.

During our discussion I received a telephone call from the head of the Navy group working on the Japanese diplomatic intercepts, informing me that the transcription "job" had been completed and that he was ready to have copies prepared. He wanted to know the number of copies we would require so that they would be ready for me to pick up early next morning.

When I told Friedman that I was to pick up copies of the transcripts next morning at the Navy, he suggested that my visit would provide a good opportunity to express General Mauborgne's views on conducting clandestine operations against a Japanese diplomatic code room. He also indicated that the reaction of the Navy cryptanalytic group working on the Japanese diplomatic intercepts would be useful background information for his discussion with Captain Safford and suggested that I report to him when I returned from the Navy next morning.

CHAPTER 19

WE EXPLOIT THE NEW SYSTEM

N EXT MORNING WHEN I went to pick up the transcriptions, the head of the Navy's Japanese diplomatic section was waiting for me. He showed me the materials which had been prepared for our use, and we carefully checked them against the photographs to ensure that nothing had been omitted. When we finished our inspection, he wrapped them into a neat package.

"Have you shown the photographs to anyone?" he asked.

"Yes," I answered. "I showed them first to Friedman, and then later Friedman and I showed them to Colonel Akin and General Mauborgne."

"What did they think of them?" he asked.

I was pleased that he asked this question, for it gave me the opening I needed for relaying General Mauborgne's message. I explained that the security arrangements were fully endorsed by General Mauborgne and that there was a great deal of concern generated over the possible damage that might have resulted if the entry had been made into an installation holding the PURPLE and RED machine systems. I then asked him if the installation that had been entered was one that held either of these two systems. I explained General Mauborgne felt that there was considerable risk that a surreptitious entry into a code room would eventually be discovered, and if so, we could then expect the Japanese to make drastic changes in all the systems held by that installation. He responded that there was no conceivable possibility that any damage would be done to our ability to exploit the RED and PURPLE machine systems, since the photographs were made at a location which did not hold either of the cipher machines.

I stated frankly that I hoped whoever was running the surreptitious entry operations had been fully apprised of the dangers of violating an installation which held the cipher machine systems. I then told him that I thought that he should make sure that the responsible Navy officials were informed of the Army's concern in this respect and that he should take immediate steps to ensure that no clandestine operations were conducted against a code room which possessed either of the two cipher machine systems. Before I finished my comments, I could see that he was getting the message that we in the Army took a dim view of mounting a clandestine operation against a Japanese code room.

"I don't understand why you feel this way," he said. "It seems to me that you would be glad to get these materials. It will be impossible to break this code system, and the only way we can read the messages in it is to photograph it."

"Do you still think that we will not be able to break this system?" I asked.

"Yes," he answered. "There is no way to break a code that complicated. You would have to recover the transposition keys for a great many messages before you would be able to get enough plain-code text recovered to enable you to break the underlying code. And you could not recover the transposition keys even if you had recovered that code. It just is not possible to solve a system that complicated."

"Did you study the technical paper I gave you?" I asked.

"Yes," he replied. "But the German Army system it dealt with is not anywhere near this one in complexity. Anyway, you only show a theoretical approach to the problem, and so far as I can tell, it will be useless against this system."

"You are wrong there," I responded. "We thoroughly tested the solution by solving German Army messages which had been intercepted during the last war. And I see no reason why these techniques cannot be successfully used on the intercepts in the new Japanese diplomatic system."

"If the Japanese do not discover that a clandestine entry was made against one of their installations, they will likely use the code until the end of its proposed life, and then a new code will be introduced," I continued. "Before you allow ONI to break into another code room, let us take a crack at solving its replacement. In fact, I will make a bet with you, and you name the amount, that we can break the replacement code cryptanalytically."

"Do you mean that you will be able to recover both the code and the new set of transposition keys by cryptanalysis, even if both are changed at the same time?" he asked.

"That is correct," I answered. "How long it will take is the only part that I am not sure about, but at the most I think we could break into the system in roughly two months. And we would not have to be concerned with the risk factors associated with a second-story operation."

"I think you believe you can do it," he remarked. "So I will not make a bet with you. You fellows are really very good, and you just might be able to do what you say."

On this note, we ended our conversation, and I picked up the package of transcribed materials and left for my office in the Munitions Building. As I walked back, I thought over the implication of my remarks and how they were received. It was now clear to me that the Navy cryptanalysts did not believe that the new system could be solved cryptanalytically. Also, I concluded that my remarks would cause the Navy to give careful thought to the risks of discovery if they attempted to enter another Japanese code room clandestinely. If I had planted any seeds of doubt about the need for another clandestine entry, I felt that I had done just about what General Mauborgne had expected of me.

When I got back to the SIS area, I went immediately to Friedman's office and gave him a detailed report on my visit to the Navy Building. He promptly called Captain Safford and made an appointment to meet with him after lunch.

"This is the first time since we started working on the Japanese diplomatic systems," Friedman remarked when he examined the transcriptions, "that we will be able to exploit a Japanese diplomatic system without having to solve it."

When I returned to my office, I made a display of the materials I had received from the Navy on my worktable. I then asked Ferner and Small to join me. When they arrived I pointed to the display and said: "Look at what the Navy has been able to achieve on the new system."

They immediately recognized that the materials had not been produced by cryptanalysis and promptly surmised that they had been clandestinely procured. While they examined the materials, I explained that we would apply the same security arrangements to the materials that we were using for the PURPLE information. I also indicated that we would follow the odd-even date formula with the Navy in the exploitation of intercepts in the system.

Possession of both the code and the superenciphering keys completely eliminated the need for any cryptanalytic effort and required only that we develop a system for reducing the intercepts to translatable plaintext as efficiently as possible. Since a considerable backlog of intercepts in the new system had been accumulated, we decided that we should give priority to the exploitation of the most recent intercepts and work on the backlog when the processing of the current traffic had been completed. This meant that practically all the cryptanalytic staff of the Japanese diplomatic section would have to be made aware of the materials we had received from the Navy.

We spent some time in discussing the steps that needed to be taken in anticipation of the replacement of the new code, which we expected to happen in about three months from its effective date. All three of us were in agreement that we should take fullest advantage of the possession of the materials by building a body of statistical information that would be of use in attacking its replacement. Small came up with a suggestion that Ferner and I fully endorsed. He proposed to use the IBM accounting machine equipment for deciphering and decoding the backlog of intercepts instead of the pencil-and-paper techniques that would have to be applied in exploiting the current intercepts. We concluded our discussion by agreeing that Ferner and Small would give priority to working out a program for a machine decoding and deciphering operation, while the remainder of the staff would devote their attention to exploiting the current intercepts, including those in the new system.

I then called in the rest of the group working on the Japanese diplomatic intercepts and informed them that we had obtained a windfall from a clandestine operation and invited them to examine the materials which were still displayed on my worktable. The language specialists were delighted with the prospects of being able to translate messages without having to recover unknown code groups. Major Harold Dowd, a language officer who had spent several years in Japan while he was studying Japanese, was especially interested in the vocabulary of the new code, and he was eager to compare it with the ones which had been recovered previously by cryptanalysis.

I cautioned the entire group to limit the knowledge of the materials to those who were present. I told them that in the Army, except for those present, only General Mauborgne, Colonel Akin, and Mr. Friedman knew about the materials. I suggested to Major Dowd, who was attached to G-2 and was under assignment to the Signal Intelligence Service, that the Chief Signal Officer would report the possession of the materials to the Director of Intelligence and that he would not need to take any action with G-2 until after the Chief Signal Officer had conferred with the Director of Intelligence. Major Dowd fully agreed with this suggestion and expressed his opinion that the closer the secret was held, the better.

We were now ready to begin the full exploitation of all intercepts in the new system. Ferner and Small distributed copies of the transcripts to the working groups and instructed each individual in their use.

∽ ∽ ∽

During the following weeks, we were able to exploit the intercepts in the new code with a minimum of effort. The Japanese language experts found it a pleasure to translate the decoded texts which our processing group provided. Major Dowd completed his comparison of the code which had been photographed with the versions of the codes which had been cryptanalytically recovered and thereby enriched our code-breaking capability. Ferner and Small pursued their researches into the statistical nature of the underlying code text and, with the assistance of Sammy Snyder, explored the use of the IBM accounting machines for decoding the backlog of messages in the new system.

The Japanese normally replaced their cryptographic systems after they had been in effect for about three months. Sometimes they extended the life of a system by introducing variations in the basic cryptographic process which could be applied by the code-room personnel without requiring a replacement of the code. The instructions for these changes were usually disseminated by a special message encoded in the system to which it applied. When these special messages were intercepted by us, we of course were able to continue our exploitation of the system without having to recover the variations by cryptanalysis. Both the Army and Navy cryptanalytic groups hoped that the life of the new code would be extended by such an arrangement, and accordingly kept a close watch on all the messages in the new system originating in Tokyo for the appearance of such a code instruction message. But we knew that inevitably the Japanese cryptographic authorities would issue a complete replacement of the system and that we could expect to be confronted with the same situation we had encountered when the new system was first introduced.

After the system had been in effect for, as I recall, almost three months, we intercepted a message from Tokyo, addressed to all holders of the new system, which stated that a replacement code was to be put into effect. We discussed the implication of this message with the Navy cryptanalysts, and we jointly concluded that we would soon be confronted with the recovery of a new diplomatic system. But from the meager information provided by the message, we were not able to make any predictions about the nature of the replacement.

When I reported to Friedman that we had intercepted a message announcing that a new code was to be put into effect, he promptly sought out Colonel Akin and relayed the information to him. Colonel Akin's immediate reaction was that we should inform the Navy that under no circumstances should any effort be made to obtain copies of the new system clandestinely. He also told Friedman that he would advise the Chief Signal Officer to get in touch with the Director of Military Intelligence and propose that G-2 express to ONI the Army's opposition to any clandestine action against a Japanese diplomatic installation at that time. He also instructed Friedman to keep him and the Chief Signal officer apprised of any developments associated with the newly announced system and especially of the Navy's reaction to the Army position in regard to a clandestine operation.

Friedman promptly acted on Major Akin's instructions by directing me to contact the Navy cryptanalytic group with which I usually dealt, while he took the matter up with Captain Safford. When I discussed the question with the Navy group, they expressed their hope that the new system could be solved without recourse to a clandestine operation, but they frankly stated their doubts that we would be able to recover the expected system by analyzing its intercepts. When I reminded them that the information contained in the transposed code system was in general only supplementary to that provided by the PURPLE intercepts, they finally conceded that there was no real urgency to exploit this class of messages and that a clandestine operation could be delayed until we had made an effort to recover the new system cryptanalytically. When I reported the results of my discussions with the Navy cryptanalytic group to Friedman, he told me that Safford considered that clandestine action to photograph the new code was undesirable. It took a little longer for G-2 and ONI to get together on this matter, but in due course we got word from Colonel Akin that G-2 had confirmed that ONI had agreed that no clandestine action would be taken to procure the replacement system without coordinating the action with the Army. The outcome of these discussions pleased General Mauborgne who had been showing a greater aversion toward any sort of a clandestine operation against a Japanese diplomatic installation each time we briefed him on the status of our efforts against the Japanese codes.

The expected code change was put into effect on the announced date. For the first few days of its use, we carefully examined each intercept that we received, hoping to find some evidence of a weakness which we could exploit to enable us to make an entry into the system. As I recall, the new system had been in effect for about a month when there was a heavy surge in the number of intercepts we received in it. Fortunately for our purposes, we found a day's traffic for which we received an unusually large number of intercepts. We were especially lucky, for Tokyo had sent a circular message to several installations, and in one of these messages, the code clerk in Tokyo had slightly altered the text by adding an additional short passage of text at the end. This slight difference in text, which amounted to something like fifty letters of code text, was all that we needed to recover the transposition key and the matrix for the key period.

After we had recovered the transposition key and the matrix, we promptly deciphered all the other intercepts in the key period, thereby reducing the messages to unenciphered code texts. Our Japanese language experts could now begin studying the code employed with the system, and we could start building our statistical banks of information for compiling the frequency characteristics of the underlying code to assist in our key recovery.

I promptly informed Friedman of our success and invited him to look over the results we had achieved. He was genuinely pleased that we had been able to make a break into the system. When I mentioned to him that

I ought to inform the Navy of our success, he asked that I defer this action until he had consulted with Colonel Akin. I reminded him of General Mauborgne's remarks about the dangers of a surreptitious entry and suggested that we ought to disclose our success to the Navy as promptly as possible to deter ONI from taking any clandestine action against a Japanese diplomatic code room. He fully agreed and promptly left for Colonel Akin's office. He soon returned, reporting that we would have wait until next morning, since Colonel Akin had left his office for the day.

〜 〜 〜

I was eager to get our group started on recovering the transposition key for another period, and I arrived at the Munitions Building next morning a good hour before the regular starting time. I had found that by arriving early I could lay out the plans for the day and also spend some time studying the more pressing cryptanalytic problems. Usually there was no one else in the office at this hour, and there were no distracting interruptions. Since I was responsible for the cryptanalytic work on the Japanese diplomatic codes and ciphers, as well as being Friedman's principal assistant on other matters for which the Signal Intelligence Service was responsible, I was finding less and less time to spend on cryptanalytic research, the work I enjoyed most.

The cryptanalysis in which we were now engaged was even more fascinating to me than the recovery of the PURPLE machine. Each key period represented a distinct cryptanalytic project, and its vulnerability could be explored in a relatively short time, in contrast with our experience with the PURPLE machine recovery where we had spent weeks, and in some cases months, searching for obscure clues. We could not expect to be successful with every key period, but we could, by a careful assessment of each day's intercepts, determine which key periods were the most likely to succumb to our attack. We were now in position to apply our planned statistical approach to unsolved key periods. It was important that we review our plan of attack to determine if there were opportunities for improving our techniques that we had not yet discovered.

When I reached the office, Small was waiting for me. He apparently had been drawn to arrive early for the same reasons that had brought me there. I unlocked the entrance to the secure area in which my office was located, and we made our way to the table on which our work sheets from the previous day were still displayed.

"Well, Albert," I asked, "What have you cooked up overnight?"

"I have given a lot of thought to mechanizing our testing procedures using the IBM accounting machines" he answered. "They were designed to do arithmetical computation, and there ought to be some way in which we can take advantage of them on this and similar projects that require a massive arithmetic treatment. I have some ideas for mechanizing our approach which may be useful."

On the blackboard he sketched a modified form of the probability chart we had designed for our transposition key recovery. After explaining the modifications to the work sheet, he then outlined an IBM card and described a novel idea for registering the information from the probability chart on it.

The central concept of his proposal was to prepare a master card for each of the twenty-six letters used in the system. One column on each card would identify the card by its letter and seventy-eight of the remaining seventy-nine columns would contain the probability, expressed as a three-place logarithm, of its digraphic relation as an initial with each of the twenty-six letters as a final. These master cards would be duplicated in sufficient quantities so that a working form of an intercept could be produced by assembling a set of cards in which the first letter of the intercept would be represented by a card corresponding to it, the second letter by its card, and so on for all the letters of the intercept. By properly wiring a tabulator plugboard, this assembly of cards could be used to print a listing which showed the probabilities of a selected set of letters, corresponding to a hypothetical column of letters in the transposition matrix as initials with the letters of the entire message as finals. While this listing would not provide us with the totals for each possible match of the hypothetical column, it would eliminate the need for our having to select the digraphic probability from our charts, by providing us with a listing of these probabilities so that we could more readily evaluate each possible matching position.

At this point Ferner arrived, and I asked Small to describe his ideas him. When Small finished his explanation, Ferner promptly endorsed his proposal.

"This idea can appreciably shorten the time required for exhaustive testing, and it certainly ought to be tried," Ferner stated. "It may lead to other ideas which might be useful for reducing the time required by our present procedures."

After further discussion of the idea, we agreed that the best way to test it would be to try it on an unsolved key period. Since our probability charts were based on a very limited amount of data, we decided that we would complete the decipherment of all the messages for which we had recovered the key periods and include the new data in our calculations.

I asked Small what he would require for testing his suggestions. "Only a few hours in the machine room and access to a key punch, reproducer, and tabulator," he answered.

"Very well," I said. "I will make the arrangements with the machine room. Before you start your tests, the intercepts in the key period we solved yesterday ought to be deciphered so that the code text frequencies can be included in the computations for the new probability charts."

At this point Friedman came into my office.

"I have just finished informing Colonel Akin of your success with the new system," he remarked. "He was pleased to hear that you had been successful in making the first break into the replacement system and sends his congratulations to the three of you. He is arranging for an appointment with the Chief Signal Officer to discuss our collaboration with the Navy. Since he expects General Mauborgne will have some questions about how you recovered the transposition key, he would like for Rowlett and me to accompany him. I expect to hear from him at any moment."

At that moment, Colonel Akin's secretary came into the office and told Friedman that Colonel Akin wanted us to report immediately to General Mauborgne's office.

General Mauborgne seemed to get a great deal of personal satisfaction out of discussing the work of the SIS. This morning he was especially cordial when he greeted us. Colonel Akin, in his usual businesslike manner, got right to the point of the meeting.

"I am pleased to report that the SIS has again performed a spectacular cryptanalytic feat," he began. "Late yesterday afternoon the Japanese diplomatic section made the first break into the system which replaced the one photographed by ONI. We have not yet informed the Navy of this development, for I wanted to obtain your views first. I have brought Mr. Friedman and Mr. Rowlett with me so that you would have the benefit of their technical opinions. Since an initial break into the new system had been made, I feel that we ought to take steps to ensure that ONI does not undertake a clandestine operation to photograph it."

"I do not want ONI to undertake a clandestine operation to procure a Japanese diplomatic code at any time and at any place in the world unless the SIS cryptanalysts are in full agreement that such action is necessary," General Mauborgne emphatically responded. "All along I have had full confidence that the SIS could break any code or cipher system the Japanese cryptographers might produce. I now feel certain that it was not necessary for ONI to go after the code they photographed. And I want my position to continue to be made clear to the Navy at all echelons of command. I welcome any suggestions you gentlemen may have to offer."

"I think it is imperative that we inform the Navy cryptanalytic group immediately of our latest success," Colonel Akin responded. "I believe this should be done first by Mr. Rowlett at his level. When he informs the Navy technicians of the break, he must emphasize that no clandestine operation is required and that it would endanger our success if one should be undertaken. Mr. Friedman should also have a discussion with Captain Safford, and at that level reiterate our objection to a clandestine operation against a Japanese diplomatic code room. I also suggest that you join with the Director of Military Intelligence and have a meeting with the appropriate Navy officials at your level. I recommend that prompt action be taken."

"Billy, do you and Frank feel that you can exploit this new system without the need for a second-story job by ONI?" General Mauborgne asked.

"I suggest that Mr. Rowlett give you a briefing on what is involved in the cryptanalysis of this system," Friedman answered. "You should be warned that it is a difficult system to deal with, and although our Japanese diplomatic section has done a remarkable job in breaking into one key period, it is my opinion that it will be virtually impossible for the group with its limited resources to achieve the same degree of success with this type of system that we have for all the other Japanese diplomatic systems. I think it is important that this point be appreciated by you as well as by the Director of Military Intelligence."

"What is your opinion, Frank?" General Mauborgne asked.

"I agree with Mr. Friedman's analysis of the situation as it appears at this point," I answered. "However, I have hopes that the outlook will improve as we become more experienced with the problem. From the cryptanalytic aspect, I feel that we will be able to break into most of the key periods where there is an appreciable number of intercepts, and this will enable us to read a fair percentage of the messages. We will have to depend largely on luck for breaking into key periods for which we have only a small number of intercepts. From the intelligence viewpoint, we are currently exploiting every PURPLE intercept that we receive. The information in the new system is supplementary to the information from the PURPLE system. Under these circumstances I would hate to see our favorable intelligence production prospects put in jeopardy by risking another clandestine operation against a Japanese diplomatic code room."

"Do you think you can take that line with the Navy cryptanalysts and make it stick?" he asked.

"From my earlier discussions with the Navy cryptanalysts, I expect them to take a pessimistic view of our prospects for exploiting this type of system," I answered. "They have repeatedly expressed their views that the system is too difficult to be mastered cryptanalytically, and I am sure they will be surprised that we have broken a key period. However, I believe they will give careful consideration to our wishes and probably will want to delay any type of clandestine operation until they have had a full opportunity to make their own cryptanalytic assessment."

General Mauborgne turned to Colonel Akin and said: "Spencer, I fully agree with your proposal. Frank, will you please promptly get in touch with the Navy cryptanalysts and brief them on your progress. Above all, impress on them that the Army is strongly opposed to any type of clandestine operation against any Japanese diplomatic code room. When you have finished your discussions with the Navy group, report immediately to Billy, so he can get in touch with Captain Safford. And Billy, I will expect you to keep Colonel Akin fully informed of all developments in this matter."

Colonel Akin rose from his chair. "Very good, sir," he said.

"Before you leave, there is one more thing I would like to say," General Mauborgne added. "Billy, I'm damned proud of what the SIS has done, and I want to congratulate everyone who was involved in this latest cryptanalytic success. Do you think you could arrange for me to spend about an hour with the group and have them explain to me just how this latest feat of magic was performed?"

"At your pleasure, sir." Friedman answered, and the three of us filed out of the General's office.

When I got back to my office, I found Ferner and Small working on the compilation of the new information for calculating the revised probabilities. I gave them a brief report on the meeting with the Chief Signal Officer, taking special pains to express the words of congratulations from General Mauborgne. I then called the head of the Navy unit responsible for work on the Japanese diplomatic codes and told him that I had some important information for him and asked him to visit me at his earliest convenience. Since it was now almost lunchtime, he proposed to join me in my office at one o'clock. This would allow Ferner, Small, and me time to organize our working papers so that we could make an effective presentation of the techniques we had employed in making the initial break into the new Japanese diplomatic code.

We completed our preparations, and I reported our plans for the one o'clock meeting with the Navy to Friedman. I also suggested that he might wish to familiarize himself with the details of our recovery of the transposition key and the matrix for the key period we had broken. He asked me to let him know when the meeting with the Navy was over and at that time he would join Ferner, Small, and me for a complete review of the work on the replacement system. At one o'clock Ferner and Small joined me in my office. When our visitor arrived, we settled around the large worktable in my office on which the materials we had selected for the briefing were displayed. He immediately picked up the sheet on which the transposition key we had solved was typed and looked at its date.

"That's not one of the new keys, is it?" he exclaimed.

"Right!" I answered. "And we didn't have to steal it," I added.

"Are you going to tell me where you got it?" he asked.

"That is why we wanted you to meet with us," I told him. "We were lucky in finding two messages in the same transposition key in which the Japanese code clerks had made slight alterations to the text of one, so that we were able to recover the transposition key and matrix for the key period. Fortunately, there was a large number of intercepts for the key period, which we are now processing. We believe that we will be able to recover other key periods and assemble enough messages in the underlying code for our language experts to reconstruct it. At this time, we are looking at the high-volume days, hoping to find another key period that we can recover. We are also working on new techniques for recovering the transposition keys and their associated matrices without having to depend on the appearance of a special case."

We spent the next half hour reconstructing our break into the key period we had solved, starting with the two messages that we had discovered with almost identical texts and following our attack in a step-by-step demonstration through the recovery of the transposition key and the determination of the matrix format.

We then outlined for him our plans for other tests which we hoped would be successful and reviewed the statistical procedures and data banks which we were in the process of developing for our exhaustive testing approach. When we had completed our presentation, he expressed his opinion that while the exhaustive testing approach might in a few cases be successful, its general application would be prohibitive because of the excessive amount of time and effort which would have to be expended in applying it. We responded that we were in general agreement with his conclusion at that time, but it was our hope that with further research and refinement the exhaustive testing approach would be feasible.

"We do not want to rely on luck exclusively for exploiting this system," we told him. "We believe that if we can sufficiently improve our techniques, we will be able to recover the keys which have been used for enciphering a large number of messages."

Being mindful of General Mauborgne's instructions, I then stated that we felt that it would be most undesirable for any type of clandestine operation to be undertaken against a Japanese diplomatic installation to photograph the replacement code.

"There is always the chance that such an operation might be detected," I argued. "And if it is discovered, it could cause the Japanese to take much greater precautions in their cryptographic security measures and, what worries me most, is the possibility that they might decide to replace all the codes held in that particular installation. Also, there is the possibility that they might be caused to undertake a complete overhaul of their cryptography. If they should do this latter, it could set us back several months or even years in our ability to provide translations of Japanese diplomatic messages to G-2 and ONI. There is also the important consideration that we are now able to read currently every PURPLE system intercept we receive. This provides G-2 and ONI with a major portion of the information carried in the Japanese diplomatic messages, and consequently the urgency for recovering the replacement code is not as great as it would be if we were not able to exploit the PURPLE system. For these reasons we believe ONI should not even consider a clandestine operation at this time."

"You make a strong case," he stated. "We have been thinking about the risks involved in this type of operation, and those of us who are working on the Japanese diplomatic traffic feel as you do. However, there are some in ONI who consider that the risk is completely acceptable and that surreptitious entries can be made without being discovered. After what I have seen and heard today, I am convinced that another second-story job against a Japanese diplomatic code room is unwarranted."

I was pleased with his remarks. I had been expecting him to argue in favor of another clandestine approach, for I knew he was understaffed, and another stolen code would enable him to keep up his share of production with a minimum of personnel. I was also aware that the Navy cryptanalytic group was being pressed hard by ONI to make better progress on the Japanese naval systems, and the Japanese diplomatic group was having difficulty in keeping its modest workforce from being raided by the group working on the naval systems.

Before we broke up the meeting, we made arrangements for briefing his staff at one o'clock the next day in his office. After our visitor had departed, Ferner and Small went back to their preparation of the information for our data banks. I promptly went to Friedman's office and reported to him that we had just finished our briefing session and that our visitor had stated that he agreed that no effort should be made to recover the new system by a surreptitious entry. Friedman seemed pleased with my report and indicated that he would promptly make arrangements to meet with Captain Safford. I then asked him if he was ready to review the status of our Japanese diplomatic work, and he agreed to join Ferner, Small, and me as soon as he had called Captain Safford.

It was not long before he joined us. "I am meeting with Captain Safford in the morning," he told us. "My schedule is clear for the remainder of the day, and we can spend the rest of the day on our review if necessary."

We spent about an hour going over the problem with him. He showed great interest in our explanation of how the initial break had been achieved. "You fellows are having all the fun," he jokingly grumbled.

When we completed our explanation of how the initial break had been achieved, he inquired about our plans for expanding it. I then told him of

Small's suggestion, and that we planned to conduct an experiment with the IBM tabulator which, if successful, would reduce the time required for computing the matching scores. I then invited Small to present his proposal. Friedman showed a strong interest in the experiment and encouraged us to give it priority over all other work on the replacement system.

"If you can arrive at a system for routinely recovering these transposition keys, it will be one of the greatest feats of cryptanalysis the SIS has yet performed," he stated. "This is an extremely difficult system to solve, and when I first examined it, I was convinced that it was beyond our capabilities. I am pleased to learn that my initial estimate needs to be revised, and that there is a chance that you may be able to develop an approach which will allow almost every key period to be recovered."

I reminded him of General Mauborgne's wishes to be briefed on our work and expressed the hope that the briefing could be deferred until we had completed our experiments on the exhaustive matching procedure. He agreed that under the circumstances a delay would be desirable and indicated that he would explain the matter to the General.

It was now the end of the working day. After Friedman returned to his office, the three of us spent some time discussing the work that was ahead of us. As we contemplated our progress for the day, we concluded that we had done more talking than cryptanalysis, and we hoped that next morning we would not be interrupted so that we could properly define just what our experiment would involve.

CHAPTER 20

WE START AN EXPERIMENT

S OMETIMES WHEN I WAS working on an interesting and difficult problem, I would retire early and sleep soundly until about two o'clock in the morning. At that time I could wake up naturally, completely rested, and mentally review the status of the problem without distraction. Often when I did this, I found that the elements of the problem became more clearly defined, and sometimes I could work out a solution to some of its parts. Sometimes it would become evident that the course of attack which we had chosen was beyond our capabilities and the futility of pursuing it would become apparent; usually when I reached this point, I would try to invent another and more promising attack on the problem.

I had such an experience that night. Around two o'clock in the morning I found myself wide awake, thinking about the experiment we had planned. As I mentally reviewed each aspect of the experiment, starting with Small's initial proposal, and examining each of the associated suggestions which had developed during the day, one emerged as being especially significant. In my experience, we had never really attacked a problem using statistical criteria to score each item in a massive array of possibilities. In every case where we had contemplated this sort of attack, we had rejected it because we did not have the manpower to expend on it. Sometimes we were able to work out some other approach, usually intuitive in nature, to circumvent the need for applying the exhaustive testing procedures. In all the previous cases where we had contemplated the exhaustive testing approach, we had never given consideration to using the accounting machines for performing the statistical computations. The concept of using the IBM tabulator was novel, and if we could devise a procedure where it would accomplish all, or even part, of the time-consuming arithmetical calculations, we might actually achieve some sort of a first in cryptanalysis. Before I finally went back to sleep, I had convinced myself that we were on the right path, and that we needed to continue our efforts.

I was up early the next morning, and arrived at the Munitions Building about an hour before the regular opening time for our office. Ferner and Small were waiting for me, for they wanted to get started on the experiment and especially to complete the computation of the probability charts which they had started the day before. While they completed the charts, I examined the accumulated intercepts, searching for a key period which would be the most favorable candidate for our experiment. By the time Ferner and Small had finished the charts, I had selected the key periods that I considered most suitable. We were now ready to begin our experiment.

We decided that we ought to review each step involved in the experiment to ensure that there were no inconsistencies which might have to be corrected later, with a consequent loss of time and effort. Using the blackboard in my office, we laid out the program and examined it in detail.

It was necessary for us to determine whether the key was odd or even in length before starting our matching procedure. When the key was even in length, all the letters of each column were either initials or finals; if it was odd in length, the sequent letters in the column alternated as initials and finals. Since the elements of the basic system were digraphic in nature, we were able to develop statistical tests that indicated whether the key was even or odd; these tests also identified whether the letters were initials or finals.

An important step in our experiment was the transfer of the probability information to IBM cards. Small was selected to oversee this operation with whatever help he required to be provided by the machine room. Meanwhile, Ferner and I made a final assessment of the intercepts in the key periods I had selected, to determine if the transposition key was odd or even in length. We would then select the most favorable periods with an odd-length key and examine each of the intercepts to select the one which seemed to be most suitable for our experiment.

By the time we selected the intercept for our experiment, Small had completed the transfer of probabilities to the IBM cards and had prepared an ample supply of these. Our next step was to assemble a set of cards for the intercept we had selected.

We were now ready to make the first test run on the IBM tabulator. We identified for Small the portion of the message that we thought would offer the best basis for statistical evaluation. He promptly started transferring this information into a wiring diagram for a tabulator plugboard. All of us hoped that we would be able to see the results of the first step of our experiment by the end of the day.

Just before lunchtime, Friedman came into my office.

"I have just returned from my visit with the Navy," he reported. "Captain Safford agrees that it would not be desirable to attempt another entry into a Japanese diplomatic code room and has promised to take the matter up with ONI to ensure that no operation of this sort is conducted without his approval. He also assured me that we will be consulted in every case where such an action is being considered. I believe the Navy cryptanalytic group is just as concerned as we are about the results of an abortive entry. By the way, he tells me that the Navy cryptanalysts working on the Japanese diplomatic intercepts are looking forward to the meeting planned for this afternoon, and I expect you will have a totally receptive audience."

We had been so busy working up the arrangements for our experiment that I had forgotten all about my promise that we would brief the Navy group on our key recovery techniques. I mentally groaned when I realized that at least one of us would have to honor our commitment.

"I wish we could hold this briefing off for a couple of days," I remarked. "We will then have a lot better information to present to them."

"The briefing should not be delayed," Friedman stated. "I know you are eager to get along with your research. Since the Navy has been so cooperative on the surreptitious-entry question, I feel that we should go ahead without asking for a delay. Couldn't one of you give the briefing while the other two carry on with the experiment?"

"I suppose so," I answered. "We are almost ready to start our first tabulator run. If Bob and Albert don't mind taking care of that, I can take care of briefing the Navy."

"Excellent," Friedman remarked, as he turned to leave the office. "When you return, let me know how the briefing was received," he said as he departed.

Since it was now less than an hour before the time we had scheduled for the briefing, I collected the work sheets and the other materials that would be needed and sealed them in an envelope. I had originally hoped that Ferner and Small would participate in the presentation at the Navy, for they had been deeply involved in the break into the replacement system. As there was so little opportunity for them to get any recognition outside of the immediate office staff for their contributions, it seemed unfair that they would not be able to participate in one of the rare occasions where their work could be professionally appreciated. However, we still had the briefing planned for General Mauborgne, and I promised myself that they would perform the star roles in that demonstration.

When I arrived at the Navy, I was surprised to find that all the members of the staff of the Navy's Japanese diplomatic group were present, as well as a few of the cryptanalysts from the Japanese naval section. Also included were three young Naval Reserve officers who had only recently joined the Navy cryptanalytic unit and were currently assigned to the group responsible for processing the intercepts in the PURPLE cipher machine system.

I started by describing how we had made the initial break into the key period that we had recovered. Next, I passed around copies of the statistical data we had prepared from the deciphered code texts and explained how the information had been derived and what it represented. Then I gave a step-by-step presentation of how we hoped to achieve a solution for another key period. In conclusion, I briefly outlined the exhaustive testing procedure, pointing out that while we had great hopes for it, we still needed to do more research on it before we would be satisfied that it would be practical. I then told them that we would welcome any suggestions for improvements or new approaches for breaking into other key periods. The briefing session took about two hours, and I was glad to answer the final question and head back for my office in the Munitions Building.

When I got back to my office, Ferner and Small were checking the accuracy of the punched cards they had assembled for our experiment. Small had finished the preparation of a tabulator plug board, specially wired for the portion of the message that we had selected as the basis of our first test. As soon as the accuracy of the cards had been confirmed, the three of us went to the IBM area.

Small took us to the tabulator he had selected for our test. He inserted the plugboard into the machine and locked it into position. He placed the stack of cards in the feeding mechanism and pressed the start button. The tabulator started printing out the data on the large sheets of fan-fold paper which were automatically fed into the machine. The printing of the first display took only about ten minutes. I asked that we have at least three copies printed so that each of us would have a copy to examine. Small suggested that Ferner and I take the first copy back to my office, and that he would join us later when he had finished preparing the other two copies.

Before trying to evaluate any of the possible matches displayed on the machine print, we checked to ensure that it was accurately prepared. When we started working with the display, we found that it would be difficult to use. Just as we discovered this, Small arrived with the other two prints. We demonstrated the difficulties to him, pointing out that we needed to make certain changes. He explained that some improvement might be achieved by rewiring the plugboard. Since it was now after closing time, we decided to call it a day, and deal with the improvements next morning.

∽　∽　∽

When I arrived at the office next morning, I found Small waiting for me.

"I think I have part of the answer," he announced as soon as we were inside the secure area.

"Do you want to give it to me now, or would you like to wait until Bob arrives and you can tell us both at the same time?" I asked.

"I would like to modify the plug-board wiring, and then I can demonstrate my ideas with another machine print," he responded. "I can have one ready in less than an hour."

We went directly to the secure area where our IBM equipment was installed. I unlocked the door for him and suggested that he lock himself in the area, since none of the regular staff had yet arrived.

I returned to my office and looked over the work which had started to pile up over the last few days. The monthly report on our activities had to be prepared, and there was a number of administrative matters which needed attention. It was clearly my job to deal with such matters, and if I did not take care of them, the work of the section would be impaired. That morning I felt a strong resentment that these administrative matters had to be dealt with. When Ferner arrived, I told him that Small was in the IBM area getting ready to produce an improved display. I asked him if he had come up with any new ideas overnight. "Not really," he answered. "But I feel that we are on the right path. If we could find some way of making the tabulator do the computations and display only the scores, we would not have to concern ourselves with the format. Possibly by making multiple runs, we could have the computations done for us by the machine."

I was in no mood for writing a report or dealing with the other administrative matters that needed attention. "Let's go down to the machine area and see what Small is doing," I suggested.

When we got to the IBM area we found Small standing by one of the tabulators, looking over a display which was being printed. When we joined him, he stopped the tabulator and pointed at the display.

"You will like this display much better than the one I gave you yesterday," he told us. "The numbers in each of these columns represent the probabilities of the individual elements which are being matched. If you read down a diagonal, you will find the probabilities listed in their correct order. Now, instead of having to prepare a clumsy pattern for each run, all we need to do is to add the values appearing down the diagonal to produce the score for the match."

"Albert, that's terrific!" I exclaimed. Ferner examined the listing carefully.

"This is a great improvement," he said. "Not only will it be faster for us to compute the score for each match, but our work will not be as subject to error. Let's finish the run and test it out."

We stood by while Small finished printing the display.

"Why don't you take this copy to the office while I make some more runs," Small suggested.

When the run was completed, Ferner and I took it to my office, where we spot-checked it for errors. The run was perfect, and now all we had to do was to compute the scores for each match.

"Let's see how long it takes us to compute the scores for a hundred matches," I suggested.

The procedure we followed was simple. I read the probabilities from the display and Ferner fed them into a comptometer. When I gave him the last value for the match, I called for the total. He then read the total to me, and I entered it at the appropriate point on the display. The operation was much simpler and a lot faster that any that we had tried before. We found that we could average about two scores per minute.

"We ought to do a little better with some practice," I observed.

"There is one thing that we can do which will speed up the computation," Ferner said. "If we use only the first two digits of the probability instead of the three which appear on the display, we can shorten the testing time."

"Fine," I said. "I'll read only the first two digits, and you can feed them into the comptometer. This time we will compute only fifty scores and compare the average times."

This time our average was a little better than three scores per minute.

"I think I might make better time just by scanning the diagonal and mentally computing the score," I said. "Adding a column of two digits is not too difficult for me, and with a little practice the addition can be done a lot faster and with about the same degree of accuracy."

"A good idea," Ferner said. "I think we ought to give it a try."

Small rushed into the office with the additional runs he had prepared.

"How is the testing working out?" he asked.

We showed him the results of our experiments with the comptometer and then told him that we were getting ready to try producing the scores by mentally summing the diagonals, using two-place probabilities. His reaction was enthusiastic.

"Let's test it right now," he suggested. "Each of us could take a message print and compute the scores for a different section. We could then get a better idea of the time required, and we might even find the score for the correct match."

We each selected a different portion of the display and started our computations. All of us were fairly adept at mental arithmetic, and I was surprised to find how rapidly I could compute each score. I purposely held myself in restraint, feeling that accuracy was more important than speed at this point. When we finished, we took a short break and compared notes. We had seen enough to realize that we had developed a procedure which excelled all the others that we had tried.

"Let's scan our results for the highest scores just to get a feel for what we might be getting out of these tests," I suggested. "For example, there is no outstanding score among the ones I calculated, and my three highest scores are all about equal."

"I have one very high score, well above all the others I computed," Ferner mentioned.

Small took his work sheets to the blackboard and listed some figures in a clear space on it.

"These are my highest scores," he said.

"And here are my highest scores," I said and read them to him.

"I have a couple which are in the neighborhood of the ones you have listed," Ferner noted and reported them for Small to tabulate.

"But here is my highest score," he added and gave Small a total which was several points above all the others that Small had listed on the blackboard.

"Maybe that is the correct match," I said. "Let's see where it is located with respect to the rest of the message."

Ferner spread out his display print on the table, and pointed out the section which had produced his highest score. Small searched through his work sheets and brought out the message print which he had used for the tabulator run.

"We assumed that the transposition key is twenty-five elements in length. Actually it may be shorter, and if so we should be able to find several more matching elements," he said.

I retrieved a copy of the probability chart from the papers on my desk.

"Read me the additional matches and I'll give you their probabilities," I proposed.

As Ferner read me the additional matches, I looked them up in the chart and gave him their values. Small and I looked over his shoulder as he tabulated them. The first few values I gave him were good ones, but as he continued to read, the values dropped. Small put his pencil on the display print and made a mark. "There is the end of the column," he stated.

"You could be right," Ferner noted.

"Let's calculate the possible key lengths, assuming the column ends where Albert has indicated," I suggested.

Ferner spent a short time making some computations. When he finished, he announced that the key would have to be seventeen elements in length.

For the moment the three of us had forgotten about carrying out the experiment, and now we were thinking only about the recovery of the transposition key. Small brought us back to the experiment.

"Shall we continue with our project, or try to break the key period?" he asked.

"If we can recover the key, so far as I am concerned, the experiment is a success," I said. "Let's try to find the column that matches with these, and if we do it will prove we are on the right track," I added.

"That might be the best way to proceed," Ferner remarked. "If we can recover the key, we will have more data to add to our probability charts and consequently improve our statistical base. We can also give more code texts to the code breakers which will help them in recovering code groups."

"I think we ought to go for recovering the key," I said. "Albert, could you give us a machine run based on the column that produced the highest score to see if we can identify another section which matches with it?"

"All I need to do is to rewire the board and run the cards through the tabulator," he answered as he gathered his papers and started for the machine room.

By this time the morning had gone and I suddenly realized it was afternoon. It seemed to be a good time to report our results to Friedman and I went to his office. He had just returned from lunch. "How is the experiment going," he asked.

"Extremely well," I answered. "Everything seems to be falling in place. Last night Small came up with an improvement which will enable us to make tests which have before now been prohibitive because of the time and effort required for the arithmetic-probability calculations. We have already used his first test run to locate a possible match in a new key period. He is now making a second test run which we hope will give us another match; if this happens, we could have another key period broken in a few hours."

"Good," he remarked. "I had a meeting with Colonel Akin this morning and reported on our conversations with the Navy. He still feels it will be necessary to have G-2 take the matter up with ONI. Personally, I do not think it is necessary to do any more than you and I have done. However, that decision is up to General Mauborgne and Colonel Akin. If your group recovers another key period, our contentions will be further validated, and I do not think we will have to be concerned about ONI conducting another clandestine operation against a Japanese diplomatic code room without seeking our concurrence."

"With luck, we will have recovered another key by the close of business today," I told him. "If we can add only two more columns to those we have matched this morning, we will be well on our way to deciphering an additional key period. I estimate this will just about double the information we have in our data bank, which of course will improve our prospects for breaking into other key periods."

"Do you think the Navy group will be able to assist in the key recovery work?" he asked.

"I am sure they will," I answered. "They are now getting familiar with the techniques we are using and are also studying the technical paper on the ADFGVX solution. I expect that in a few days they will be successful in recovering a key period. One reason I would like to expand our data is to provide both of us with better statistical criteria, which will of course make the initial matching process easier.

"It looks like you have a lot of work ahead of you," he commented. "I wonder if you will be able to accomplish all that you have set out to do."

"I am still hopeful that we can," I answered. "I believe the research work that this new system has caused us to undertake will in the long run more than repay for the effort we have expended."

"I agree," he answered. "But I am still not very optimistic about our ability to keep up with the processing and exploiting of the intercepts in this system," he added.

As I started to leave his office, he got up from his desk and walked over to the door with me.

"You know, Frank," he said to me very seriously, "I think you sincerely believe you will master this system. And I won't be surprised if you do. Good luck!"

I went back to my desk feeling rather good about his last remarks. I picked up the display print that I had been using earlier that morning for computing the scores. If we could mechanize this step, and do it reasonably efficiently, we would have developed a cryptanalytic process of exceptional power, not only for the new Japanese diplomatic system, but for a great many other code and cipher systems which required an exhaustive testing attack. It would indeed be a great achievement.

My speculative mood was interrupted by Ferner and Small entering the office.

"I made only one print to save time," Small explained. "We can separate it into three parts, one for each of us."

"Good enough," I said. "Let's get going."

Small separated the print into three sections and distributed them. He and Ferner worked at the large table while I sat at my desk. Suddenly, Ferner got up and went to the blackboard. He did a short arithmetic computation and wrote a number on the board.

"Anyone who finds a score higher than that gets a prize," he announced.

CHAPTER 21

SOME ENCOURAGING IMPROVEMENTS

T O BECOME A SUCCESSFUL cryptanalyst, one must learn not only to be able to concentrate for long periods of time on a routine search for information but also to keep his mind fully alert for recognizing anything which might be significant while the search is being conducted. As I computed the scores for each match, I could not avoid recognizing the mechanical nature of the routine we were following. Each test was made up of three separate operations: add the probabilities, record the total, move to the next testing position. We were merely repeating a simple process over and over and over. These three steps had to be repeated for each successive match as I moved forward through the message. I was not acting like an intelligent human or a skilled cryptanalyst; I was performing a purely mechanical operation, doing a simple process over and over. The only time I acted intelligently was when I found a total close to the figure written by Ferner on the blackboard, and that was not often. There just had to be some mechanical contrivance which would automatically perform the simple tasks of adding, recording, and advancing. As this thought occurred to me, I began mentally to review all the machines known to me which might perform these operations; only the IBM tabulator seemed to have the qualities needed. We had used it to perform all the desired operations separately, and all we needed was to devise some way of having it perform them in succession.

Suddenly I became really bored with the routine I was following. I stopped working on the display print so that I could review my thoughts. "Yes," I concluded, "the IBM tabulator has all the elements needed to perform these routine operation, and what we must do is to figure out how to make it do them."

My thoughts were interrupted when Small let out a sharp whistle. He went to the blackboard and recorded a number. It was higher than any other we had found in the new display run and only slightly different from the highest score that we had found for the previous run.

"Shall we test it?" Ferner asked.

"By all means," I answered.

Small found the work sheet on which we had entered the two columns from the morning's work and entered on it the column he had just scored. When he extended the match several letters beyond the portion included in the machine run, we found that, as in the previous case, only a few of the additional letters gave reasonable probabilities.

"That looks good," I remarked. "Let's look for the four-letter combination possibilities and see if we can develop hypothetical columns to precede and follow these three columns."

It took only a few minutes for us to identify the four-letter possibilities in the three columns which had been entered on the work sheet. Fortunately, there were enough of these to allow us to make tentative assumptions about letters in both the preceding and succeeding columns. While Small and I were identifying the four-letter groups, Ferner examined the location of the third section in the message to see if it conflicted with our assumption that the transposition key was seventeen elements in length.

"This new section fits nicely into the pattern for a key length of seventeen," he reported.

"Let's block out the remainder of the columns on a message print," I suggested. "That will make our search for the additional matching columns a lot easier."

Ferner selected a message print and identified the three columns we had tentatively matched. He blocked the remaining portions of the message into sections of approximately equal length, so that there was a total of seventeen sections. It was reassuring to note that the three columns we had chosen fitted nicely into the pattern for a seventeen-element key.

From this point on, the key recovery effort went smoothly. We had no trouble locating passages of ciphertexts in the message to satisfy the requirements of the hypothetical columns we had developed to precede and follow the three columns we had assembled. We ignored the underlying Japanese language and worked only with the plain-code text using a combination of hypothetical four-letter groups and high-frequency digraphs to expand our break. Finally, we added the last column which fit nicely into the pattern and completed the matrix. Only the location of the blanks in the upper levels of the matrix remained to be recovered. These were easily determined by deciphering a few short messages in the same key period and adjusting the positions of the letters appearing in the upper levels so that they formed acceptable plain-code texts for the beginnings of the messages.

We were now ready to decipher all the intercepts in the key period. While Ferner and Small started to organize the deciphering program, I went to Friedman's office to inform him of our success.

"We made the initial entry by using Small's machine displays," I reported. "After we got the first three columns lined up, we finished the recovery by a combination of intuitive and analytic techniques."

"Congratulations!" he responded. "I think you should report this to the Navy without delay. What are you planning to do next?"

"We are starting a project to decipher all the messages that use this key," I answered. "Then we will incorporate the new deciphered code texts into the work books used by the code breakers and update their index books by preparing new listings. But the most important aspect is that we can enrich our statistical bank with the new information. We are planning to compute revised probability charts when the information from this new key has been included."

"You fellows have been working pretty hard for the last few days," he said. "Don't overdo it."

I returned to my office and put in a call for the head of the Navy group working on the Japanese diplomatic intercepts.

"We just opened up another shipment," I reported. "When would you like to examine it?"

"It arrived sooner than we expected," he answered. "How about first thing tomorrow morning?"

"Just give me a call before you leave for my office," I suggested.

"Will do," he responded.

Small and Ferner were still working in my office. Together, we reviewed the situation. The format for the new matrix was being reproduced, and when copies of it were distributed, the decipherment process could be started. The additional deciphered code texts would greatly assist the Japanese linguists in the recovery of the more frequently used plain-language elements such as punctuation, numbers, and the fifty kana, thereby setting the stage for the recovery of the less frequently appearing elements. Also, a revised set of probability charts would have to be constructed. And I still had the monthly report of the section to finish.

"Before starting work on a new key period, I think we need to spend some time studying our techniques and see if we can improve them," I proposed. "We have the PURPLE system well under control, and as long as we keep current with it, G-2 and ONI will keep off our backs. It is unlikely that we will find a better opportunity to continue our work on the exhaustive testing approach. We have some excellent ideas which need further study, and I am sure that other ideas will be developed before we are finished with our experiments. I feel that we should quit worrying about trying to keep current with the intercepts in the transposed-code system, and spend all the time we need in improving our techniques. The most important task now is to get the IBM machines to compute the scores for us automatically."

"I have been thinking about that possibility," Small remarked. "The difficulty is that we cannot get the tabulator to scan progressively across the fields of information punched into the cards as they move across the reading brushes. If we could devise some way of achieving this, we could selectively feed the probabilities into a counter where they could be totaled. But at this time there seems to be no way of having the tabulator scan different fields as the cards pass through the machine."

"I would like to continue the experiments with the ideas we have been pursuing and especially to work on how to get the tabulator to compute the scores automatically," I stated. "Also, we ought to reexamine our techniques for employing the probability values based on our data bank and see if they can be improved."

"I believe it would be an improvement to use two-place equivalents for the probabilities," Ferner observed. "The third digit did not really help us in identifying the high scores in the tests we have just completed."

We then reviewed the personnel assignments for the section and designated the individuals who would fill in for Ferner and Small while they devoted full time to the research on the exhaustive testing effort. I then called a meeting of the staff of the Japanese diplomatic group and made the needed temporary work assignments.

The next day, which was a Friday, was a good day for catching up with my administrative matters. I started the day by working on the monthly report, hoping that I would be able to finish the first draft before my visitor arrived. I felt it would be a good report, for it would record our successes on the transposed code effort as well as the status of our work on the PURPLE machine system and the other systems used by the Japanese foreign office. The section of the report which detailed the number of intercepts received in each system, the number of messages decoded and translated, together with personnel data, was automatically compiled on the last day of the month, from the appropriate daily registers which were kept in the section. Colonel Akin had instructed that the monthly reports be submitted by the end of business of the first working day following the end of the month. It really would not require much time and effort on my part to prepare the report, but with my fascination for the research which we were conducting I felt some irritation that I had to spend any time at all on its preparation.

I soon received a call from the Navy indicating that our expected visitor was about to depart for my office. When he arrived, he did not seemed to be much surprised that we had been able to recover another key period. He carefully looked over our work and shook his head when we explained to him how we had discovered the first matching pair of columns.

"Why didn't you use the technique that gave you a break into the last key period you recovered?" he asked. "That would be a lot less trouble than compiling all these stacks of cards and wiring up boards for the tabulator. My group has been searching through all our intercepts for another pair of messages with repeated texts, and while we have not yet been successful, we think it is only a matter of time until we break into a key period. But all this business with the stacks of cards and plug boards seems a lot of work."

We responded by pointing out that the technique we had used previously was dependent on special conditions, and if these did not exist, they could not be relied upon to produce results. We felt that a more general approach was needed, and if the exhaustive testing procedure could be made to work, it could replace all the other techniques known to us.

When we finished our briefing, he gave us a report on the work of his group. The Navy cryptanalysts assigned to the PURPLE watch were working on the system in their spare time, thus augmenting the force available for study of the new system. His entire group had been making an exhaustive search of all intercepts, looking for pairs of messages with repeated passages of plaintext, but no favorable case had yet been discovered. Considerable work had been done on a key period for which there was a large volume of intercepts. Statistical tests indicated that the key was an even number of elements in length, and it could be either sixteen or twenty-four elements in length. Ferner, who kept close track of each key period, brought out our file for this key period. Although there was an unusually large number of messages in it, we had not chosen it for our experiment because our tests had indicated an even-length key.

After our visitor left, we spent some time discussing his remarks. Instead of being discouraged by them, they served to increase our determination to continue with our research on the exhaustive testing procedures. We also speculated on how we might successfully deal with an even-length key and tentatively worked out a routine for applying the exhaustive testing procedure to determine the number of columns in such cases.

Reluctantly, I closed the discussion and turned my attention to completing the draft of the monthly report. By the time I had finished it and my other administrative chores, the middle of the afternoon had passed. I took the opportunity to check on the progress of the Japanese diplomatic section. I found that all the current intercepts had been processed except for the messages in the transposed code system. The catalogs and the message prints for the transposed code system were being produced in the IBM machine area, and we hoped they would be delivered to the language group early on Monday morning. Ferner and Small were recomputing the probability charts in terms which would be more suitable for our exhaustive testing experiments. With the affairs of the Japanese section in good shape, it seemed to be a good time to give a verbal report to Friedman.

I found him in a receptive mood. After my report, he expressed his satisfaction with the progress which had been made. When I asked if he had any suggestions for improving our recovery of the transposition keys used in the new system, he replied "I have been giving a great deal of thought to this problem. I am delighted that you have made so much progress on such a difficult system. But I have no technical suggestions to offer. All I can contribute is to encourage you and your team to continue your efforts. I think you are wise in giving priority to research on new techniques. I sometimes feel that we lose sight of the importance of exploring new fields in our anxiety to exploit the bonanzas we have discovered."

That day I left the Munitions Building feeling really pleased with the way things were going in the Japanese diplomatic section.

～ ～ ～

Over the weekend I kept thinking of the problems associated with the new system. I felt we would be able to exploit it only if we had additional skilled cryptanalysts to assign to it full time. We could now routinely process all the intercepts in our most important intelligence-producing system, the PURPLE machine system. From a cryptanalytic-research standpoint and if there was no requirement to produce timely intelligence information, we would in due course develop the new techniques required for the exploitation of the transposed code system. But from the standpoint of intelligence production, where we were required to process the important intercepts on the same day they were received, the outlook for the transposed code system was far from being a favorable one. At some time in the future, with additional staff assigned to the key recovery of the transposed code system, we might be able to exploit high-volume key periods in a reasonable time, but for the key periods in which there were small numbers of intercepts our techniques simply were not adequate. And it was most unlikely that additional skilled cryptanalysts would be made available.

In spite of my discouraging conclusions about our ability to exploit the new system fully, there was one thought which kept demanding my attention. The concept of using the IBM tabulator to perform the onerous and time-consuming tasks of the exhaustive testing procedure continued to intrigue me. Small's device of using a deck of specially prepared cards to represent the ciphertext of a message had opened up a new domain which had to be further explored. If we could devise a method or scheme whereby the tabulator would selectively scan a new set of columns as each card passed through the reading position, we could accumulate the arithmetic data in the banks of counters in the tabulator and have the machine print the totals. I finally concluded that this possibility ought to be thoroughly explored as the first order of Monday's business and that we should ask the customer service representatives of the local IBM office for assistance if our machine-room experts were unable to satisfy our requirements.

Early Monday morning the three of us assembled in my office. I presented my conclusions on the selective scanning idea, and both Ferner and Small agreed that it would improve our prospects, but promptly admitted that they knew of no way to have the tabulator operate in such a manner. Small volunteered to explore the problem with our machine-room experts, which Ferner and I encouraged him to undertake promptly. Since there was still considerable work to be done on the probability calculations, I took Small's place working with Ferner while Small checked out the tabulator capabilities.

About an hour later Small returned and reported that he had canvassed the "experts" in our machine room and not one of them knew of any way by which the tabulator could perform the desired scanning operation. He added that he had made a call to the IBM service office, and that he expected a representative to visit him after lunch.

In due course we finished our work on the probability charts. Our next step was to prepare new punched cards using the revised data. Small undertook this task while Ferner and I examined the new intercepts which had arrived over the weekend. My aim was to select another key period for attack, and I wanted to make sure that we chose the most favorable case.

Two key periods stood out above all others in terms of long messages. One of these was the key period which the Navy was studying. The other was a more recent one, in which Tokyo had sent two long circular messages, each composed of several parts. Using our revised statistical data, we tested all the long messages in these two key periods to determine if the key lengths were odd or even. Our tests showed that the keys for both days were an even number of elements in length.

Since none of the other key periods contained as many messages as these two, we decided not to attack the one on which the Navy group was working, but instead chose the other. We would have preferred to work on a key of odd length, for we had successfully used our techniques for solving this type of key, and we had not yet recovered an even-length key. After some discussion, we decided that sooner or later we would have to tackle a key of even length and that we might as well go ahead with this one. We selected the most promising intercept for the key period and started preparing a work sheet so that when Small finished the new master cards we could assemble a message for him to process through the tabulator.

Unfortunately, the IBM service representative who called on Small that afternoon had nothing to suggest for having the tabulator perform the selective scanning operation we needed. In fact, he flatly stated that it would be impossible for this type of operation to be performed by the tabulator or any other machine built by IBM.

When Small reported this information to us, we reluctantly concluded that we would still have to rely on the visual inspection of the machine display print for computing the scores. By closing time we had completed all the preparatory work for our attack on the key period we had selected so that Small could start producing the tabulator displays next morning without delay.

Next day we arrived at the office fresh and eager to get started on our project. Small promptly headed for the machine room, and while he was producing the displays, Ferner and I reviewed the procedures we had planned to use to ascertain if there were any improvements we might introduce. We gave considerable thought to how we might improve our computation of the scores, but finally concluded that we would have to work our way through the displays, mentally computing each possible match and recording only the highest scores. We hoped that the correct match would be high enough to be clearly recognized so we would not have to spend time needlessly computing the remainder of the scores.

When the first display run was ready, Ferner and I started working on it. Occasionally one of us would find a high score which we would post on the blackboard, but none of these seemed to be significant. We finally improved our technique by first scanning the diagonal, and if it contained several low values, we merely passed over it without computing the score. This simple trick cut our processing time almost in half. When Small returned with the display prints for the second run, he joined us in our task.

We spent the remainder of the morning computing scores, always hoping to discover an outstandingly high one. When lunchtime arrived, we welcomed it, for even though we were conditioned to long periods of routine work, this particular task seemed unusually trying.

After lunch, we continued our score computations. We had accumulated several favorable scores, but not one of them was outstanding enough for us to believe that it represented the correct match. By closing time we were still hoping for a distinctive score and, feeling somewhat disappointed with our progress, decided to call it a day.

The lack of positive results for the day's work was discouraging to me. The approach which we had developed and which had seemed to be so promising now appeared to be inadequate for producing the desired results for the message on which we were working. The theory underlying it seemed sound, but there must be something which, for the message we were studying, was denying us the results we were expecting.

That we had successfully attacked other key periods by using these techniques still stood out as the most important consideration. In my experience as a cryptanalyst I had learned that some messages were more difficult to break into than others, and as a practical consideration it was better to keep looking for an easier message to solve, assuming of course that it could be identified, than to spend time and effort on a message that was resisting attack. I finally concluded that we must have selected an unfavorable message and that I ought to look over the other intercepts in the key period to see if I could find one which might be easier to break.

Next morning, while waiting for the arrival of Ferner and Small, I reassessed the other long messages in the key period which we had rejected in favor of the one we had chosen. I also carefully searched through the intercepts which had arrived after we had made our selection to determine if any additional messages in the same key period had been received. Here I was in luck, for in the intercepts which had been picked up by our station near San Francisco were two messages from Mexico City to Tokyo in the same key period that we were studying. One was exceptionally long; in fact, it was the longest message that I had seen in the new system. Evidently the Japanese code clerk in Mexico City had disregarded Tokyo's instructions to transmit very long messages in several parts, each of which was to be enciphered separately. Instead of sending the long message in two or three parts, he had avoided the extra work and had produced an unusually long code message. When I applied the statistical tests to determine whether the key was of odd or even length, the results were encouraging, for the tests produced a more positive indication that the key was even than had been shown by any of the tests we had conducted on the other messages in the same key period. This piece of evidence also led me to the conclusion that the cryptographic text of the message might also be more responsive to our statistical matching procedure than was the case in the message on which we had been working. I promptly started to prepare a work sheet for the message so that Small could process it through the tabulator.

When Ferner and Small arrived I showed them the intercept and the results of my tests on it. I suggested that we defer testing the sample we had previously selected and start work on the Mexico City intercept instead. Evidently they also had felt discouraged with our progress of the previous day for they offered no objections to my proposal. Small promptly started rewiring a tabulator plug board while Ferner and I completed the other preparations for attacking the Mexico City message. In about two hours Small had finished the first display run, which Ferner and I divided between us and immediately started to compute the matching scores.

While the long message provided us with the advantage that the scores we computed would be more reliable, since they were composed of a greater number of matched elements, we soon discovered that the arithmetic process was more cumbersome and took longer to complete than had been the case in the previous examples we had processed. Summing over twenty two-digit numbers several hundred times would be a time-consuming process.

"If these were single-digit probabilities, we would be able to finish this chore a lot faster," I casually observed.

Ferner interrupted his computations and looked at me thoughtfully.

"With this much data, maybe a single-digit probability would be sufficient," he remarked.

"Let's give that idea some thought," I answered. "If we used a single-digit value, we might be able to make a preliminary computation to identify the location of the best scores and then recompute each high score using the two-digit probabilities."

My remarks seemed to trigger his imagination.

"Instead of using base-ten logarithms for our probabilities, maybe we ought to use a different bas,e which would spread the logarithmic probability values over a scale from one to nine," he remarked. "If we equated the highest frequency in our arithmetic chart to the digit nine and distributed the other arithmetic frequency values over a logarithmic scale from one to nine, and used these instead of the base-ten logarithms, we might cause the highest score to be more visible."

"And it would also make it possible to scan the data on the display sheet more rapidly," I added. "Why not try it?"

While Ferner and I were discussing this new idea for our testing procedure, Small returned with the second tabulator run for the Mexico City intercept. We brought him into the conversation and explained what we were considering. His reaction was enthusiastic, and he was ready to start immediately on the computation of the improved one-place probabilities. There was, however, the consideration that we would have to delay any matching until the new charts were computed and a new set of master cards prepared. Also, all the work which we had just done on the Mexico City intercept would be lost. On the other hand, if the revised one-place probabilities prove to be practical, we would have the most powerful tool we had yet devised for the exhaustive testing technique, and the recovery of all keys would be facilitated. We chose to start work immediately on preparing the revised materials instead of continuing our work on the message.

It took several hours for us to compute the values for the new chart and to prepare the master cards based on it. We also had to assemble another set of cards for the Mexico City intercept. Although we worked at top speed, and fortunately without any interruptions, it was past midafternoon before the first display print was ready.

While Small continued working with the tabulator, Ferner and I started to work on the display print, computing the scores for each possible match.

It was a pleasure to work with the new display, for with a single-digit print-out we found that we could place a straight-edge diagonally over the columns of the print and read the values down the diagonal identified by the straight-edge. Also, by merely inspecting the diagonal for high values, we could discard a great many possibilities without having to perform the addition; only when there was a preponderance of high values did we have to compute the score. Not only was the new display faster and easier to use, but also it provided us with what appeared to be the most reliable results of all the schemes that we had tried. Small soon finished the second display run that we required and joined us in the computation of the matching scores.

Closing time arrived before we were ready for it. We reluctantly secured the area and left. None of the scores we had obtained seemed significant, and although we found several which looked favorable, we were unable to find any confirming evidence that they were valid.

CHAPTER 22

THE "GEE-WHIZZER" DEBUTS

T HAT NIGHT I REVIEWED our current position for recovering the key periods and the steps we had taken to reach it. I concluded that the use of single-digit logarithms to represent the probability values was a significant forward step, although it had to be tested further. Small's inquiries into the possible use of the tabulator for performing the required addition of the probability values had established that there was no known procedure for mechanically obtaining the results we needed by using the IBM equipment available to us. Unless we could discover some way of speeding up the arithmetic process, it appeared that the exhaustive testing procedure would be too costly in time and manpower requirements for us to continue to use it on the transposed code system. Finally I got tired of thinking about the problem and went to bed.

I woke up about two o'clock and started to think through the problem again. Using the format of our latest message display as a base, I considered each element of it in the light of the process we had been following. The data on the display sheet were presented in a series of columns, with each card contributing several items of data as it passed through the tabulator. Small had cleverly arranged the plug-board wiring so that the data for each test could be selected from the display by simply starting with a given level in the first column for the first value, then progressing to the second level and the second column for the next value, the third level and the third column for the next, and so on until the last value was taken from the last column in the array; the sum of the values so selected gave the score for the match. To obtain the next score, we merely advanced the column being matched by one position, and, starting with the first value, progressed simultaneously down and to the right one level at a time until the last letter of the column was reached. Each subsequent score was produced by advancing to the next matching position and duplicating this process. If we could somehow cause the tabulator to duplicate this simple pattern and accumulate the desired values in one of its counters, we could command the counter to print the total when the final item had been fed into it. The only way I could think of to achieve this result was to change the wiring of the plugboard each time a card passed through the machine. But it was patently impracticable to rewire the plugboard each time a card was read. If there was an auxiliary mechanism which would automatically shift the connections on the plugboard, and if this mechanism operated in synchronism with the tabulator, the desired effect could be achieved. Whatever form this auxiliary mechanism might take must be one which would not require a modification of the tabulator, for these were rented from IBM and our contract with IBM specified that all alterations of the equipment would be performed only by IBM service personnel.

The more I thought about an auxiliary mechanism, the better I liked the idea, and I started to visualize what mechanical or electrical form it might take. I was at that time very familiar with the operation of the telephone selector switches since we had used these as a basis for the construction of the cryptographic mazes in our versions of the both the PURPLE and the RED machines. Before I finally dropped off to sleep, I had worked out the general scheme of a switching device that would automatically perform the desired column scanning operation and could be wired into the tabulator plugboard. In the morning I would reduce the concept to drawings and ascertain if the tabulator would provide a properly timed impulse for controlling the selector switches.

When I awoke early next morning, I could hardly wait to get to the office. When I arrived there, I started to sketch out the circuits for the auxiliary switching mechanism. These would have to be completely laid out before we could evaluate the practicability of the apparatus to ensure that it would be fully compatible with the normal functioning of the tabulator. I would also have to determine the type of impulse I would require from the tabulator to energize the master control relay in the auxiliary switching mechanism. So far as I knew, no one had ever thought of automatically changing the wiring of a plug board between the card cycles of an IBM machine, and there were several technical questions which would have to be answered before we attempted to connect the apparatus to the tabulator.

By the time Ferner and Small arrived, I had completed the sketches of the circuitry and was preparing a list of materials which would be needed for building the apparatus. The major components would be easy to get; these were the telephone selector switches and the master control relay. And, because it was our practice to accumulate the required parts so that we could construct an additional machine when it was needed instead of building spare PURPLE machines and holding the completed machines in secure storage, I would simply borrow these items from the supply of parts.

When Ferner and Small joined me in my office, I described to them my concept of having an auxiliary device operating in synchronization with the tabulator. Together we went over the ideas I had developed and we examined each aspect to ensure that not only would the machine perform the desired scanning operations but also that it was electrically and mechanically sound in design. So far as we could ascertain, the contemplated device seemed to satisfy our scanning requirements, and the only question that remained unresolved was that of how to obtain an impulse to energize the master relay at the proper instant in the tabulator cycle. Small suggested that the wiring diagrams which were in the manual issued with the tabulator might provide us with the information we needed and left for the IBM area to locate a copy. When he returned with it, the three of us made a careful study of the circuits available through the plugboard to determine if any one of them might provide an appropriate impulse. But all the impulses which we could obtain from the plugboard were emitted during the operation of the reading cycle of the tabulator and consequently were not satisfactory for our purposes. We finally concluded that we would have to look inside the machine itself for a control impulse, since the diagrams included in the manual did not show the internal circuitry of the machine.

"Something tells the tabulator when to start feeding a card," I observed. "If this is an electrical impulse, maybe we can wire our master control relay into the circuit which provides it. There must be a diagram which shows this circuit."

Small remarked that there were a number of wiring diagrams for the IBM machines in the machine area which were for the use of the IBM technicians who kept the machines in repair, and he volunteered to examine these to determine if they could provide us with information about the control circuits. In a short while he returned with a master diagram for the tabulator and an associated chart which gave the timing and duration of certain impulses in the operational cycle of the tabulator. Our examination of this chart showed an impulse that seemed to be ideal for our purposes. Our problem now was to identify the location of the terminals inside the tabulator which would provide us with access to the impulse.

"Can you locate this circuit inside the tabulator?" I asked Small.

"I'm not sure," he answered. "We have always avoided meddling with the internal wiring of the IBM equipment. But if we remove the covers from the tabulator, we might be able to identify the location of the terminals which provides the impulse that controls the card feed mechanism."

"That would be great," I said. "I could temporarily connect the control relay to the terminals to see if it would operate. If the relay operates normally without interfering with the tabulator circuits, then we can be reasonably sure that the auxiliary mechanism will function satisfactorily. Why don't the two of you go to the IBM area and, if the IBM service representative is not there, remove the covers from one of the tabulators and start looking for the circuit. Meanwhile, I will select a relay from our supply area and we will be ready to test any of the circuits that seem promising."

"If we damage the tabulator, someone will have to answer to IBM," Small cautioned. "Their service representatives are mighty sensitive about anyone except IBM employees working on their equipment."

"I am reasonably confident that we will not damage the machine unless we have an accident," I answered. "And if we have an accident, I am sure I will be able to find some plausible explanation for it. I will select the relay which draws the least amount of current and we will have to be especially careful when we connect it to the tabulator circuits to ensure that we do no damage."

I went to the area where we kept our spare parts for the PURPLE machines and selected the relay which I thought might be suitable for our test. I also picked up a spool of wire, a pair of wire-cutting pliers, and a screwdriver. I was so excited about the prospects of our test that I felt no trepidation about the clause in our contract with IBM regarding alterations to the rented equipment. The stakes were too high for this consideration to keep me from making a test which was so important to us in our attack on the Japanese transposed code system.

When I entered the IBM area, I found that Ferner and Small had removed the metal protecting covers from a tabulator. Small was sitting on the floor, a flashlight in his hand, peering into the interior of the machine.

"I think I've found the circuit we want," he announced. "It looks as if it will be possible to get access to it without disturbing any of the other parts of the machine. In fact, we may be able to test the relay by merely touching the connecting wires to two exposed terminals."

I got down on the floor alongside him, and took a careful look at the terminals which he identified for me. Fortunately for our purposes, IBM used screw connections in the construction of their machines. If the terminals identified by Small were the right ones, it would be a simple matter to connect the relay to the terminals. But for the moment Small's advice was good; we could determine if the relay would be energized properly by merely holding the connecting wires to the screw heads on the terminals he had selected.

I cut two pieces of wire long enough to allow us to place the relay on the floor alongside the tabulator and reach the two screw contacts inside the machine. I connected one end of each of these wires to the coil terminals of the relay. While Small directed the flashlight beam on the two terminals that we wanted to test, I practiced holding the bare ends of the two wires connected to the relay coil against them. When we had satisfied ourselves that we could make a temporary connection good enough electrically to test the operation of the relay, Small plugged the tabulator into the power outlet and loaded it with a supply of cards. Ferner stood at the machine ready to press the starting switch when we gave him the signal. Small again illuminated the two terminals with his flashlight and I got ready to touch them with the naked ends of the wires leading to the external relay when Ferner started the tabulator.

"I'm ready," I announced and suggested that Ferner start the machine.

I let the tabulator run for several cycles before I felt I was ready to touch the bare ends of the wires to the terminals we had selected.

"Now!" I exclaimed. "Watch the relay to see if it operates," I said to Small as I touched the bare ends of the two wires to the screw heads of the terminals. I was afraid to take my eyes off the screw heads which the wires were touching for fear I would let them slip.

"It's working," Small reported, excitedly. I continued to hold the ends of the wires on the terminals until several more cards had been fed through the tabulator.

"Are you sure?" I asked.

"I am sure," Small answered.

I then carefully removed the wires and Ferner stopped the machine. We replaced the protective covers on the tabulator, and the three of us returned to my office. We were well pleased with the outcome of our experiment, and we all were in agreement that the construction of an auxiliary switching device was an urgent matter. "Before we start building the device, we ought to determine how many card columns it will have to scan to provide us with dependable scores," Ferner cautioned. "For example, your preliminary sketches show that only ten columns will be scanned, and this is a smaller number than we used in the cases where we were successful. We ought to examine our scoring procedure and confirm that this number of columns will provide us with enough information to identify the correct match. If we should need more information, the machine should be designed to provided it."

"If we have to let a contract for building the machine, we will have plenty of time for examining our scoring procedures," Small remarked, facetiously.

"Yesterday we computed the single-place logarithmic probabilities and transferred them to a supply of master cards," I reminded them. "If we had the auxiliary device, the simplest way to test our procedures would be to connect it to a tabulator and make some runs. The data from these runs would indicate whether or not our procedures are sound."

"If we had the auxiliary device, that would be the best way of proceeding," Ferner conceded. "However, we do not have the device, and it will take some time to build one, especially if we have to place a contract for its construction."

"I have some ideas that may enable us to have a device in a short time," I answered. "Building an auxiliary scanning device would be a lot simpler than building another PURPLE machine. Also, we have enough stepping switches and relays in our supplies to construct a pilot model."

With his usual spontaneity, Small showed the first reaction to my remarks.

"How long do you think it will take to build it and have it ready for us to operate?" he asked.

"With luck, I might be able to build one over this weekend," I answered. "I think the three of us ought to go over carefully what we want the auxiliary apparatus to do for us, and I will try to construct it so that it will at least do the essentials. The first model ought to be as simple to build and operate as we can possibly make it. The next thing we ought to do is work out the detailed wiring connections between the auxiliary device and the counters in the tabulator. The input into the auxiliary device is easy; we simply plug the input wires into the appropriate positions on the tabulator plugboard. But what is done with the impulses after they leave the auxiliary device is a more complicated matter, and I think we ought to work it out in detail before we start building the device."

"I completely agree," Ferner remarked. "Since we have never tried anything like this, it might be a good idea to review the entire concept in a step-by-step manner to ensure that we have not overlooked anything of importance."

"I would like to see the whole idea laid out on the blackboard," Small noted.

"Very well," I agreed.

I went to the blackboard and laid out the proposed auxiliary device in full detail. As I sketched each element of the device, I explained its function and identified the type of component I planned to use in constructing it. In essence, the device was fairly straightforward in concept; the most noteworthy aspect was its novelty — none of us had ever encountered such a piece of equipment. I concluded my remarks by describing the functioning of the device in detail and noted that a total would be printed each time a card was fed through the tabulator. At this point, I turned to Small.

"Now please describe to us what will happen inside the tabulator," I suggested to him.

"There are twenty counters in the tabulator," Small explained. "If we considered these as two sets of ten, and loaded the sets alternately, we would not have to read the counters each time a card is fed through the tabulator. Instead, we can read out the totals when each tenth card passes through. This would shorten our running time appreciably, for we would have to stop the machine only once for each ten cards."

"Then I will provide for twenty output leads instead of the ten I had planned," I answered.

When this modification was agreed on, Small went on to explain how he planned to store the information in the tabulator, and he described in full detail the wiring of the plugboard. When he finished his presentation, we concluded that our concept of the device was adequate for our immediate purposes and that I should construct one. We also concluded that, for purposes of simplicity in construction and operation, the first device would be built to scan only ten columns.

We decided not to continue our attack on the Mexico City message. If the device could be ready by Monday morning, any effort we expended on the manual computation of scores would be wasted. Also, we needed to review the work on the other Japanese diplomatic systems to see if it was going smoothly. Since the three of us had neglected our more routine responsibilities in favor of the greater excitement of working on the transposed code system, I felt that we ought to spend the rest of the day on our regular duties. Fortunately, we found that the work of the section was going smoothly, and I was able to leave the office before the usual closing time. On my way home, I purchased the angle iron and metal screws I needed for constructing the mounting rack for the relays. I was now prepared to start building the auxiliary device.

At this time my wife was expecting our second child, and her mother was staying with us to help out with caring for our four-year-old son and to provide the needed feminine supervision of our household while my wife was in the hospital. When I got home, I found my wife and her mother impatiently waiting for me, for there were indications that the new baby would soon be arriving. I immediately took my wife to her doctor's office. After examining her, he told us that she would have to be admitted to the hospital the next day.

∽   ∽   ∽

After dinner, I started to work on the auxiliary device. By bedtime I had fashioned the mounts for the stepping switches and had fastened these to a baseboard. I felt I had made a good start on building the device and decided to call it a day. The next day, Saturday, was a busy one for me. The grocery shopping for the coming week had to be done, and some last-minute items for the new baby had to be purchased. The lawn had to be cut and I needed to attend to other chores. Shortly after lunch the doctor called and told us that he had made arrangements for my wife to be admitted to Georgetown University Hospital at five o'clock that afternoon.

After I got back home from taking my wife to the hospital and had finished dinner, I started work on the device. It was almost midnight before I finished assembling the components, and all that remained to be done was to complete the wiring of the selectors and to connect them to the terminal strips I had provided. I felt I had done enough for the day, and decided to leave the wiring until tomorrow.

Before I left the workshop, I took a critical look at my handiwork. "That surely looks like a Rube Goldberg contraption," I thought. "Anyone who sees it will think we're crazy to expect that mess of wires and switches to help us break a sophisticated transposed code system."

It was after ten o'clock next morning before I was able to get started on the wiring. I decided that I would do this part of the job on the screened-in porch where I could keep an eye on our four-year-old, who had discovered his mother was missing and was giving his grandmother and me a rough time. It was a lot easier to keep him in hand on the porch than in the basement workshop. When I started to work on the wiring, he began to take an interest in what I was doing. I gave him some simple tasks to perform, such as holding a pair of pliers for me while I was soldering a wire to the terminal strip. Before long, he lost interest and started amusing himself by playing with his toys, thus enabling me to give full attention to my work. I wanted to finish the job by noon so that I could spend some time with my wife when the hospital's afternoon visiting hours started.

Just before lunchtime our family doctor called and reported that my wife had given birth to a boy and that both mother and child were doing well. He advised us to wait until late in the afternoon to visit the hospital.

Although I soon completed the wiring job. I could not operate the device without a source of direct current so there was nothing more I could do with it until the next morning.

The next day, Monday, I was delayed in arriving at the office. Small and Ferner were working there and they curiously eyed the cardboard box I was carrying.

I removed the device from the box and placed it on the worktable near an electrical outlet.

"Here it is," I said. "It has not been tested yet, and I would like to do that at once."

The Munitions Building at that time used direct current for its lights and office equipment. We had designed the PURPLE machines to operate from the building power supply, and since the stepping switches I had used were spare parts for the PURPLE machines, they would operate satisfactorily off the same power source. I plugged the device into the electrical outlet and threw the power switch. As I had hoped, nothing happened. I then took a wooden pencil and with the eraser end pressed the relay armature toward the coil, simulating the operation of the relay when it was energized. When the relay contacts closed, there was a loud click, signaling that the coils of the selector switches were energized. I then allowed the relay armature to return to its normal position, and, when the relay contact was broken, the wipers of the selector switches advanced. I continued to depress the relay armature until the stepping switches had gone through a complete cycle.

"It seems to be working perfectly," Ferner observed.

"When can we try it out on the tabulator," Small asked.

"Immediately," I answered. "But first we ought to make sure the IBM service man is not in the machine area."

"I'll let you know in a moment," Small said as he left the office. In a short time he returned, reporting that the coast was clear.

I repacked the device into the cardboard box, and the three of us left for the machine room area, carrying the box with us. When we arrived, we removed the covers from the tabulator we had tested the week before, and I made the connections to the two terminals we had selected. Before I attached the two wires to the auxiliary device relay, I asked Small to verify that I had selected the correct terminals in the tabulator. When he confirmed that the connections were correctly made, I connected the free ends of the wires to the auxiliary device. I gave it a final check and then plugged its power cord into an electrical outlet. Small had reconnected the tabulator to the power source and was standing by with a stack of cards which he was ready to feed into the tabulator. We were now ready to determine if the stepping switches of the auxiliary device would advance in step with the cards as they were fed through the tabulator.

It was a most exciting moment for me, for we had never tried such an experiment before. The tabulator was an expensive piece of equipment, and I still felt some nervousness about possibly damaging it. As a final precaution, I again looked over the device and the connections we had made to the tabulator to determine if anything was out of place. When I was sure that nothing was wrong, I felt we were ready to start the test.

"Everything seems to be in order," I remarked. "Go ahead and turn on the tabulator," I added, as I threw the power switch on the device.

Small started the tabulator, and, after letting it run for a short time, inserted a small supply of cards into the card feed mechanism.

As each card was fed into the tabulator, the selector switches advanced, apparently in perfect synchronization with the card feed. We watched the device operate until the card feed was empty and the last card had passed through the tabulator.

"We're ready for the showdown test," I said. "Can you connect the device into the plugboard?" I asked Small.

Nodding his head in assent, he stopped the tabulator and disconnected it from the power outlet.

By this time the curiosity of the machine-room staff had been raised to the point where they could no longer resist forming a circle around the tabulator and the auxiliary device.

"What is that apparatus you're attaching to the tabulator?" one of them asked.

"That is a 'Gee Whizzer'," I jokingly answered. Then, in a more serious vein, I explained that it was an experimental device we had built to improve the operation of the tabulator in the hope that it would help us in our work on the Japanese diplomatic systems. I also cautioned them not to reveal to the IBM representatives that we had attached an auxiliary device to the tabulator.

When Small finished connecting the device to the plugboard, he explained in detail to Ferner and me what he had done and asked us to check his work. After we had examined each of the connections and verified them, he announced that he was ready to make the first run. I checked the stepping switches to ensure that they were set to the correct positions as Small loaded the cards we had assembled for the Mexico City message into the tabulator. We were now about to learn if the plugboard wiring of the tabulator could automatically be changed each time a card was fed into it. The next test we planned would determine if the counters would operate satisfactorily with the auxiliary device and provide us with the desired totals.

Small threw the power switch on the tabulator and, after an appropriate wait, pressed the start button. Each time a punched card passed through the machine, a line of digits was printed. After a couple of hundred cards had been fed through the tabulator, Small stopped the tabulator. Ferner had retrieved the display print which had been prepared the week before for the same cards before the device was built. Small removed the new display sheet from the carriage of the tabulator and placed it alongside the old display print. Just as we had hoped, the digits which had appeared on the diagonals of the old print now were listed in columns on the new print.

"This print is perfect," Ferner observed. "We can now make a run to test if the counters in the tabulator will provide us with the totals we want."

Small continued to study the print for a short time before he made any remarks.

"I can have the tabulator print the totals, but first I will have to run the cards through the reproducer and punch a signal in every tenth card," he replied. "This signal will cause the tabulator to print out the totals stored in the counters. It will probably be an hour before we will be ready to make the next test run."

As excited as I was about the experiment, I thought I had better get back to my desk and look at the intercepts which we had received over the weekend. Before I left the machine area, I cautioned both Ferner and Small to keep a close watch on the "Gee Whizzer" to ensure that the stepping switches were operating properly, reminding them that occasionally we had trouble with the PURPLE machine because one of the switches failed to advance.

When I returned to my desk, I found that I had been called by the head of the Navy unit working on the Japanese diplomatic intercepts. When I returned his call, he asked me if I could meet with him in his office, stating that he had "something important" for me. The first thought that occurred to me was that ONI had made another surreptitious entry. If this was the case, I wanted to confirm it as soon as possible. "I'm on my way," I replied.

As I walked to the Navy Building, I speculated again about the possible undesirable results of an abortive second-story job against a Japanese diplomatic code room. Except for the newly introduced transposed code system, all the other Japanese diplomatic code and cipher systems currently in use were completely exploitable by us. If the device we were now testing met my expectations, the need for a clandestine operation to photograph the transposed code system would be eliminated. Also, G-2 and ONI were well pleased with the intelligence that was now being produced. President Roosevelt was personally interested in reading certain of the translations. If the Japanese changed their systems as a result of an abortive entry, there would really be "one hell of a flap."

The head of the Navy Japanese diplomatic unit and three of his staff were waiting for me.

"Do you recall the key period I discussed with you the last time we met?" he asked. "The PURPLE watch was not very busy over the weekend, and they were able to recover the transposition key and the matrix."

I mentally heaved a sigh of relief.

"Congratulations," I said. "Did you develop any new techniques in recovering it?"

"Nothing spectacular," he answered. "We set up two teams to work on the period, one assuming that the key was sixteen elements in length and the other twenty-four. The key was actually twenty-four elements in length. Fortunately, we found a three-line repetition between two of the messages which made the recovery possible. Incidentally, the key they recovered from the repetition was reversed, and it took some time for them to discover this. We have our work sheets here and we would like for you to look them over if you can spare the time."

We spent almost an hour reviewing the recovery process, and I found it informative, for all our solutions had been for keys of odd lengths. I demonstrated for them a statistical test which I thought would be useful in establishing the correct version of the key in the early stages of its recovery, thus avoiding the ambiguous situation they had encountered. I then gave a brief resume of our research on using the single-digit probability values and identified for them the key periods on which we were currently working.

I did not tell them about the "Gee Whizzer" I had built, for I felt it would be better to wait until we established that it would be practicable. I thought it would be a good time now to restate our views on the possible dangers of a clandestine operation against a Japanese diplomatic code room.

"You gave me a bad moment this morning," I remarked. "When you told me that you had something important for me, I immediately assumed that ONI had done another second-story job on a Japanese embassy. I must say that I am much more pleased with the news that the PURPLE watch has recovered one of the transpositions keys than I would have been if you had told me that you had photographs of the new code. I believe it would be a disaster if the Japanese overhauled their cryptographic systems."

Their reaction to my remarks clearly revealed the attitude of the Navy cryptanalysts.

"I agree with you completely," the head of the group answered. "I have discussed this point with Captain Safford and Commander Kramer, and we are all in agreement. I don't think you have to worry about this matter any longer. Our position has been made clear to ONI, and they have assured us that no further clandestine entry will be made into a Japanese diplomatic code room without our prior approval."

I was eager to get back to my office to learn what Ferner and Small had been able to do with the "Gee Whizzer". I found them in the machine area, still working at the tabulator.

"We are having some trouble getting the tabulator to print the totals," Ferner reported. "Evidently there are not enough counters to provide the twenty totals we require."

He explained the difficulty they had encountered, while Small continued working on the plugboard, which he was rewiring. The type of run we had planned required twenty counters, and the machine we were using had only twelve. As a stop-gap measure, they had worked out a scheme for making two runs, using ten counters for each run. They were now making preparations for testing the scheme. I quickly reviewed for them my meeting with the Navy and suggested they go ahead with the test while I informed Friedman that the Navy cryptanalytic group had recovered a key period.

Friedman was pleased to hear about the success of the Navy in recovering a key period. He was amused when I told him that the Navy cryptanalysts had first tried to decipher the intercepts with a reversed key and mentioned that the cryptanalysts of the AEF in their work on the ADFGVX system had had similar experiences. I also reported that we were continuing our experiments in using the IBM equipment to compute the matching scores, but we still had more work to do before we would be able to evaluate our techniques. I did not tell him about the "Gee Whizzer" for I was afraid he might forbid us to experiment with the IBM equipment.

When I finished reporting to Friedman, I returned to the machine area. Ferner and Small were still busy with the tabulator, making the final adjustments to the wiring of the plugboard and checking out the operation of the counters. I decided I would be more in their way than a help to them, and I returned to my office, where I looked over the fresh intercepts in the transposed code system, which by now had been sorted out and were ready for our examination.

I was especially interested in finding a favorable key period with an odd-length key. I visualized that if the "Gee Whizzer" worked satisfactorily, we might be able to recover the entire transposition key automatically. The first run would identify a pair of adjacent columns, and each succeeding run would add another column at a time until the entire key was recovered.

I searched the intercepts for the longest messages in the transposed code system. In our previous selection of key periods to attack, we wanted a large number of messages as well as a long one, for we needed to build up a large body of plain-code messages for our data banks and our code recovery work. For the purposes I had in mind, I felt that a long message was more important than a large number of intercepts. In the traffic I was examining I found two key periods with long messages, and I decided to test these two periods to determine if the keys were odd or even. I tested the longest message first, and the statistics I computed indicated strongly in favor of an odd-length key. I did not bother to test the other period, but started at once to prepare the message in work-sheet form so we could prepare the cards for running it through the "Gee Whizzer". I had scarcely started the preparation of the work sheet when Ferner and Small came charging into my office carrying a machine display.

Ferner usually did not display much excitement, but this time he was as jubilant as Small. He placed the run on my desk and pointed to a column of figures circled in red. "That is the highest score we found, and there is no other even close to it," he announced.

"This may turn out to be like shooting fish in a barrel," Small said, excitedly. "Now all we have to do is to scan the totals printed by the tabulator, and when we find the highest we have identified the match."

"Did you have any problems with the "Gee Whizzer"," I asked.

"None at all," Small answered.

"It might get out of step without being noticed," I suggested. "Maybe we should spot check each run to verify that it worked properly."

"Yes, we ought to check at least one total at the end of the run and maybe one near the start of the run," Ferner agreed.

"We also ought to check the highest total to ensure that it is correct,"

Small remarked as he searched for the probability chart he had used for preparing the cards.

It was with some relief that I noted that the values in the machine listing corresponded exactly to the ones we had selected from the probability chart and that the totals produced by the machine exactly duplicated the ones we had calculated. Obviously, the "Gee Whizzer" was performing just as we wanted it to.

"Maybe we will be able to determine the length of the transposition key," Ferner suggested.

"Let's try that and then call it a day," I proposed. "Also, we must remove the 'Gee Whizzer' from the machine area and store it in a secure place for the night. We ought to be able to remove the plugboard to which it is connected from the tabulator without disturbing the wiring. Also, the wires connecting the master relay should be disconnected and the covers replaced on the tabulator."

"We can store it in one of the metal supply cabinets in the machine area," Small answered.

"Make sure the cabinet can be locked," I suggested. "We should keep the key where only the three of us can have access to it for the time being."

While Ferner and Small set about determining the number of elements in the transposition key, I prepared to leave. I rapidly went through my incoming basket and was pleased to find nothing that needed early attention. Before I left the room, I checked to see if the key length had been determined.

"Our results are inconclusive," Ferner reported. "We will have to wait for the results of another run before we can make a judgment about the length of the key."

A busy evening was ahead of me. I stopped at the hospital to look in on my wife and to take my first look at the new baby. She was feeling really good and she related to me all that she observed about our new son. The high point of the visit arrived when the nurse brought the baby in for his feeding. It was a great moment.

After dinner, I drove my wife's mother and our older son back to Georgetown so that she could visit with my wife and take her first look at her new grandson. By the time we got back to my home in Arlington, I was ready for a good night's rest.

CHAPTER 23

THE DEVICE PROVES A SUCCESS

S MALL WAS WAITING FOR me when I arrived at the office the next morning. I unlocked the machine area for him, and we connected the "Gee Whizzer" to the tabulator. He immediately started preparations for making the second run. Since we were attacking an even-length key period, we had to select a different hypothetical column for our match. I secured the entrance to the machine area when I left and unlocked the area where our offices were located. Ferner soon arrived and he came directly to my office.

"Since the auxiliary device limits us to ten values, I think it would be useful to make a study of the scores we are producing as we make each run," he suggested. "These are all listed on the display sheets, and it would easy to make a distribution showing their range and the number of times each numerical score occurs. We could then fit a probability curve to the distribution and evaluate the likelihood of a high score's being spurious. While such a test might not be needed for exceptionally high scores, it could be useful in cases where the correct match produces a total that lies in the range of spurious matches."

He then outlined on the blackboard the procedure he had planned for collecting the data on which the study would be based. We then made a distribution of all the scores on the runs that had been produced by the auxiliary device. As we had expected, the distribution had the characteristics of a bell-shaped curve, but showed a pronounced skewness that we had not anticipated. While we were speculating about the cause of the skewness, Small arrived with the results of the run he had just finished.

"I have two candidates for another match," he announced as he entered the office. "There are two high scores, either of which can be correct."

He placed the display on the table and identified the two high scores. Ferner and I compared them with the range of scores on the chart we had just finished compiling. They were indeed high enough to be possible matches. Although the score from the first run was considerably higher than the two highest ones from the second run, the latter were within the upper range of the scores we had tabulated from the first run.

"If we can determine the length of the key, we may be able to identify the correct matches," Ferner suggested.

We were lucky, for only one even-length key seemed acceptable. If our work was correct so far, we had matched two pairs of columns and had determined the length of the transposition key. We could now roughly identify the portions of the message which corresponded to the remaining columns of the transposition matrix. If our matches were correct, we were now well along the road to our first recovery of an even-length key. Without the "Gee Whizzer", our next step would be to identify the location of the remaining columns by an anagramming process; but with the device, we could continue our statistical approach and be able, we hoped, to identify correctly all the remaining pairs of columns.

"Which should we do," I asked, "start our anagramming process or continue with the tabulator runs?"

"Since the cards are assembled," Ferner answered, "I would like to have the scores from at least two more runs. I would like to compare the distributions of scores from these runs with the distribution we completed this morning."

"I agree," Small remarked. "I would like also to get some more experience with the tabulator procedures, particularly on an even-length key."

"Before we start the tabulator runs, we ought to look at some intercepts which I selected yesterday for our next attack," I said. "I think I have identified an unusually favorable key period. It has an odd-length key and may be ideal for determining if we can automatically recover an entire key by using only the auxiliary device. But I think we ought to finish recovering the even-length key before starting another."

"Why not work on both key periods simultaneously," Small suggested. "If the two of you will assemble the cards for the odd-length message, I will finish the runs for the even-length Mexico City message. Then I can begin the runs for the odd-length key period while you recover the matrix and transposition key for the even-length key."

We readily agreed to Small's suggestion, and before he left for the machine room we identified two columns consisting of initial letters to be used for the next two runs. Ferner and I began the assembly of a set of cards for the longest message in the key period which I had selected for our next recovery effort. Fortunately there were no interruptions to our work and by the time Small had completed the runs on the even-length Mexico City message, Ferner and I had finished the assembly of the cards for the message I had selected.

The two machine displays Small had produced each showed a distinctive high score, and we decided that, instead of making additional runs for the message with the even-length key, he should instead start processing the cards we had assembled for the message with the odd-length key. We were becoming more and more eager to prove that we could automatically recover a key by using the "Gee Whizzer." Before he left for the machine area, we reviewed the procedure which ought to be followed with the recovery of the odd-length key. We decided that we would use the final section of the intercept as the basis for our first run. The high score from the first run would identify the portion of the intercept which would be used as a basis for the second run. In turn the high score from the second run would identify the part of the intercept to be used as a basis for the third run, and so on, until the relative positions of all the columns of the message were identified. At Ferner's suggestion, Small made an estimate of the time required for such a procedure.

When Small informed us that he might be able to complete all the required runs in approximately three hours, we decided that the experiment was worth doing. Under the most favorable circumstances we had not been able to recover a key in such a short period of time.

While Small worked on the runs for the odd-length key period, Ferner and I attacked the message with the even-length key. Our first step was to join the columns identified by the tabulator runs into pairs. The next step was to identify and match the remaining columns of the message into pairs. From this point on, we would have to rely on our ability to anagram the two-letter and four-letter groups for determining the arrangement of the matched pairs of columns. When we finally arrived at the exact arrangement of the pairs of columns, we fitted them into a hypothetical matrix and determined the location of the blanks in the matrix. We then deciphered a few short intercepts to ensure that we had correctly recovered the key.

"I wonder how Small is doing," I remarked. "It has been almost three hours since he left for the machine area."

"Maybe we ought to pay him a visit," Ferner suggested.

When we got to the machine room, we found Small busy at wiring a plugboard, and the tabulator was standing idle.

"I am on the twelfth run," he explained. "When I finish wiring this board I will show you the results."

"How is the Gee Whizzer operating?" I asked.

"No problems there," he replied. "But our scoring statistics are not good enough to give us automatic answers. However, I thought a modification of the procedure might be used to advantage. In the first five runs, I found significantly high scores, but when I made the sixth run, instead of finding a single high score, I found three. Here is the print from that run, and if you examine the scores you will note that any one of three portions of the message might be selected as a basis for the next run. However, if you take into account the location of the three portions in the intercept, you will find that only one is acceptable because of the limitations of the length of the key. I used it instead of the other two and continued the runs. If all my work is correct, the transposition key is nineteen elements in length, and I have identified and tentatively matched thirteen of the columns. Actually it would be quicker and easier to anagram the remaining columns instead of continuing to run the tabulator."

After a short discussion, we concluded that when the current run was finished, we would halt the work on the tabulator and complete the recovery of the key by using the anagramming procedures which we had successfully used in recovering the other keys we had solved. I suggested that the three of us meet in my office when the run was completed.

When the run was finished, we assembled in my office to check the results of the runs Small had made. In less than half an hour we had verified the correctness of the columns he had matched, and within an hour we had added the remaining columns and recovered both the transposition key and the matrix. For the first time since we had started our experimentation with the exhaustive testing procedure, we felt that we had brought it to a practical basis for recovering the keys for the transposed code system.

Normally I would have made a report of our success to Friedman at this point. In his absence, I usually reported such successes to Colonel Akin, who was always affirmatively interested in our achievements and who enjoyed receiving such reports. But at this time both were away from their offices and not expected to return for several days. I felt it was important to report the results of our work with the "Gee Whizzer" to the Navy cryptanalytic group. In the absence of both Friedman and Akin, it was up to me to take this action.

I called the head of the Navy group responsible for the work on the Japanese diplomatic systems and informed him that I had something of importance to discuss with him and suggested that he arrange to spend at least three hours in my office. Since it was close to the end of the working day when I placed the call, we agreed to meet early next morning. I was pleased with the delay, for it would give us time to set the stage for what I hoped would be an impressive demonstration. When I informed Ferner and Small of the planned meeting, we discussed how we might best present the application of our newly developed machine procedure. We concluded that the fairest, as well as the most impressive, way to demonstrate the "Gee Whizzer," would be to apply it to an unsolved key period. We also decided to select an odd-length key, since the last two keys we had recovered showed clearly that it was a lot easier to recover an odd-length key than one of even length. At this point we decided to wait until the next morning to make the selection of the message to be used for the demonstration.

I was beginning to feel some concern about devoting so much time to the work on the Japanese diplomatic transposed-code system. Friedman lately had been spending little time in the office, and, in his absence, I had to attend to certain of the other technical responsibilities of the Signal Intelligence Service, especially in the work on communications security. It was now a critical time in the development of the new cipher machine which we had joined with the Navy in producing, and the latest pilot models of the new device were expected to be delivered soon. There was a strong feeling of urgency about getting the new machine into production. We had to anticipate that the U.S. would sooner or later be drawn into war, and it was imperative that we have enough cipher machines on hand for distribution down to division level in the Army. There was also the requirement for producing training manuals for the new machine, which would have to be written and printed when the final specifications for it had been approved.

Personally I wanted to continue working on the cryptanalytic research problems full time. It was extremely satisfying from an intellectual standpoint to participate in the development of new cryptanalytic techniques and to realize the greater cryptanalytic potential we had achieved when our research efforts paid off, as we had found in our work on the Japanese transposed code system. Within in our group we had many times discussed the need for a device which would automatically perform a mass of arithmetic computations, and actually to accomplish this goal through a combination of refinement of established statistical methods and the development of a mechanism was a most gratifying experience. In contrast, the prospect of having to spend more time on administrative matters and less time on research was one which I did not anticipate with pleasure.

꧁ ꧁ ꧁

The next morning we gave our full attention to preparing the demonstration for the Navy cryptanalysts. Ferner and I searched through the unsolved intercepts for long messages which we might use as examples while Small ensured that an adequate supply of message cards was available and that the tabulator and the "Gee Whizzer" were in working order.

When our visitor arrived, I first informed him that we felt we had achieved a significant advance in our procedures for recovering the keys for the Japanese diplomatic transposed code system and that we were prepared to give him a demonstration of the new techniques on an unsolved key period.

As the first step in our demonstration, we made statistical tests on messages from three different key periods, to establish whether the keys were odd or even. One key period favored an odd-length key, and we selected the most promising intercept from it as our example, explaining that we had found the recovery of odd-length keys to be much easier than solving even-length keys. We then demonstrated our procedures for assembling the specially prepared cards from the text of the message. While Ferner and Small completed the assembly of the cards, I explained that we had constructed a special piece of equipment to be used with the IBM tabulator which would perform automatically the arithmetic procedures that we had found so time-consuming. When the cards for the message were assembled, we took our materials to the IBM machine area, where the tabulator and the auxiliary device were ready for our use.

Small arranged the wiring of the plugboard and adjusted the "Gee Whizzer" in preparation for the first run. He loaded the message cards into the feeding mechanism of the tabulator and started the run.

While the run was in progress, Small explained the function of the tabulator, pointing out that the purpose of the run was to determine which columnar matches produced the highest totals. After the run was finished, we examined all the high totals and were able to confirm that the highest was statistically valid. Small rewired the plugboard and reset the Gee Whizzer and started the second run.

During the second run our visitor's attention was attracted to the auxiliary device. I gave a detailed explanation of it, pointing out that the tabulator had not been designed for performing all the operations we required and that we had designed and assembled an attachment that expanded the tabulator's capabilities to meet our special requirements for the column matching process.

"It looks like a part of the PURPLE machine," he commented.

"Except for the stepping switches, it really is not anything like the PURPLE machine," I answered. "Their function is not cryptographic at all; instead they merely rearrange the wiring of the plugboard according to a regular pattern each time a card is passed through the tabulator."

"And all you need to do, once you have prepared the cards for the intercept, is to keep making these runs through the tabulator," he observed. "The tabulator and this device are taking the place of the cryptanalyst."

"It's a marvelous idea, if it works," he added as an afterthought.

When the second run was finished, Small prepared for the third run while we verified the validity of the high scores appearing in the first run. We then selected the one which seemed most promising and identified the column associated with it as a basis for our third run. The third run produced only one exceptionally high score, and when we consolidated the results of the three runs, we found that only one key length was possible. On the assumption that we had determined the correct key we could now tentatively identify the other portions of the intercept which would correspond to the remaining columns of the transposition matrix.

"If your work is correct up to this point, all you need now is to arrange the columns in the correct order," our visitor observed. "Wouldn't it be easier to complete the key recovery by the anagramming process than by using the tabulator?"

"That is likely," I answered. "I think we ought to continue for at least two more runs, since this procedure is new and we still have to develop a better understanding of its effectiveness. However, it would be an interesting experiment if you and I tried to complete the key by the anagramming process while Ferner and Small make additional runs. This would provide us with a better base for comparing the anagramming technique with the procedure using the IBM equipment."

"I would like to see the outcome of such a competition," he answered.

The two of us returned to my office, where we started the anagramming process without delay. Unfortunately for us, the columns we were using as the starting point of our recovery operation did not contain any of the letter combinations which formed the four-letter supplementary code groups and we had to rely on our other techniques for identifying the additional columns.

After about an hour of trying to find a matching column by the anagramming procedure without success, we concluded that our only recourse was to apply the statistical techniques. When we reached this point, it was evident that for this particular message the machine process was superior to the anagramming approach. We returned to the machine area and reported our lack of success to Ferner and Small.

By this time they had finished three additional runs and had located three more columns in the transposition matrix. Another run was in progress; if it was successful, a section of eight columns would have been produced.

"From now on, it will probably be easier to apply the anagramming procedure for locating the remaining columns," I suggested.

"It probably would," our visitor answered. "But now I am so impressed with the machine approach that I would like to see how well it works in recovering the remaining columns."

I felt his response was a good endorsement of our machine techniques. There seemed to be no point in my remaining in the machine area, since there was little that I could contribute. I excused myself and returned to my office.

It was almost lunchtime before the group joined me. Our visitor was enthusiastic about what he had seen and asked if we could arrange a similar demonstration for his cryptanalysts.

"The members of our PURPLE watch have been working on a key period, but they are having trouble getting a break into it," he explained. "It would be interesting to see if this process of yours would be successful on the message they have been testing."

"If you like, we can start immediately after lunch," I promised.

"In that case I had better get back to the Navy Building and inform the group of our plans," he answered, as he prepared to leave.

Ferner and Small had checked the newly recovered key by applying it to another message in the same key period. When they reported to me that the accuracy of the key had been confirmed, we spent some time discussing the import of the day's work.

"If there was any doubt about the effectiveness of our procedures, it is now removed," Small observed. "For the first time we have recovered a transposition key by using a combination of statistical techniques and machine procedures."

"Do you have any suggestions for the demonstration I promised for this afternoon?" I asked.

"I hope our procedure works as well this afternoon as it did this morning," Ferner observed. "If we are able to recover another key today, we can decipher enough additional intercepts to justify the preparation of another catalog and message print for the code recovery work. If we are successful this afternoon, I suggest that we start the updating process tomorrow morning. We can also include the new data in our probability charts, which should make them more reliable.

"I was amazed at how well our procedures worked this morning," Small remarked. "The scores we obtained for each run seemed exceptionally high, much higher than I expected them to be."

"The Mexico City message also gave good scores," I remarked. "Where did the message we worked on this morning originate?"

Ferner sought out the copy of the intercept.

"It also was from Mexico City," he calmly announced.

"Maybe we should make a statistical study of the text of the Mexico City messages," I suggested. "Possibly the subject matter is uniquely different from that sent by other Japanese installations. Or maybe the code clerk in Mexico City has unusual encoding habits which could cause his messages to give better scores."

"There seemed to be an unusually small number of four-letter groups in the message we worked on this morning," Small noted. "If the Mexico City code clerk has a bias against using the four-letter section of the code, this bias could be reflected in accentuated frequencies for the groups representing the kana sounds. This in itself could account for the high scores we found in the Mexico City messages."

"That is an intriguing possibility," Small remarked. "If there is a bias in the Mexico City messages, why shouldn't there be a bias in the Washington messages or the Tokyo messages. It would be an interesting exercise to make a special frequency study of each of our high-volume originators to determine which is the most favorable for our purposes."

"I can visualize two sets of data," I remarked. "One set would be comprehensive and would be based on all the messages we have deciphered, regardless of source. The other set would consist of several subsets, one for each high-volume originating office, such as Tokyo, Washington, London, Mexico City, Rio de Janeiro, and the other holders of the transposed code system. If we were trying to recover the key for a message originating in Washington, we would use the probabilities based on the Washington intercepts. If the message originated from an office for which we had not prepared a subset, we would use the data from the comprehensive set."

"It would be a very simple matter to produce the various sets of data you have described," Small remarked. "I think it is worth trying."

When the Navy group arrived for the demonstration, we looked over their preliminary work on the key period they had chosen and selected the message which seemed to us to offer the most favorable prospects for attack. When the cards for the message were assembled, Ferner and Small took the group to the machine area, while the head of the group and I remained in my office. We reviewed the prospects for the work on the transposed code system and explored the possibilities for a division of effort in the exploitation of the transposed code system. We concluded that the odd-even formula for division of effort which had been initiated shortly after we had recovered the RED machine and which we were currently following for all other work on the Japanese intercepts, including recovery of the daily keys for the PURPLE machine, could also be applied to the recovery of the daily keys for transposed code system. When we reached agreement on this point, we discussed the requirements for additional tabulators and the auxiliary-device construction possibilities. He suggested that the Navy Yard facilities might be able to build additional auxiliary devices, and I promised to provide the necessary drawings and explanatory material.

When I expressed my concern that IBM might learn that we had made unauthorized connections to the tabulator circuits, I was assured that this information would be adequately protected.

Since we both were eager to learn how the demonstration was progressing, we decided to join the group in the machine area. When we arrived there, Small was operating the tabulator, and the remainder of the group was clustered around it, watching the scores being printed. Ferner stepped out of the group and explained that the first run was still in process. When we inquired if there had been any significant scores displayed, he answered in the negative.

As we watched, the stack of cards in the feeding mechanism of the tabulator grew smaller and smaller. I was beginning to fear that we might not find a significant score when there was a flurry of excitement around the tabulator.

"There is the highest score we have yet seen!" one of the Navy cryptanalysts announced.

As the tabulator continued to run, Ferner entered the letters corresponding to the high score on a work sheet he had prepared. He then validated the machine score and announced that an acceptable match had been located. By this time, the run was finished without producing another comparable high score. Since it was obvious that the demonstration was going well and holding the full interest of our visitors, I excused myself and left to attend to other matters which needed my attention.

The most pressing management problem I had was to select and assign qualified personnel to carry on the recovery of the transposition keys, using the procedures we had developed and were now testing. It now seemed to be a good time to review the status of our work and determine which of the personnel could be reassigned for training in the new techniques.

I first checked with Major Dowd, who was coordinating the work on the recovery of the code employed in the new system. He seemed to be somewhat discouraged with the progress that had been made. I tried to reassure him and promised that we would soon have a considerable volume of new messages to add to his work file. I also informed him that we had been discussing the key-recovery effort with the Navy and that they would soon be in production on the odd-day messages.

"I don't know whether that is good news or bad news," Major Dowd remarked. "Our Japanese language staff is overworked. We will need to hire some more Japanese language experts if we are expected to keep up with the current translation load and also recover this unsolved code."

After my conversation with Major Dowd, I spent some time with the cryptanalysts working on the key recovery for the PURPLE machine system. Here we were in excellent shape and, as a general rule, by closing time we were able to decipher all the intercepts received during the day; in fact, most of the more important PURPLE intercepts were being translated and delivered to G-2 and ONI before they had been processed by the Japanese embassy code clerks. For example, a message from Tokyo to the Japanese Ambassador in Washington in the PURPLE system would regularly be in

G-2 and ONI several hours before it was available to the Japanese Ambassador. And if the President or the Secretary of State had expressed an interest in a particular subject, priority would be given to processing messages having a bearing on it, and sometimes translations would be available to Mr. Roosevelt or Mr. Hull before the Japanese Ambassador had seen them. All other systems used by the Japanese diplomatic service, except for the transposed code system, were being exploited on the same basis as the PURPLE intercepts; since their subject matter was generally of lower interest to G-2 and ONI, they were usually given lower priority.

In bringing myself up to date on the status of our work, I spent some time with each unit, discussing the work and dealing with any problems that had arisen. I also took the opportunity to report any information that I thought might be useful to them and generally to review any new developments in the Japanese diplomatic communications. I found this practice to be stimulating both to the members of the staff and to me, for it helped in developing a strong feeling of team cooperation.

When I finished my rounds within the Japanese diplomatic section, I returned to the machine room to see how the demonstration was going. The Navy group was still assembled around the tabulator. When I joined them, I asked what they thought of the procedures we had developed.

"I never expected that the recovery of the transposition keys could be reduced to such an automatic procedure," a member of the Navy group observed. "We have almost completed matching all the columns. This could have taken us days to accomplish by using the methods we were following."

I examined the work sheets displayed on a table near the tabulator. The results certainly looked good, and it appeared that the remainder of the key could be easily recovered. I suggested that the group might wish to take the work sheets back to the Navy Building and to complete the recovery there by using the more conventional methods. This suggestion was promptly declined.

"This is a rare opportunity for us to get some first-hand experience with the IBM equipment," one of the group observed. "Normally, our IBM processing is conducted by the machine room staff, and we are not permitted to participate in it. I much prefer the arrangement you follow, where the cryptanalyst can use the equipment as a tool. Also, if we wished to have one of these auxiliary devices constructed, we would be required to place a requisition on the Navy Yard. I understand this device was built and connected to the tabulator without any outside help."

"We are fortunate that we have little administrative restraints on our technical activities," I answered. "This entire installation of IBM equipment is for the sole use of the Signal Intelligence Service. Ordinarily, we give priority to our cryptographic requirements, but in special circumstances, we can give precedence to our cryptanalytic work."

"Who sets the priorities for the IBM machine usage?" he asked.

"Normally, Mr. Friedman allocates the machine-support effort," I explained. "In his absence, I am responsible. Usually when a conflict in priorities occurs, we have a meeting of the concerned parties and work out a solution. To my knowledge, this type of decision has never been made outside the SIS."

After the demonstration was over and the Navy group had departed, Ferner and Small joined me in my office. They were obviously tired, for they had been working since early morning. I asked them for their impressions on how the demonstration had worked out.

"Perfectly," Ferner responded. "We couldn't have put on a better one. There were enough high scores to demonstrate the theory and enough ambiguous ones to establish the need for caution in applying the procedures. The Navy cryptanalysts want to adopt our procedures, but they are not sure that they will be able to arrange for the full-time use of a tabulator. In fact, I am afraid that we made the key recovery look so easy that they will be discouraged from applying any other approach."

"I am sure that they will be provided with a tabulator in due course," I remarked. "But until one is available to them, we can allow them to use our equipment if they need it. Also, I think it would be wise for us to have another of the auxiliary devices on hand. Before we construct another model, we should give some thought about how it might be improved."

"The auxiliary device seems adequate," Small remarked. "But it is important that we have more counters installed in the tabulator we have been using. Once the additional counters are available, we can shorten the time required for each run."

"We have another tabulator on order and it will be delivered in a few weeks," I observed. "It is not too late to have the order amended to ensure that it has an adequate number of counters for use with the auxiliary device."

"We ought to have at least two tabulators with full counter capacity," Ferner remarked.

"I am sure we can arrange for that," I answered.

I then told them about my discussion with Major Dowd, describing his frustration in getting a satisfactory start on recovering the new code. I sensed that the three of us also felt some of the same frustration, but because our knowledge of the language was so limited, there was little we could do to help in the code recovery. We had designed and provided the language group with message prints and catalogs which made their code recovery work much easier, but these ancillary aids were no substitute for proficiency in the language. At best, we could provide some meager assistance in the recovery of the more frequent kana sounds, numbers, message instructions, and punctuation, but so far as the more esoteric aspects of the language was concerned, we had nothing to offer.

The next day we selected the members of the staff who were to be trained in the transposition key recovery techniques. Ferner took charge of the training program while Small worked with the procurement office on amending the order for the new tabulator and arranging to have one of the tabulators on hand modified to meet our requirements. I was kept busy with a variety of other projects since Friedman was spending more and more time away from the office. Our code and cipher production program was at a critical stage, for we were at the point of putting into final form the specifications for the new cipher machine which was being built under a joint Army–Navy contract.

There was one interesting development which contributed substantially to our code recovery and, at the same time, afforded Ferner, Small, and me some diversion. Early one morning, Louise Prather, who along with her other duties supervised the handling and logging of all intercepts, called to my attention a long message which had originated in Tokyo. She pointed out that the message carried the same external number as a circular message which had been sent out by Tokyo shortly after the transposed code system which ONI had photographed was first put into use. She had located a copy of the earlier message in our files, and, since it was almost exactly the same length as the new intercept, she concluded that the two messages represented different encipherments of the same plaintext.

It took only minutes to verify that Louise was correct in her assumption. The new version of the message was addressed to an embassy that had only recently been activated. Evidently Tokyo felt that the new embassy needed the information contained in the previously transmitted circular message, and, since the embassy did not have a copy of the old code in which the message had originally been transmitted, the code room in Tokyo had enciphered the text in the new code. I was delighted with the discovery, for if we were able to recover the transposition key for the message, its code text could be matched with the text of the earlier message and the equivalents of all the code groups appearing in it would be accurately identified.

Ferner, Small, and I promptly started the recovery of the key for the message. By this time we had refined our techniques to the point where they could be routinely applied with an almost certain chance that the key would be recovered by making only eight to ten runs through the tabulator. The message Louise had identified responded to our attack, and by noon the transposition key and the matrix had been fully recovered. When we compared the basic code texts of the two messages, it was clearly evident that we had an exact repetition of the same plaintext in two different codes. The earlier version was in the code which ONI had photographed, and the later version was in the code which was now being recovered by our Japanese language experts.

I was eager to inform Major Dowd of the repeated texts, so that he and the other linguists working on the code recovery could take full advantage of our stroke of good luck. Unfortunately, it was after twelve o'clock on Wednesday, and I found that Major Dowd had closed his desk for the day and had taken the afternoon off for his War Department-mandated exercise period. When I checked with the other members of the language staff, I found that they were fully occupied with translating the day's decipherment of PURPLE messages; from the amount of PURPLE intercepts which still had to be processed, I concluded that they would have little, if any, time to devote to code recovery work that day. I was curious to learn how useful the repeated texts would be, so I decided that Ferner, Small, and I might just as well go ahead and equate the code texts of the two messages. By the end of the day we had completed our exploitation of the repeated texts and were ready to provide Major Dowd with an impressive number of confirmed code recoveries when he arrived next morning.

Overnight, I was seized with a puckish idea. Major Dowd had not known of the repeated text before he left the office for his afternoon of exercise, and he would therefore be entirely unaware of how we had made our recoveries. Also, there was a continuing spirit of friendly professional competition between the Japanese language experts and the cryptanalysts. "Why not," I thought, "have some fun out of the situation and present Major Dowd with the recoveries, merely identifying them as the results of a code recovery effort by the cryptanalytic group?" And the more I thought of the idea, the more I got carried away with it.

The next morning, I told Ferner and Small of my idea of giving Major Dowd the recoveries without explaining how we had obtained them. I proposed that we would merely present him with a copy of the recovery chart which we had prepared and ask him for an evaluation of the accuracy of each of the entries. We would then suggest that he inform us at his convenience of his evaluation of our code-recovery efforts. Ferner and Small gleefully endorsed the idea.

When Major Dowd arrived, we gave him enough time to get settled at his desk before the three of us paraded into his office. He was in the process of completing the required report of exercise for the previous afternoon.

I interrupted him and handed him the code-recovery chart we had prepared from the texts of the repeated messages.

"Yesterday afternoon we spent some time on code recovery work," I explained. "We believe we made some progress and have prepared a chart showing the groups we recovered. We would be grateful to you if you would take a look at our recoveries at your convenience and let us know what you think of them."

Major Dowd, who was always a very considerate person, accepted the chart and remarked that he would check our recoveries at a later time. As we left his office, he noted that we should not feel too bad if many of the values we had given him turned out to be wrong, pointing out that this code seemed to be an exceptionally difficult one to break. Had he not made these last remarks, I might have weakened and told him how we had arrived at the recoveries, but with this last observation he had set the stage for a really good bit of fun. So we returned to my office without giving him any hint about the real source of the recoveries.

It was almost two hours before we heard from Major Dowd. He came into my office where Ferner and Small were still working. His attitude was serious and he looked perplexed.

"This is unbelievable!" he exclaimed as he waved the chart we had given him earlier at us. "Every one of the values on this chart is absolutely correct. I have not found a single mistake on it. And the most amazing part of it is that you have recovered at least a dozen meanings which none of us linguists could ever have identified. If you fellows can do this well in one afternoon, you don't need me." With these last words he flung the chart on my desk and started to stalk out of the office.

I had not expected this kind of reaction from Major Dowd. I knew that he was disappointed with the progress that had been made on the code, but I had not expected him to react so strongly. I had to make amends immediately.

"I did not tell you the full story," I said. "We had a lucky break yesterday. Just take a look at these work sheets."

I showed him the copies of the work sheets on which we had equated the code texts of the two messages with the underlying plaintext and explained how we had arrived at the recoveries.

"We just couldn't resist playing a joke on you," I apologized.

When Major Dowd learned how we had been so successful in making the code group recoveries, his good nature again showed up.

"I knew there had to be a catch in it somewhere," he remarked, good naturedly. "Those recoveries you fellows gave me were just too good to be true. With this start, the code recovery ought to proceed nicely."

By the end of the month the new system was well under control. The new workers we had assigned to the transposed code system soon mastered the machine techniques under Ferner's guidance and started producing solutions of transposition keys on a regular basis. The procurement office validated our order for additional items in the tabulator on order, and the Washington IBM office gave priority to the installation of additional counter capacity in the machine we were using for transposition key recovery.

One important modification which Ferner and Small developed for our machine technique provided for the suppression of all scores below a set level, so that the tabulator listed only those scores which were significant. Not only did this modification cut down on the number of scores the cryptanalyst had to examine, but also it shortened appreciably the time required for each run.

The Navy group soon was able to procure a tabulator for full-time use on the transposed code problem and arranged for the Navy Yard to build an auxiliary device for it. When our additional tabulator was delivered, we put another of the auxiliary devices into operation with it. From this point on, we were able to recover all the keys used in the transposed code system, except for a few in which there was no message of sufficient length to provide us with enough statistical information for our machine techniques to be successful.

EPILOGUE

F RANK ROWLETT quit writing his memoirs in the middle of his story —even before the United States entered World War II. He no longer remembers why. But the book could not be published as Rowlett left it; its abrupt ending would leave readers puzzled and unsatisfied. So, with the permission of the author, the approbation of the publisher, and in the desire to pay tribute to a great cryptologist, I have tried to round out Rowlett's story, carrying it through Pearl Harbor and into World War II.

Nothing can replace what Rowlett would have written. This loss is a great pity, because it deprives the world of the record of how a leading cryptanalyst and administrator saw the technical, organizational, and personnel problems that faced him, how he resolved them, what results his unit achieved, and his views of their relative importance and how they helped the Allies win the war. But to wish that he had written this is to wish for a chimera. Rowlett's memory, weakened by time, can no longer fill the blanks. His oral-history transcript tells no consecutive story and misses much essential information, particularly for World War II.

Of course he deserves a complete history of his own. However, this would require heavy research in the archives and extensive interviewing among his surviving subordinates. Limitations of time and space prohibit my doing this. So, for this brief but, I hope, compendious addendum, I have restricted my investigations to the notes of some of my earlier interviews with Rowlett and others and to the annual report for fiscal year 1944 (July 1943 to June 1944) of the Signal Security Agency's Cryptanalytic Branch, Branch III, which Rowlett headed at that time and for much of the war, and I have restricted my writing to all-too-few pages. I hope that this may give readers at least a glimmering of the significance of the work of a man whose contributions saved perhaps thousands of lives. I pray that some day Frank Rowlett will get the full history he deserves.

〜 〜 〜

Unlike the Kryha or the Army's M-94, which Rowlett described in his memoirs, the Japanese PURPLE machine was electromechanical, and in a way Frank Rowlett was destined from his youth to be the man to lead the solution. As a boy, he had been fascinated by things electrical. "I ate the stuff up," he said. He built radios. He was also interested in chemistry. Using some nitric acid and potassium permanganate that a passing salesman had brought, he set up a chemistry lab in the family's smokehouse. Then, at Emory & Henry College in southwestern Virginia, he studied chemistry and physics. But he got "sidetracked," he said, into mathematics, which he found "more purely intellectual. You could think about it in the middle of the night." One day, one of his mathematics professors, with whom he got along quite well, showed him a federal civil service test for a mathematician. He urged Rowlett to take it, saying it would give him confidence even if he didn't want the job. Rowlett passed. After graduating with a Bachelor of Science degree on 11 June 1929 and then marrying Edith Irene King on 13 September 1929 in Blountville, Tennessee, he took a job as a high school math and chemistry teacher in Rocky Mount, Virginia; his wife taught 250 miles away at Stickleyville School in Lee County. Then the civil service test bore fruit — on its results, and because he had studied German, Rowlett was offered a job as a junior cryptanalyst at $2,000 a year. He hadn't the faintest idea what a cryptanalyst was, but the amount was more than he and his wife were making together. And so on 1 April 1930 he reported for duty at the War Department. Abraham Sinkov and Solomon Kullback arrived some 10 and 20 days later, making Rowlett the senior junior cryptanalyst.

Japan was the main target for the cryptanalysts, as it was for the nation's war planners. In 1932, after the three young cryptanalysts had got what they could from studying Yardley's Japanese files, they attacked Japan's diplomatic codes as their first nontraining cryptanalyses. But, exciting as it was to crack the real thing, the results were disappointing. The systems encrypted only insignificant messages. The more important information was apparently protected by a cipher machine. The Signal Intelligence Service realized this, and one day in 1936, while Friedman was on duty at Fort Monmouth in New Jersey, Rowlett and Kullback attacked a cipher machine that the Japanese Foreign Office called its "Type A" cipher machine. They cracked it clean in a couple of days, Rowlett said, adding that "nobody else was involved," although John Hurt provided some linguistic information and translated the results and the Navy claimed that parallel work provided an assist.

The solution of what the S.I.S. called the RED machine gave the United States access to more and better information than ever before. This included advance information starting in March 1937 about Italy's possible adherence to the German–Japanese anti-Comintern pact of the previous November. The intercepts revealed the early indications that Italy might join, the start of negotiations, the discussion over whether Italy should accede to the existing treaty or sign a separate agreement with Japan, a statement that Hitler wanted Japan to participate in the existing agreement, Italy's apparent acceptance, the emperor's approval, and part of the text of the treaty, which was signed 6 November 1937.

U.S. diplomats had not begun reporting until October on this rapprochement between three aggressive nations to the east and to the west of the United States — and even then their information was far less specific than the intercepts. These intercepts seized the attention of officials in Army and Navy intelligence, in the State Department, and in the White House. In large part owing to Rowlett, cryptanalytic intelligence began going, for the first time in history, to the White House, probably to the president, Franklin D. Roosevelt.

Rowlett became expert in cracking RED, sometimes even sight-solving RED messages. But it was an electromechanical device, and its mechanisms started to wear out. Messages began appearing in the Japanese traffic about a new machine and, on 20 February 1939, the Japanese introduced it. More complex than RED, the Japanese called it their "Type B" machine; the Americans, PURPLE. Messages in RED gradually disappeared. Japan's major diplomatic messages had become unreadable. Faced with the loss of the nation's most paramount intelligence, the Signal Intelligence Service mounted a concentrated attack to solve the new machine. Friedman put Rowlett in charge, while he himself exercised overall supervision.

In the absence of any American spies almost anywhere in the world, these half-dozen cryptanalysts believed they might be able to provide the United States with its best secret intelligence on Japan, as relations with that nation, which persisted in its aggression against China, deteriorated. They plunged into their work in Rooms 3416 and 3418 in the Munitions Building. While Rowlett has told this story in typically dramatic fashion, an addendum might be noted: Though there is no reason to doubt Rowlett's statement that the first PURPLE messages were intercepted 20 March 1939, the machine was introduced on 20 February 1939. RED was finally discontinued on 21 August 1941.

〜 〜 〜

Rowlett breaks off his narrative at the recovery of a Japanese diplomatic code with a transposition superencipherment — probably one of the J codes with one of the K transpositions. He does not tell about the continuing growth of his agency or of the Navy unit, nor about the increasing volume of their solutions of Japanese code messages. From the early trickle of a few messages every few days, their output reached the remarkable figure of 50 to 75 a day — all, it must be emphasized, diplomatic, not military or naval. Army and Navy officers bore the more important ones in locked briefcases to the president and to high officials of the White House and the State, War, and Navy Departments.

The intercepts revealed the reports from and instructions to Japanese diplomats, in Washington and elsewhere, disclosing the diplomatic intentions of the empire of the Rising Sun. These clearly showed late in 1941 that a crisis was approaching and, during the first week in December, as the Americans solved messages telling the Japanese embassy in Washington to destroy its codes, that a rupture in relations was imminent. Yet, because the Japanese diplomats were not told of the plans of the Imperial army or navy, no intercept said anything about a declaration of war or an attack upon the United States. Rowlett and the other cryptanalysts, Navy as well as Army, fought to produce as much intelligence as possible to enable their superiors to predict what the Japanese would do. They were sure that war would come, but they didn't know how or when or where. Around the clock they attacked new keys, solved messages, translated them, went home, came back, sometimes in a daze, and started over again.

On the morning of December 7, 1941, Rowlett, who had worked all night before finally going home, was so tired he couldn't sleep. His wife suggested that he take his sons, Frank Jr. and Tom, for a walk, which she said would make him feel better. Upon returning home, he listened to the radio. Hearing the newscast report that the Japanese had attacked Pearl Harbor, this courteous, soft-spoken Southern gentleman cursed to himself, angry that his efforts had not prevented the surprise. But the war was on. He went back to work.

‿ ‿ ‿

The Signal Intelligence Service was divided at the time into four branches. The A Branch devised and managed Army codes and ciphers — communications security. C Branch intercepted foreign messages, mostly by radio. D Branch operated the IBM tabulators and other devices that helped make American cryptosystems and break foreign cryptosystems. B Branch broke foreign codes and ciphers. Its three sections were headed by Friedman's original three cryptanalysts. Solomon Kullback attacked German cryptosystems. Abe Sinkov dealt with Japanese military codes and ciphers; he later went to Australia to head General Douglas MacArthur's codebreaking Central Bureau. Rowlett handled all other cryptosystems, of neutrals as well as enemies, plus Japanese diplomatic cryptosystems.

As the war progressed the S.I.S. expanded, adding hundreds of men and women. Outgrowing its little offices in the Munitions Building, it moved into a former girls' school called — from the suburb in which it stood — Arlington Hall. The S.I.S. became the Signal Security Agency. And it reorganized. What had been B Branch had, by the fall of 1943, elaborated into an Administrative Office and several numbered sections. Section B-I indexed all intercepts, decryptographed intercepts in solved cryptosystems, disseminated important solutions in a daily bulletin, and ran an information service for the other sections. B-II encompassed the vast effort against Japanese army codes. B-IV was now the IBM unit.

B-III was the Cryptanalytic Branch, under Rowlett, by then a lieutenant colonel of the Army reserve. Having absorbed some functions formerly run by other elements, it attacked the military codes of nations other than Japan and the diplomatic and other codes of all nations. Within it, the cryptanalytic problems were grouped as much as possible by language, regardless of their cryptography. Sometimes technical problems overrode this preference, however. Thus all machine-cipher systems were attacked in a single subsection.

The constant changes in foreign cryptosystems — in the opportunities they presented, in the political situation, in the contribution of allied cryptanalytic agencies, and in intelligence needs — impelled constant reorganization of B-III. For example, work on Japanese diplomatic and military attaché systems and the addition of 11 new language problems grew enormously, while the effort on Italian, Spanish, Swiss, Belgian, and Giraudist French systems shrank.

Unlike B-II, B-III faced a spectrum of problems. Its targets consisted of 31 governments and factions (Vichy French, Free French, Giraud French), with their diplomatic, commercial, and military aspects and vocabularies, in more than 35 languages, some exotic as Thai and Ethiopian, encrypted in a great variety of cryptosystems — transposition ciphers, machine ciphers, and codes, both enciphered and plain, among others. Of the 576,566 intercepts it received in fiscal 1944, B-III solved 89,467 — a rate of 15.5%, or a little better than one message of every seven. This doesn't mean the failure rate was 85%. Though some messages could indeed not be solved, many were not attacked because their origin or length made them seem unlikely to be carrying information valuable enough to spend time on, and many were plaintext messages that needed no solution.

The unit also worked on new and unknown cryptosystems that produced no solutions. In March of 1944, for example, B-III spent 13,899 of what its chronicler called "the most intensive, the most demanding" man-hours — "the hours of the hardest work, the hours of false leads and disappointments at every turn save the right one, and the hours of constant goading by the excitement of real success" — on 15,471 intercepts in 38 cryptosystems. Of these, the nature of seven could not be determined, eight were introduced so late or used so rarely that progress was slow, cryptanalytic progress had been made on 19, and four — including two Iraqi monoalphabetics — were readable. Not one solution from all this work appeared in the daily Bulletin. But, by yielding experience, knowledge, and "new ideas for new attacks," the chronicler said, this time was "some of the most fruitful spent."

B-III assembled under its Administrative Office four units that benefited all the subsections. The Training Program instructed in the particular problems of the section and, through individual attention, helped assign new cryptanalysts to where their talents could best be employed. Some languages were also taught. The Recorder's Group wrote up papers to preserve the knowledge and experience of the section. The Traffic Coordinator compiled the List of Cryptanalytic Short Tiles and the System Identification Book, with its 500 trigraphs, each the short title of a system followed by external identifying characteristics and the radio circuits it used.

The Research Group, the most interesting of the units, engaged in some imaginative studies. It developed a photographic cryptanalysis for solving German Enigma messages. At the time, the technique for solving these required assuming the plaintext of an intercept; this could come from a guess or from information from the solution of a cryptogram in another system. For success, the assumed plaintext had to be exactly the same as the real plaintext. This was not always available or conjecturable. The Research Group sought a statistical method of solution that would not require such a crib. Its film method, wrote the B-III historian, "consisted of photographs of the entire set of cipher alphabets generated by the Enigma from nine high-frequency plaintext letters. A large number of alphabets, from 17,576 to 2,743,416 depending upon the problem, are photographed on one continuous film and then matched against the first 36 letters of the cipher messages. At the point where the highest number of the 36 cipher letters are identical to the letters on the generatrices of the nine high-frequency plaintext letters, a photo-cell receives the maximum amount of light and signals that the correct beginning generatrix has been found. Preliminary experiments in this method have been successful, and it is planned to have the necessary equipment constructed." The Research Group also devised a statistical method that solved for the first time — or so it claimed — "an unknown transposition of an unknown code by purely statistical means."

One of B-III's major efforts dealt with its cryptanalytic machines — an effort in which Rowlett's hand can be seen. As the historian of the section wrote, "Perhaps no development in cryptology has produced a greater revision in theory and application than the growing use of machines in cryptography and cryptanalysis. Throughout the branch this development is recognized as the most far-reaching in implications in recent years, and throughout this report the repeated references to machine techniques emphasize the importance of these ramifications."

The RAM (Rapid Analytical Machinery) subsection not only cryptanalyzed intercepts but researched improvements in the speed and efficiency of its machines. In August of 1943, the subsection had but one machine, used to find the index of coincidence between messages, and two tape readers. By the fall of 1944, it included a mechanism called the tetratester that counted repetitions at from 10,000 to 100,000 positions per second to overlap messages, a 70-millimeter machine that worked at the same speed to count exact coincidences, the photometric device, and other, more ordinary devices such as tape readers and National Cash Register differencing machines, presumably for the stripping of additives from enciphered codes.

The subsection also improved what it called the 003 but whose British original was known as a bombe. This was the mechanism used with a crib to recover the keys of an Enigma message. The 003, built by the Western Electric Company, could crack problems not resolvable on a bombe. One such problem was the case in which the indicator was missing or garbled. In some nets, 40% of the messages came through that way. The unit used the 003 with a new statistical approach to read such messages. Similar was the case in which the enemy cipher clerk used the setting of the Enigma rotors left at the completion of one message as the setting for the next message. B-III developed a solution using the 003 that exploited the relationship between the settings. So successful was it that the British, who had been unable to solve those messages, quit work on a new type of bombe to attack them.

The work of B-III eventuated, of course, in the reading of intercepted foreign cryptograms. These encompassed messages in 35 languages encrypted in hundreds of cryptosystems.

Success was great with the 241 cryptosystems in Romance languages that it attacked. Of the 100 French systems, 55 belonged to the Vichy government and 45 to the French Committee of National Liberation. It removed a complex system of digraphic substitution in five phases from one of the Vichy codes. A complicated route transposition was solved with the help of some documents discovered by accident. Ten French codes were reconstructed; four more were being broken at the end of the fiscal year. A Vatican code introduced in September 1943 was broken in two months. Dozens of Portuguese-language and Spanish-language systems were read. Forty-six Italian systems were being worked on successfully until Mussolini's fall in July 1943, and Italy's leaving the war ended the urgency of this work. Still, the volume and value of just this subsection is shown by the fact that in May of 1944, 3,426 messages in its systems — more than 100 a day — were published in the daily Bulletin, and 107 were printed in the much more selective Magic Summary.

The non-Romance languages likewise covered a wide spectrum. Swedish, Greek, Czech, Afghan, Iranian, Iraqi, Egyptian, Trans-Jordanian, and other Near Eastern cryptograms were solved. A double transposition used by the Yugoslav resistance under General Draja Mikhailovitch was broken. Finnish intercepts, many enciphered on a Hagelin machine, were regarded as "consistently valuable." The cipher systems used by Arabian princes on a midwar visit to the United States were solved completely within two hours. The Chinese unit solved the two most elaborate encipherments in Chinese, which appeared to be the most secret systems used by the foreign minister, Dr. T.V. Soong. A Thai cryptosystem used from China was solved within 30 minutes of its appearance. The main diplomatic code of Turkey, whose intercepts were "by far the most important as regards the volume of traffic, the number and complexity of systems, and the intelligence contained in the messages," was solved in a month.

German and Japanese combat military and naval intercepts did not go to B-III. These were solved elsewhere — in theater cryptanalytic units, by Navy codebreakers, by the British. But B-III continued to read PURPLE messages, and it solved German Foreign Office and German army high-level and intelligence cryptosystems. One of the latter, also used by a special diplomatic net, employed an Enigma with a complex rotor motion. Another high-level army system utilized an Enigma with a pluggable end-plate complicated by variable wiring in one of the rotors. The section developed new ways of solving the teletypewriter encipherment device called "Fish" by the British. And it obtained useful intelligence from its solution of three Foreign Office enciphered code systems. The most valuable of these was a double additive system that B-III designated "GEC" and Britain's Government Code and Cypher School called "Floradora." In addition, the section was attacking a one-time pad diplomatic system on the supposition that the pad had been used more than once.

What information emerged from all this work? An American spying for Japan, Mrs. Velvalee Dickinson, was uncovered because her secret information, disguised as innocuous letters offering different kinds of dolls for sale, was spotted as an open code. Turkish solutions gave information about the disposition of German troops in France. A Vatican message gave details of the protracted negotiations concerning exports of wolframite to Germany, perhaps leading to prevention or preclusive buying of the material. Argentine traffic revealed that Argentine vessels were carrying platinum and other contraband goods to Germany, enabling Britain to stop the ships at Gibraltar. Finnish messages disclosed the course of Finnish–

Russian negotiations. One group of messages in the most secret Japanese military attaché cryptosystem contained information — not specified — of such urgent importance that it was flown to President Roosevelt and Prime Minister Churchill in conference at Teheran. Solutions of German diplomatic cryptograms proved that German missions abroad were directing espionage, in violation of international law. In one case, solutions of Argentine traffic indicated that an Argentine consular official, one Hellmuth, was in league with the Germans. On his way to Barcelona, the British arrested him in Trinidad. This led to an investigation of German spy rings in Argentina, to a breaking of relations between Argentina and Germany, and eventually to a declaration of war.

PURPLE solutions continued to provide enormously valuable information. Much of it dealt with the Eastern Front, since the messages of the Japanese ambassador in Berlin, General Hiroshi Oshima, often revealed Hitler's plans. Some of these concerned discussions of negotiations between the Japanese and the Russians for a separate peace. Another cryptogram intercepted by an American post in the former Italian radio station in Asmara, Eritrea, reported on a tour that Oshima took of the Atlantic Wall in November of 1943. In his message, Oshima provided extraordinarily detailed information about the German defenses. As one example, he reported that the German antitank ditches, in the shape of a V, were 3.5 meters deep and 5 meters wide at the top. Rowlett, who to a large measure was responsible for this success, has called it the greatest intelligence coup of all time. Whether history will sustain that judgment or not, there can be no doubt that this trove of information, translated into action by Eisenhower and his subordinates, saved hundreds of American lives — thereby alone justifying all the time and labor of American cryptanalysts before the war.

But spectacular as codebreaking is, sensational as the stories it produces, thrilling as its victories over human ingenuity, Rowlett did not consider his successes in cryptanalysis his major contribution. He believed it was his codemaking. Signal security is not as dramatic as signal intelligence, for it does not change history. It merely preserves the status quo. But Rowlett explained its significance. It is more important, he said, to keep your own secrets than to obtain those of the enemy. Thus he feels that his invention of the SIGABA, called the ECM, or Electric Code Machine, by the Navy, was his most important work in cryptology. During the war, neither German nor Japanese nor Italian cryptanalysts ever solved a message encrypted by using the SIGABA. The Germans may have given him their greatest accolade when they wrote, in the war diary of the codebreakers of Army

Group C, that, because statistical tests showed that no breaks were possible, they had decided to stop even intercepting U.S. Army five-letter (SIGABA) messages. Congress recognized Rowlett's contribution when it awarded him $100,000 for his cryptologic inventions.

After World War II, Rowlett continued his cryptologic work, transferring for a time to the Central Intelligence Agency. Modest and constrained to silence though he was, in the shadows he stood as a giant. During the war, his work saved lives. After it, he helped make American cryptology central to the preservation of peace. Our debt for this contribution cannot be repaid, but we must remember, with gratitude, the life and work of Frank B. Rowlett.

DAVID KAHN

Many of the books published by the U.S. Government and related by Frank B. Rowlett in his memoirs have been reprinted by AEGEAN PARK PRESS. The reader is invited to write for a free catalog containing these books.

AEGEAN PARK PRESS
P.O. Box 2837
Laguna Hills, CA 92654-2837